MANAGING HUMAN RESOURCES IN GLOBAL ENVIRONMENT

A M Sarma
Former Member of the Faculty,
Tata Institute of Social Sciences,
Deonar, Mumbai.
arsola1939@hotmail.com

First Edition: 2013

Himalaya Publishing House

MUMBAI • NEW DELHI • NAGPUR • BENGALURU • HYDERABAD • CHENNAI • PUNE • LUCKNOW • AHMEDABAD • ERNAKULAM • BHUBANESWAR • INDORE • KOLKATA • GUWAHATI

First Edition : 2013

Published by	:	Mrs. Meena Pandey for **Himalaya Publishing House Pvt. Ltd.,** "Ramdoot", Dr. Bhalerao Marg, Girgaon, **Mumbai - 400 004.** Phone: 022-23860170/23863863, Fax: 022-23877178 **E-mail: himpub@vsnl.com; Website: www.himpub.com**
Branch Offices	:	
New Delhi	:	"Pooja Apartments", 4-B, Murari Lal Street, Ansari Road, Darya Ganj, New Delhi - 110 002. Phone: 011-23270392, 23278631; Fax: 011-23256286
Nagpur	:	Kundanlal Chandak Industrial Estate, Ghat Road, Nagpur - 440 018. Phone: 0712-2738731, 3296733; Telefax: 0712-2721215
Bengaluru	:	No. 16/1 (Old 12/1), 1st Floor, Next to Hotel Highlands, Madhava Nagar, Race Course Road, Bengaluru - 560 001. Phone: 080-32919385; Telefax: 080-22286611
Hyderabad	:	No. 3-4-184, Lingampally, Besides Raghavendra Swamy Matham, Kachiguda, Hyderabad - 500 027. Phone: 040-27560041, 27550139; Mobile: 09390905282
Chennai	:	No. 8/2, Madley 2nd Street, Ground Floor, T. Nagar, Chennai - 600 017. Mobile: 09345345055
Pune	:	First Floor, "Laksha" Apartment, No. 527, Mehunpura, Shaniwarpeth (Near Prabhat Theatre), Pune - 411 030. Phone: 020-24496323/24496333; Mobile: 09370579333
Lucknow	:	House No 731, Shekhupura Colony, Near B.D. Convent School, Aliganj, Lucknow - 226 022. Mobile: 09307501549
Ahmedabad	:	114, "SHAIL", 1st Floor, Opp. Madhu Sudan House, C.G. Road, Navrang Pura, Ahmedabad - 380 009. Phone: 079-26560126; Mobile: 09377088847
Ernakulam	:	39/176 (New No: 60/251) 1st Floor, Karikkamuri Road, Ernakulam, Kochi - 682011, Phone: 0484-2378012, 2378016; Mobile: 09344199799
Bhubaneswar	:	5 Station Square, Bhubaneswar - 751 001 (Odisha). Phone: 0674-2532129, Mobile: 09338746007
Indore	:	Kesardeep Avenue Extension, 73, Narayan Bagh, Flat No. 302, IIIrd Floor, Near Humpty Dumpty School, Indore - 452 007 (M.P.). Mobile: 09301386468
Kolkata	:	108/4, Beliaghata Main Road, Near ID Hospital, Opp. SBI Bank, Kolkata - 700 010, Phone: 033-32449649, Mobile: 09883055590, 07439040301
Guwahati	:	House No. 15, Behind Pragjyotish College, Near Sharma Printing Press, P.O. Bharalumukh, Guwahati - 781009, (Assam). Mobile: 09883055590, 09883055536
DTP by	:	HPH, Editorial Office, Bhandup (Sunanda)
Printed at	:	Geetanjali Press Pvt. Ltd., Nagpur, On behalf of HPH.

Preface

As more firms move outside their domestic world of international business, the globalisation of world markets appears to be gaining momentum. The globalisation of business is forcing managers to grapple with complex human resource issues as they seek to gain or sustain a competitive advantage. Faced with unprecedented levels of foreign competition at home and abroad, companies are beginning to recognise that human resources are of critical importance to implement their international or global strategy. As our companies expand globally, the human resource challenges become more pronounced. Managing people typically focuses on helping employees to understand and effectively handle cultural requirements by building sensitivity to languages, national customs, legal and regulatory environments, and other country and regional differences. Among the various dimensions of international business, the people aspect with all its cross-cultural complexities and issues assume greater significance and pose major challenges to managing employees globally. IHRM as a discipline plays a vital role in success or failure of a business venture since businesses are essentially driven by people. It examines the way in which international organisations manage their human resources in the different national context in which they operate.

The intention of this book is to portray different dimensions of IHRM, including different issues pertaining to all categories of staff operating in an international sphere. The material for this textbook came from many sources which have been identified and duly acknowledged. Reference books which are particularly valuable for this subject have been listed in bibliography.

A M Sarma

Acknowledgements

I am grateful to many learned authors whose contributions to the subject have inspired me to write this book. I would like to record my appreciation and gratitude to the staff of Himalaya Publishing House Pvt. Ltd., Mumbai for their sincere efforts in bringing out this book in time. Also, I extend my sincere thanks to all my colleagues and friends who have assisted me in this task. Finally, I would like to thank my family members for their loving support.

I would be grateful to the readers if they can send me their comments and suggestions to improve the usefulness of the book.

A M Sarma

Contents

Preface *iii*

Acknowledgements *iv*

1. **The Environment of International Human Resource Management (IHRM)** **1**
   - Introduction
   - Globalisation of Business
   - International Operations
   - Internationalisation of HRM
   - Concept of IHRM
   - IHRM Functions
   - IHRM Manager
   - HRM in Multinational Enterprises
   - Standardisation and Adaptation of Work Practices
   - Domestic and International HRM
   - Enduring Context of IHRM
   - Summary
   - Review Questions
   - References

2. **Organisational Context of IHRM** **24**
   - Introduction
   - Stages of Internationalisation
   - Organisational Structure
   - Changes in Organisational Structures
   - IHRM Approaches
   - IHRM Strategy and Model
   - Control Mechanisms
   - Mode of Operation
   - Summary
   - Review Questions
   - References

3. **Strategic IHRM** 35

- Introduction
- Features of Strategic Planning
- Features of Global Strategic Management
- International Business Strategies
- International Strategic Management Process
- MNCs Business Strategies
- Collaborative Strategies
- Organisational Strategies
- HR Business Competency
- Summary
- Review Questions
- Reference

4. **Staffing for International Assignments** 48

- Introduction
- International Assignments
- Major Considerations for Selecting Expatriates
- Expatriate Failure
- Adjustment of Expatriates
- Staffing Policies
- Recruitment
- Selection
- Retaining, Developing, and Retrenching Staff
- Dual-career Couples
- Women as International Managers
- Case
- Summary
- Review Questions
- References

5. **Training and Development in International Context** 68

- Introduction
- Training Cycle
- Training of Expatriates
- Areas of Global Training and Development
- Components of Pre-departure Training
- Developing International Staff

- Cross-cultural and Ethics Training
- Summary
- Review Questions
- References

6. **International Compensation System** **85**
- Introduction
- Objectives
- Complexities
- Compensation Plan
- Influencing Factors
- Key Components
- Managing Pay Variations
- Varied Approaches
- Global Reward Strategy
- International Taxation
- Compensation Practices
- Summary
- Review Questions
- References

7. **International Performance Management** **101**
- Introduction
- Objectives
- Challenges
- Evaluation Criteria
- Who Should Appraise the Performance?
- Process of Performance Appraisal
- How to Make Performance Appraisal Effective?
- Case 1
- Case 2
- Summary
- Review Questions
- References

8. **Expatriation and Repatriation** 117

- Introduction
- Selection Criteria
- Female Expatriates
- Staffing the Local Subsidiary
- Process of Repatriation
- Making Repatriation Succeed
- Career Perspective
- Responsibilities of IHRM in Repatriation
- Summary
- Review Questions
- Reference

9. **International Industrial Relations** 128

- Introduction
- Concept and Scope
- Key Issues and Concerns
- Trade Unions and Approaches of MNCs
- Country-specific Labour Relations Practices
- Labour Relations Practices of MNCs
- Employees' Participation in Management
- Employee Participation Across Countries
- Emerging Trends
- Summary
- Review Questions
- References

10. **International Mergers and Acquisitions HR Perspective** 150

- Introduction
- Principles of Acquisition
- Communication Framework
- Responsibilities of HR
- Personnel Considerations
- Anticipation of Employee Problems
- Pre-merger Considerations
- Case 1
- Case 2

- Summary
- Review Questions
- Reference

11. Cultural Dimensions of IHRM **162**
- Introduction
- Concept of Culture
- Strategic and Cultural Values
- Cultural Sensitivity and Cultural Shock
- Cultural Differences and Similarities
- Hofstede's Framework
- Kluckhohn-Strodtbeck Framework
- Workforce Diversity
- Strategies for Managing Diversity
- Behaviour Variations Across Cultures
- Case
- Summary
- Review Questions
- References

12. Cross-cultural Communication and Negotiation **185**
- Introduction
- Verbal and Non-verbal Messages
- Dimensions of Human Communication
- Barriers to Cross-cultural Communication
- Cross-cultural Negotiation
- Summary
- Review Questions

13. Global Occupational Health **195**
- Introduction
- History of Occupational Health
- Concept and Objectives
- Principles
- Issues
- Systems
- Services
- Measures to Improve

- Role of International Organisations
- Future Challenges
- Summary
- Review Questions

14. Global Ethical Environment 208

- Introduction
- Ethical Decisions
- International Business Ethics
- Corporate Ethics Code
- Bribery
- Social Responsibility
- Ethical Dilemmas of MNCs
- Intra-company Ethical Issues
- Guest Workers and Immigrants
- Ethics Programme
- Summary
- Review Questions

15. Leadership and Motivation in a Global Context 221

- Introduction
- Leadership Across Cultures
- Universalism in Leadership
- Cross-cultural Differences in Leadership
- Leadership Styles
- Theories on Motivation
- Motivational Issues
- Summary
- Review Questions

16. IHRM Issues, Trends and Future Challenges 233

- Introduction
- Organisational Capability
- Understanding and Building Centres of Excellence
- Streamlining HR Support Functions
- Outsourcing or Insourcing HR
- Managing Talent
- Global Knowledge Management

- Management Through Global Networks
- Managing International Projects: HR Perspective
- HR Ethics and Corporate Social Responsibility
- Summary
- Review Questions
- References

Glossary 247

Bibliography 253

Index 255

1

The Environment of International Human Resource Management (IHRM)

Objectives

- To explain the term IHRM and its functions.
- To differentiate between domestic HRM and IHRM.
- To describe the global work environment and the enduring context in which IHRM functions.

INTRODUCTION

International organisational activity has existed in one form or another for many hundreds if not thousands of years. Each generation across history has brought with it different challenges and requirements in managing international organisations and in managing employees. The current approach to international business is to have a global strategy but with the capability to act locally. Human beings grow and develop in a particular cultural context and while there will be many similarities between every culture there are also many differences. It can be very difficult for any international organisation to arrange its affairs consistently across diverse operating locations. To be commercially successful, organisations that operate across borders need to be able to create effective and efficient methods of work; achieve operational, procedural and systems consistency; and uniformity in management approach. The more diverse the organisation, the more difficult it becomes to achieve these requirements.

GLOBALISATION OF BUSINESS

Globalisation refers to a growth of trade and investment in international business operations resulting in integration of economies around the world. It is the shift towards a more integrated and interdependent world economy. Globalisation has four components *viz.*, the globalisation of markets, globalisation of production, globalisation of investment, and globalisation of technology. Globalisation is the trend toward a more integrated global economic system. Global companies plan or venture not only on national markets, but also venture globally and act globally. As our companies expand globally, the human resource functions become more and more complex. Managing people in a global environment is a challenging task that typically focuses on helping employees to understand and effectively handle cultural requirements by building sensitivity to languages, national customs, legal and regulatory environments, and other country and regional differences.

Rapid globalisation requires organisational flexibility. Flexibility is more important because global companies increasingly work with partners around the world. Coping with international competition requires flexibility that traditional organisations often do not possess. Flexible organisations require flexible people. Managers need to understand the characteristics of flexible organisations, and determine the organisational design and capabilities required to achieve business objectives. Fortunately, the revolution in information technology permits many organisations to develop the needed flexibility.

Global companies target investments according to the unique merits and requirements of each regional/local market and operation. Although successful globalisation strategies are not easy to implement, many organisations have effectively moved outside their domestic markets. For example, Ford, Merck & Co., IBM, and Hewlett-Packard have strong profitable operations in Europe. McDonald's, Walt Disney, DuPont have successful Asian operations. Global companies adapt to the market requirements of multiple countries and cultures, although they challenge their conventional wisdom of business practices in different settings.

Technology, specially computer-based information technologies, continue to revolutionise as to how: (a) tasks are performed; (b) organisations are structured; (c) customers are served; (d) human resources are led and managed; (e) planning and control systems operate; (f) employees communicate and network with one another and external stakeholders, such as customers, suppliers, competitors, and government agencies; (g) individuals and organisations learn to innovate and adapt; and (h) many other tasks are performed. Technological change may have positive effects, including higher quality products and services at lower costs. But it may also have negative effects, including erosion of personal privacy, computer-related stress, and health problems.

Next stage in the evolution of business organisations is the creation of cybercorps. Internet and intranets are monitored by cybercorps. The internet is a worldwide collection of interconnected computer networks through an array of computer-based information technologies; the internet directly links the organisation and its employees to customers, suppliers, information sources, the public, and millions of individuals.

INTERNATIONAL OPERATIONS

There are many different forms that international activity can take, all of which have different implications for the HRM activities and approaches required. They include:

1. *The export of goods and services*: This form of international activity has very little HRM implications as in most instances the organisation itself is based in one location. Consequently, the HR policies and practices adopted will be based on the home country norms, and hence no need to cater or incorporate other country variations. The exception would be the need to provide HR policies and practices to those employees dealing with exports or visiting other countries on business deal.
2. *Sales agents*: Requires less specialist HRM support than direct exporting as the agent would usually be paid commission for sales achieved but would not be a direct employee.
3. *Licensing or franchising*: It involves an agreement between the company and licence or franchise holder to run a 'mini-business' in a particular location in return for a fee or proportion of the profit. There would be a need to ensure the provision of appropriate HRM advice and support to its local licensees or franchisees.
4. *Management contracts*: This involves running something on behalf of someone else in return for a fee. It would be necessary for the contractor to have an ability to recruit, train and generally manage employees in each location where they hold a management contract.
5. *Technical assistance agreements*: In practice, these are similar to the management contracts, but they tend to be used for consultancy or knowledge transfer situations. There would be a need for providing service to the expatriates and helping them to develop.
6. *Contract manufacturing*: This type of arrangement involves the subcontracting of part of the organisation's process to a local business. For example, a car manufacturing company might subcontract engine making to a company based in another country with cheaper labour. In HR terms this type of arrangement has little direct impact other than the requirement to train company staff as how to negotiate deals across cultures, understand the demands of customs and trade systems, and monitor local labour practice.

7. *Partnership/Joint venture direct investment*: It involves working with local partners or through joint ventures with other companies entering another country. Any local partner should have expertise in local HRM policies and practices. There is a need to ensure an appropriate balance between local and home company HR practices as it is possible that the local partner might seek to 'shift the balance' in favour of local conditions.
8. *Directly owned investment*: This type of investment involves the company investing directly in another country. It involves the HR specialists in understanding the local conditions and in creating an HRM framework that matches the needs of local and home company conditions.

INTERNATIONALISATION OF HRM

Adler and Ghader (1990) identified four different phases of internationalisation of organisations that wish to operate globally. These are: domestic, international, multinational, and global. This classification is primarily based on the influence of national and corporate culture.

In the first stage, management's attitude can be explained as ethnocentric. At this stage, the host country's potential in terms of human resources is not utilised optimally and the organisation heavily depends on the support from the headquarters. In the second stage, the organisation adopts a polycentric perspective. The cultural differences and customer expectations are considered carefully. Establishing production unit in the host country or the region is a common feature. In the third stage, the MNC tries to gain cost advantage by considering the differential price factors in the respective countries, and utilisation of available human resources in the host countries. At the last stage, the MNCs not only try to understand their potential client's needs, but also translate them into products and services by trying to provide those things on a low-cost basis as far as possible; and eventually deliver them in a culturally appropriate manner and as per the scheduled time.

The impact of internationalisation and globalisation are reflected as to how IHRM needs to play a more active role in international business by building, sustaining, and developing through transnational networks; and also how to manage a workforce effectively across borders. The key determinant of MNEs effectiveness is the extent to which their various operating units across the world are to be differentiated and at the same time integrated, controlled, and coordinated.

CONCEPT OF IHRM

Managing international resources in the global context is indeed a complex process. In the words of Harzing and Ruysseveldt (1998) a better way to understand the philosophy of human resource management in international context demands a thorough understanding about the evolution of the concept itself. In late 1980s, the economic and technological developments not only led to a major shift in international division of labour, but also, expanded the relative sizes of various sectors. In 1990s, several factors such as liberalised government policies of various countries; changed export-import structure; country-specific labour legislation; proximity to advanced technology; and availability of skilled workforce encouraged the MNCs to widen their business horizons. Obviously, the focus of managing human resources shifted from traditional day-to-day personnel administration to managing and developing human capital.

P. Morgan[1] defines IHRM as the interplay among human resource activities (*viz.*, procure, allocate and utilise), types of employees (*viz.*, host-country nationals, parent country nationals and third country nationals), and countries (*viz.*, host-country, home country and others).

According to Paul Sparrow,[2] "global management of human resource (in other words IHRM) is a possession of the skills and knowledge by formulating and implementing policies and practices that effectively integrate and cohere globally dispersed employees, while at the same time recognising and appreciating local differences that impact the effective utilisation of human resources".

IHRM is about the worldwide management of human resources. The purpose of IHRM is to enable the multinational enterprises to be successful globally. This entails on its part to be: (a) competitive throughout their presence in the world market; (b) efficient; (c) locally responsive; (d) flexible and adaptable within the shortest of time periods; and (e) capable of transferring knowledge and learning across their globally dispersed units.

International HRM is performing HRM activities by a domestic organisation that employs foreigners along with nationals and by international/global/multinational/transnational organisations. Broadly defined, international human resource management (IHRM) is the process of procuring, allocating, and effectively utilising human resources in a multinational corporation.

Among the various activities of HRM, the following are the most common ones:

- Human resource planning
- Staffing (recruitment, selection, and placement)
- Performance management
- Career management
- Training and development
- Compensation and benefits
- Health and safety
- Labour relations

IHRM deals with all the above functions of HRM and also certain functions exclusively meant for expatriates. These additional functions include resolving the disputes between domestic and foreign employees, cross-cultural management at varying levels, and collaborating domestic employees and foreign employees.

IHRM Policies

An MNE's IHRM policy and practice are the interaction of its home HRM system, firm characteristics, and host societal characteristics. Hence, while devising IHRM policies, both firm-specific factors and host-contextual factors are to be considered. Firm-specific factors include international strategy, organisational structure, organisational culture, stages and model of internationalisation, and international exposures. The host-contextual factors include political, legal, economic and socio-cultural factors.

Evans and Lorange (1989) have proposed two sets of logic which are to be considered by the MNCs while formulating HRM policy in the international context:

(a) *Product market logic*: Here, the stage of product life cycle is the key factor on the basis of which HRM policies about recruitment, training, compensation, and so on, are decided.

(b) *Socio-cultural logic*: Here, the main emphasis is on socio-cultural differences, and their related work styles.

According to Paauwe, J. and Dewe, P. (1995), there are two dimensions which need to be considered while designing HRM policies and activities in the context of domestic and international operations of a firm. The first dimension is the product, market, and technology; and the second is that of socio-cultural and legal. While the former represents the economic and market realities encountered by a company to compete in the domestic and international market, the latter refers to the socio-cultural and prevalent value systems that determine the elements of fairness, legitimacy, and distributive justice determining the relationship between employer and employees. Hence, the focus is not on the individual market players, but on interest groups such as government, trade unions, and other relevant institutions.

IHRM Dimensions

According to Morgan (1986), international HRM is the interplay among three dimensions, i.e., human resource activities, types of employees, and countries of operation. Morgan presents a model of international HRM (shown in Fig. 1.1) that consists of three dimensions:

1. The three broad human resource activities – procurement, allocation, and utilisation.

2. The three broad international HRM activities – the host-country where a subsidiary may be located, the home (parent) country where the firm is headquartered, and other countries that may be the source of labour or finance.

The three types of employees of international firm – host country nationals (HCNs), parent country nationals (PCNs), and third country nationals (TCNs).

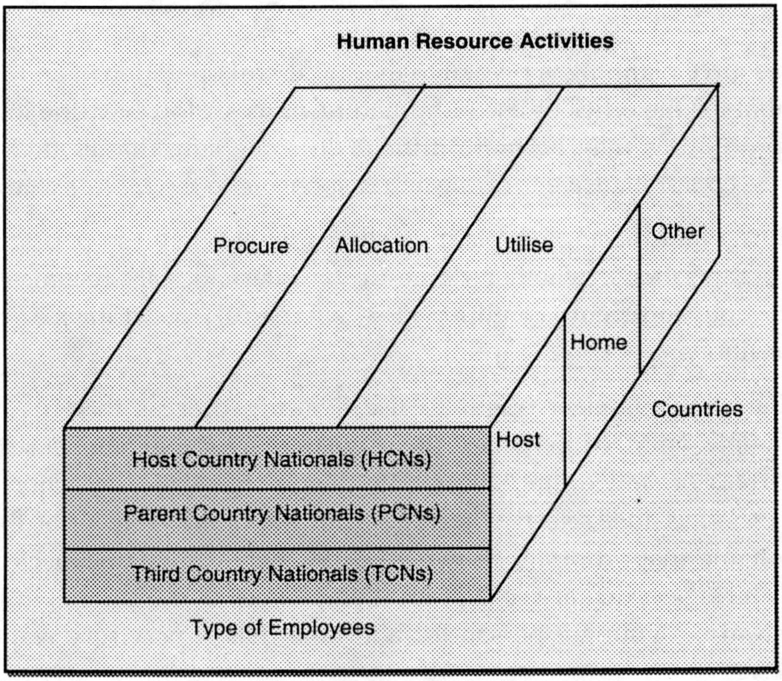

Fig. 1.1: Model of International HRM

Source: Adapted from P.V. Morgan, 1986, *International Human Resource Management.*

IHRM FUNCTIONS

The significant IHRM functions include:

Job analysis: It is a systematic process for gathering, documenting, and analysing data about a job to be performed. It consists of task analysis, skills analysis, and abilities analysis. The three outcomes of job analysis are: job description, job specification, and job evaluation. According to McCormick (1976), job analysis usually concentrates on:

- *Work activities* – to identify precisely what tasks are to be accomplished.
- *Performance standards* – to identify the expected output in terms of both quantity and quality.
- *Work technologies* – to identify appropriate machines, tools, and other job technologies.

- *Job-related tangible and intangibles* – to identify the knowledge to be applied, materials to be processed, products to be made, or performance to be performed.

Planning: Human resource planning from international point of view is rather more difficult and complex. This is due to the fact that international human resource planning normally takes into consideration a number of additional variables like language, culture, spouse and family adaptability in addition to job skills, and talent and knowledge requirement.

Human resource planning is pivotal to the successful operation of an MNC. Planning in MNCs is essential for the efficient use of human resources. However, the implementation of HR planning procedures may be more difficult in some subsidiaries than in others. Such planning must be comprehensive in scope and responsive to the MNC's characteristics.

Hiring: Hiring and placing people in positions where they can perform effectively is a goal of most organisations, whether domestic or international. Technical competence is necessary but not sufficient condition for successful performance of international management positions.

A subsidiary HR manager ought to use a hiring process that fits the local labour market. For example, an MNC may need the services of a local personnel selection agency to identify the sources of skilled employees. The development of a selection system may be complicated by the fact that selection tests used in the home country of the MNC may be culturally biased and inappropriate elsewhere. Also there can be unexpected disadvantages associated with hiring particular types of local employees. For example, in Japan, it may be inappropriate to hire a younger person for a job that has supervisory responsibilities over older employees.

One of the major problems associated with hiring in less developed countries is that the skill level of individuals may be less than desired. In such circumstances, it is important to invest considerable time and effort in the selection process and to provide increased training to local employees when they take up the job. In such a case, appropriate training materials have to be prepared and training methodology to be followed across cultures.

Staffing: Staffing is a major IHRM practice that MNEs have used to help coordinate and control their far-flung global operations. MNEs remain concerned about the best way to identify and select expatriates. On the way to developing a global workforce and cadre of global managers, MNEs need to open their recruitment process and enhance the attractiveness of global assignments. Perl Mutter (1969) has categorised MNCs staff management's choices towards staffing as ethnocentricity, polycentricity, and geocentricity.

Appraising performance: Culture helps to determine what aspects of performance should be appraised and how that appraisal should be conducted. Individual performance assessment is common in the U.S., a very individualistic society. By contrast, in Japan or China, group performance is critical, and singling out individuals for praise or criticism is highly threatening. Apart from this, there is considerable variation as to the system of performance assessment across countries. Therefore, the development and application of suitable performance appraisal systems for expatriates require extreme care. In addition, the active involvement of the expatriate, home country supervisor, and host country supervisor is very essential.

While the expatriate is on assignment, the individual performance must be appraised. For the expatriate, in contrast to domestic, MNEs need to evaluate not only the dimension of performance, but also several other job-related factors such as cross-cultural interpersonal qualities, sensitivity to foreign norms, laws and customs, and adaptability to uncertain and unpredictable conditions. Units within a large MNE may pursue different strategic missions, face different legal conditions, and encounter far different competitive situations. Consequently, MNEs must account for these environmental conditions when constructing appraisal formats.

An effective performance management system also has to deal with the challenges of comparing subsidiary managers in different countries. For example, it is difficult to compare the performance of an Indian subsidiary manager with that of a Russian manager because each manager works under quite different environmental conditions. Also, it is equally challenging to evaluate the performance of the various subsidiary employees.

Compensation and benefits: The key components of international compensation include base salary, foreign service inducement/hardship programme, allowances, and benefits. As a starting point, multinational firms need to match their compensation policies with their staffing policies and general HR philosophy. Compensation policies within each subsidiary must be consistent with the local market, wage legislation and regulations, union influences, and cultural preferences. At the same time, the subsidiary's compensation system must provide an adequate level of strategic consistency within the MNC's overall business strategy. Besides dealing with a pay system tailored for host country employees, the subsidiary HR manager must deal with a separate system applicable to home country expatriates and third country nationals working for the subsidiary.

Most expatriate compensation plans are designed to achieve four major objectives:

1. Attract employees who are qualified and interested in international assignments.
2. Facilitate the movement of expatriates from one subsidiary to another, from home to subsidiaries, and from subsidiaries to back home.
3. Provide a consistent and reasonable relationship between the pay levels of employees at headquarters, domestic affiliates, and foreign subsidiaries.
4. Ensure cost-effectiveness by reducing unnecessary expenses.

There are a variety of factors that affect compensation systems within MNCs. MNC compensation systems are influenced by internal business factors such as varying wage costs, levels of job security, and differing business strategies. Besides, the cultural preferences may influence the type of compensation system that is appropriate to the organisation. In high power distance cultures, compensation systems should reflect hierarchical divisions within the firm; if we relate specific cultural dimensions to pay systems. In contrast, compensation systems in low power distance cultures should be more egalitarian, with relatively minor differences between the top and bottom earners. In individualistic cultures, compensation systems should reward individual achievement, and in collective cultures, pay should be group-based or seniority-based.

Some of the key issues in compensating the expatriate are:

- How can MNEs develop pay structures that are cost-effective, fair, and adaptable to different employee groups?
- How can MNEs develop more culturally sensitive compensation schemes that recognise country differences, yet are equally motivating and still equitable?
- How can international-assignee compensation be better linked to the strategy and industry characteristics of a given MNE?

Training: To maximise training efficiency, the international HR manager should select and develop training programmes that best fit the particular assignment and individual. Four aspects are to be considered in selecting the type of training programme needed: (1) business strategy, (2) job requirements, (3) cultural similarities and dissimilarities, and (4) communication with local nationals. The difficulty and degree of communication with local nationals must also be considered in deciding the necessary level of cross-cultural training.

Labour relations: In international labour relations, it is important to realise that it is difficult to compare industrial relations systems and behaviour across national boundaries. A labour relations concept may change considerably when translated from one industrial relations context to another. The concept of collective bargaining, for example, in the United States is understood to mean negotiations between a labour union and local management; while in Sweden and Germany the term refers to negotiations between an employers' organisation and a trade union at the industry level. Cross-national differences also emerge as to the objectives of the collective bargaining process and the enforceability of collective agreements. Many European unions view the collective bargaining process as an ongoing class struggle between labour and capital, whereas in the U.S. union leaders tend toward a pragmatic economic view of collective bargaining rather than an ideological view. The trade union structure also varies from one country to that of another. Hence, the multinationals advocate for flexible industrial relations policies to adapt to local requirements.

IHRM MANAGER

When compared with domestic human resource management, IHRM requires a much broader perspective for even the most common HR activities. This is particularly so for HR managers operating from the multinational corporation's headquarters location. The number and variety of IHRM activities are increasing day-to-day. International HR manager must deal with varying issues like international taxation; international relocation and orientation; various other administrative services for expatriates; selecting, training, and appraising local and international employees; and managing host government relations in a number of countries around the world. Even when dealing with one particular HR functional area such as compensation, the international HR manager is faced with a great variety of national and international pay issues. He must coordinate pay systems in different countries with different currencies that may change in relative value to one another over a time period.

Human resource managers in MNCs must integrate human resource policies and practices across a number of subsidiaries in different countries, so that overall corporate objectives can be achieved. At the same time, the approach to HR functions must be sufficiently flexible to allow for significant differences in the types of HR policies and practices that are most effective in different business and cultural settings.

The role of a subsidiary HR manager is to develop HR practices that are acceptable within the local culture, and also to the management at the MNC's headquarters. The balancing of these two requirements is a difficult task. The procedures and policies developed must be consistent with the host country's legal requirements and cultural traditions. Cross-cultural interpersonal skills; sensitivity to foreign norms and values; and ease of adaptation to unfamiliar environments are just a few of the managerial characteristics when selecting international managers.

In their international manager, a company normally looks for the leadership skills; the intellect, flexibility, courage, and imagination; a broad knowledge of the history, culture, law and language; and the willingness to be a team-member who can work with multinational project groups in different countries and varying cultures.

Exhibit 1.1

Characteristics of International/Global HR Manager

- Strategic awareness
- Aaptability to new situations
- Sensitivity to different cultures
- Ability to work in international teams
- Ability to manage change and transition
- Open-minded and flexible in thought and tactics
- Resilient, resourceful, optimistic, and energetic
- Honesty and integrity
- Ability to learn and transfer knowledge
- Cross-cultural communication skills

→

- International negotiating skills
- Open and non-judgemental personality
- Awareness of cultural background
- Intellectual ability
- Self-esteem
- Relationship building skills
- Managerial skills
- High task and result orientation
- Language skills
- Understanding international marketing

HRM IN MULTINATIONAL ENTERPRISES

A multinational corporation is defined as an enterprise that has an interlocking network of subsidiaries in several countries. Human resource departments in most MNCs administer the human resource functions keeping in view their own social, cultural, legal, economic, political, and historical characteristics.

The growing importance of MNEs and the use of complex global business decisions have generated a linkage of IHRM with the strategic needs of the business and developed a strategic perspective of IHRM. IHRM policies and practices relevant to the needs of MNEs include those related to planning, staffing, appraising, compensating, training and developing, and labour relations. To illustrate, an MNE might have an HR policy that indicates that better performance will be rewarded. Within the framework of this general statement, each MNE unit could be free to develop its own specific practices that are simultaneously consistent with local conditions and the general policy.

One of IHRM task relates to selection and repatriation of international assignees as well as how to compensate these employees. Apart from this, it focuses on managerial training and development, largely to develop a global management cadre. Accordingly, the resources devoted to and the location of IHRM operations can be expected to vary considerably across MNEs. The question for the multinational firm is how to maintain and leverage its human resources so that suitably trained and internationally oriented personnel are available to support its strategic responses and contribute to its core competencies.

STANDARDISATION AND ADAPTATION OF WORK PRACTICES

The International Labour Organisation (ILO) has identified a number of workplace related principles that should be adhered to by all nations. In 1997, the ILO adopted a code of conduct for MNCs. From this it is obvious that corporate culture and practices that have been successful elsewhere cannot be transplanted in the host country just like that. This depends on the receptivity of the local workforce to the corporate norms of behaviour, the effectiveness of expatriates as agents of socialisation, and whether cost considerations have led multinationals to localise management prematurely. MNCs have to learn how to deal with people of other cultures of the world and how to manage them.

In both the domestic and international environment, it is important to understand the current state of the environment and to monitor and predict changes. When a company sets itself in a new location, it emphasises on learning the local customs, laws, values, and so on. The expatriates, who become fluent in the host country language, provide subsidiary staff with access to information in their own language so that the language barrier is overcome. The four major areas of international environment are economic, politico-legal, socio-cultural, and technological.

- *Economic*: The internal organisation must be concerned with various aspects of international trade, such as the extent of control on imports and exports, and on foreign investors.
- *Politico-legal*: While contemplating involvement with a foreign country, MNCs are primarily concerned with the stability of its political system, the economic and political philosophy of the party in office, the attitudes of powerful opposition parties, and the prevalence of red-tapism in country's bureaucracy.
- *Socio-cultural*: To be successful, the business manager must be aware of and adapt to potentially large number of diverse societies. In addition to everyday cultural characteristics, it is helpful to be familiar with the country's social structure.
- *Technological*: The managers must be aware of the level of technological advancement in the host country. Even with the enthusiastic backing of the host government, the introduction of new technology may not always be immediately successful.

Any business is done in environments of different textures – social, cultural, economic, political, and technical. International business is not an exception to this impingement of environment. International firms and their management need to understand the impact of the economic development in the international business environment. Differences in the living standards between the developed and the developing countries have far reaching implications on the business growth and opportunities among them. The context in which international human resource management has to function, therefore, is decided by these environment flows. IHRM professionals have their hands full with the different types of influences they are supposed to face while carrying out their responsibilities. Hence, having the right people in the right place at the right time emerges as the key to a company's international growth.

DOMESTIC AND INTERNATIONAL HRM

In broad terms, international HRM involves the same activities as domestic HRM, though domestic HRM is involved with employees within one national boundary. HR managers working in a domestic environment generally administer programmes for a single national group of employees who are covered by a uniform HR policy. HR managers working in an international environment face the problem of designing and administering programmes for more than one national group of employees. They need to take broader view of issues. The HR department must ensure that the expatriate employee understands housing arrangements, health care, and all aspects of the compensation package and benefits provided for the assignment.

Major external factors that influence international HRM are the type of government, the state of the economy, and the generally accepted practices of doing business in each of the various host countries in which the multinational operates. As the international business involves considerable interaction and movement of people across national boundaries, an appreciation of cultural differences is important and essential.

As indicated by Morgan, the main characteristics of IHRM lie in the complexities of operating in different countries with different categories of employees. Though on the face of it HRM activities remain the same both in the domestic and international arenas, there are varying degrees of intensity with which the complexities arising out of IHRM activities have to be addressed. P.J. Dowling[3] (1988) attributes these complexities to: (i) more HR activities; (ii) more heterogeneous functions; (iii) more involvement in employees' personal lives; (iv) change in emphasis as the workforce mix of PCNs and TCNs varies; (v) risk exposure; and (vi) more external influences.

More HR Activities: In order to operate in an international environment, the HR department must involve itself in a number of activities that would not be necessary in a domestic environment such as, international taxation, international relocation and orientation, administrative services for expatriates, host government relations, and language translation services.

International taxation: Among the various laws one has to abide by in a foreign country to continue the company's operation there, income tax laws are those that cannot obviously be evaded or avoided. At the same time, the expatriate cannot afford to do away with taxation in his country of origin. Sometimes, this may lead to double taxation. This is a disincentive for anyone to take up a foreign assignment. Therefore, IHRM has to take care of compensating the individual adequately so that he does not feel the pinch of double taxation. This may give rise to anomaly in the salary structure of employees in the home country. A tax equalisation policy has to be designed by the IHRM personnel.

International relocation and orientation: Whenever a transfer of an employee takes place within the country, the HR professional is not burdened with the additional responsibility of arranging the employee's passage from one location to another. His job simply is to provide transfer expenses to the employee as per rules and regulations of the company. But in the case of an expatriate, the job of arranging passports, visas, tickets, immigration and travel details, accommodation, recreation, and schooling information falls on the IHRM professional; not only for the concerned expatriate, but also for his/her spouse and family. Finalising compensation details such as delivery of salary overseas, and determination of various overseas allowances are the extra responsibilities added on to IHRM. Further, the training of the expatriate to prepare him to cope with the new environment and culture is an added activity. For domestic HRM personnel this is not an issue because the cultural impact of workers/employees will be homogenous. Once the expatriate reaches foreign soil, the orientation that has to be given is certainly different from what it is at home.

Administrative services for expatriates: A multinational firm needs to provide administrative services for expatriates in the host countries in which it operates. Providing administrative services can often be a time-consuming and complex activity because policies and procedures are not always clear-cut and may conflict with local conditions. For example, if in the host country (which is not secular) there is a requirement that a place of worship has to be provided for the employees, but in the parent country (which is a secular state) there is no such provision. HRM has to address this dichotomy administratively to suit local diktats. These issues add to the complexities of providing administrative services to expatriates.

Host government relations: This aspect is an important activity for an HR department, particularly in developing countries where work permits and other important certificates often are obtained more easily when a personal relationship exists between the relevant government officials and multinational managers. Maintaining such relationships helps resolve potential problems that can be caused by ambiguous eligibility and/or compliance criteria for documentation such as work permits but this can at times become quite volatile.

Language translation services: This service for internal and external correspondence is an additional international activity for the HR department. Morgan notes that if the HR department is the major user of language translation services, the role of this translation is often expanded to provide such services to all foreign operation departments within the multinational.

More Heterogeneous Functions: Effective performance of different IHRM functions definitely requires more diverse and in-depth understanding of various countries' culture, government policies, and needs of more heterogeneous employee groups.

It is well known that HR managers working in an international environment have to deal with more than one national group of employees (e.g., PCN, HCN and TCN). Therefore, narrow domestic walls have to be removed and parochialism, regionalism or even nationalism cannot, or should not, find its way into the operation and administration of programmes for the multinationals. For designing and administering programmes for more than one national group of employees, the HR managers need to take a broader view of issues. For example, a broader and more international perspective on expatriate benefits would endorse the view that all expatriate employees, regardless of nationality, should receive a foreign service or expatriate premium when working in a foreign location. Even in domestic HRM, partialities due to regionalism should be shunned. All the more so, IHRM should be bereft of this attitude and embrace a broader perspective for the employees.

More Involvement in Employees' Personal Lives: In the domestic environment, the HR department's involvement with an employee's family is limited. But in the international environment, the department should be sufficiently involved in order to provide the level of support required and to know more about the employee's personal life. For example, despite the best effort of a company to avoid any discriminatory selection process, a married person may be rejected just to escape some of the stringent legislations in the matter of immigration into the country of posting. Even if the employee has to be sent single to the host country, the family's requirements in the absence of the employee need to be taken care of by the HR department. These can range from housing, education of children, health benefits, and so on. Sometimes, the HR department has to take care of the children left behind in boarding schools when both husband and wife stay together in the host country on an assignment from parent country. For a domestic assignment, most of these matters either would not arise or would be primarily the employee's responsibility rather than that of the HR department.

Change in Emphasis as the Workforce Mix of PCNs and TCNs Varies: As foreign operations mature, the emphasis put on various human resource activities change. For example, as the need for PCNs and TCNs declines and more trained locals become available, resources previously allocated to areas such as expatriate taxation, relocation, and orientation are transferred to activities such as local staff selection, training, and management development. The latter activity may require establishment of a programme to bring high-potential local staff to corporate headquarters for development assignments. The need to change emphasis in HR operations, as a foreign subsidiary matures, is clearly a factor that broadens the responsibilities of local HR activities.

Risk Exposure: Frequently, the human and financial consequences of failure in the international arena are more severe than in the domestic business. For example, expatriate failure (the premature return of an expatriate from an international assignment) is a potentially high-cost problem for international companies. Direct costs (salary, training costs, and travel and relocation expenses) per failure to the parent firm may be as high as three times the domestic salary plus relocation expenses, depending on currency exchange rates and location of assignments. Indirect costs such as loss of market share and damage to international customer relationships may be considerable.

Risk exposure is high in domestic HRM. Depending on the countries where the MNC operates, the headquarters and subsidiary HR managers may also have to worry about the physical safety of the employees. In many countries, kidnapping and terrorism are common and international HR managers must learn to live with them. In the recent past, Taliban activities in Afghanistan took an Indian engineer hostage and killed him to press their demand that all Indians should leave their country within twenty-four hours. Terrorism poses a great risk to international operations.

More External Influences: Major external factors that influence international HRM are the type of government, the state of the economy, and the generally accepted practices of doing business in each of the various host countries in which the multinational operates. Morgan proposed an additional factor, risk exposure which differentiates domestic from international HRM. According to him, business operation in an international context exposes an organisation to more political and financial risks.

Countries like the US and UK are now-a-days careful about outsourcing their activities for the fear that personnel from countries like India or China will displace their own workforce and create unemployment. Also, they are imposing various restrictions on foreign nationals in their own countries. The legal framework of the host countries are another parameter within which HR managers need to operate. The subsidiary HR manager must spend more time for learning and interpreting the local ways of doing business and the general code of conduct regarding activities such as giving gifts. It is also likely that the subsidiary HR manager will become more involved in administering benefits either provided or financed by the multinational such as housing, education, and other facilities not readily available in the local economy.

International HRM differs from domestic HRM in five major dimensions:

Wider nationalities: IHRM deals with the employees drawn from a number of nationals in contrast to domestic HRM, where employees are drawn from one nation. People from different nations come with a variety of cultures, values, ethical interpretations, religious beliefs, and the like. Behaviour of people does also vary based on geographical regions.

Broader relations and complexities: Organisations seek the information on broader aspects of employees and their family members while recruiting and selecting employees from foreign countries. These aspects include age, health, educational qualifications, driving skills, criminal record of employee and his/her family members. Organisations arrange work permit, visas and resident permits for employees and their family members. In addition, organisations also arrange for socialisation of employee and family members with the local community and also various welfare amenities for them. Domestic HRM is not concerned with this relationship as the relationship among the people of the same nation or community have already been built and developed.

Influence of international environment: International environment has become complex, highly competitive, dynamic, vibrant and interdependent. The emergence of World Trade Organisation, increased phase of globalisation of all facets of business, widening scope of regional integrations and strides in information technology transformed the domestic environment of most of the countries into international environment. In other words, the gulf between domestic environment and international environment is narrowing down. The domestic HRM practices are mostly influenced by its economic, political, technical and social factors while IHRM is influenced by environmental factors of host country/domestic country as well as various foreign countries, thus, delineating the distinction between IHRM and domestic HRM.

Enduring complexities of IHRM activities: Expatriates in case of MNCs comprise of home country nationals, host country nationals, and third country nationals. Expatriates in case of a purely domestic company include foreigners. Thus, IHRM deals with expatriates and nationals, whereas domestic HRM deals exclusively with nationals.

Variety of functions and approaches: International human resource managers perform certain additional functions as compared to domestic human resource managers. Domestic HR managers in purely domestic companies perform usual HR functions unlike international HR managers who normally carry-out certain additional functions with different approaches and magnitude. The international HR manager has to follow different approaches for different nationals unlike the domestic HR manager who normally follows a uniform approach as the employees belong to one nation.

Apart from the complexities involved in IHRM more than in domestic HRM, P.J. Dowling[4] enumerates four other variables that contribute to the differences between domestic and international HRM. These are: (1) the cultural environment; (2) the industry/industries with which the multinational is primarily involved; (3) the extent of reliance of the multinational on its home country domestic market; and (4) the attitude of senior management. These four additional variables are discussed below:

The Cultural Environment: The word 'culture' many a time is confused with nation but it should not be assumed that national differences necessarily represent cultural differences. Culture normally describes a shaping process; that is, members of a group or society share a distinct way of life with common values, attitudes, and behaviours.

Any one travelling abroad, either as a tourist or business person, experiences situations that demonstrate cultural differences in language, food, dress, hygiene, and attitude to time. They experience culture shock — a phenomenon experienced by people who move across cultures. Normally, there is a tendency to believe that what has worked successfully for so long in one culture should work in another environment also. This is what researchers call an '*etic*' approach to culture. According to them, the '*emic*' approach, on the contrary, is culture specific. However, each culture is unique in nature and the employee should adapt himself/herself to the new culture rather try to change it to suit oneself. Being aware of the local culture and adapting oneself to it enables one to cope with the requirements of the local market with much better responsiveness than a person who thinks what is done back home is the best way of doing it. This naturally leads to global efficiency and organisational learning.

Industry Type: Porter[5] suggests that the industry or industries (if the firm is a conglomerate) in which a multinational firm is involved is of considerable importance because patterns of international competition vary widely from one industry to another. The global industry is not merely a collection of domestic industries but a series of linked domestic industries in which the rivals compete against each other on a truly worldwide basis.

Depending on the industry, global competition varies and accordingly HRM activities also vary. What is most talked about these days as a blue chip industry is information technology (IT) which has suddenly taken Indians all over the world. This industry has definitely earned India pride of place in the global arena. Nevertheless, the same cannot be said of all other industries, though Indian presence is felt all over the world in diverse industries. Each of these industries has its own way of managing their human capital.

Reliance of the Multinational on its Home Country Domestic Market: It is often assumed that a global market perspective would be dominant in a firm's culture and thinking because of the large size of its operations. But size is not the only key variable when looking at a multinational; the extent of reliance of the multinational on its home country domestic market is also very important. A very large domestic market influences all aspects of how a multinational organises its IT activities. Such a market will also influence the attitude of senior managers towards their international activities. Processes that have succeeded in the domestic market are likely to find favour in the international market as well.

Attitude of Senior Management: It is likely that if senior management does not have a strong international orientation, the importance of international operations may be under-emphasised in terms of corporate goals and objectives. In such situations, managers may tend to focus on domestic issues and minimise differences between international and domestic environments. They may assume that there is a great deal of transferability between domestic and international HRM practices. This failure to recognise differences in managing human resources in foreign environments frequently results in major difficulties in international operations.

ENDURING CONTEXT OF IHRM

Just as HR professionals are strategic partners in business in domestic HRM, so also are they in IHRM. It becomes, therefore, a necessity for IHRM to live up to the vicissitudes of the global environment. This environment is fraught with perils, political events, and economic changes. These at times can be facilitators of internationalisation and at times barriers to the same. The balancing act is done mostly by human beings and so they have to be managed more effectively. The concept of the world becoming a global village is only indicative of the interdependency among countries. The complexities arising out of this are also enormous.

Trade agreements such as the World Trade Organisation (WTO) and regional integration of countries such as the European Union (EU) have accentuated this interdependency.

Division of Labour

Since human considerations are more important than financial ones in international business, we shall look at the increased relevance of the division of labour, which developed as a concept some centuries ago. In the existence of a sprawling global network, carrying on business single handedly is difficult indeed. Even at the unit level in a single location, demands for specialisation are common today, especially due to the existence of the sophisticated technology.

Adam Smith is more typically referred by economists for his contributions to classical economic doctrine. His discussion in *The Wealth of Nations* (1776) included a brilliant argument on the economic advantages that organisations and society would reap from the division of labour. Smith used the pin manufacturing industry for his example. He concluded that division of labour raised productivity by increasing each worker's skill and dexterity, by saving time that is commonly lost in changing tasks, and by encouraging the creation of labour-saving inventions and machinery.

Division of labour which started at a micro level three centuries back, is now part of practical experience in the international arena as well as in domestic business. As the world has shrunk due to the development in telecommunication links and electronic media, interdependence on various disciplines is a necessity. Now-a-days, we do not stop with specialisation but go into super specialisation.

Forces for Change

The international firm, irrespective of size and geographic reach, faces continuing forces for change that affect its characteristics and operations, which in turn plays certain demands on its management. The key trends that are generally accepted to be forces for change in the current global workplace are: (a) global competition, (b) growth in mergers, acquisitions and alliances, (c) organisation restructuring, and (d) advances in technology and telecommunications.

Working life has changed rapidly since the 1980s ended the era of a stable economy dominated by the manufacturing industry. A new step in the progress of globalisation was taken with the closure of the General Agreement on Tariffs and Trade (GATT). Its successor, the World Trade Organisation (WTO) was given a special mission to promote free trade and simultaneously generate agreements and rules for global economic operations. Globalisation was also promoted by the worldwide introduction of new information and communication technologies that have radically changed the time and space dimensions of global economies, including work life.

The impact of globalisation is universal. The process of globalisation affects every workplace in the world either positively or negatively. Numerous positive effects (for e.g., growth of world trade, new employment opportunities, closure international collaboration, and vulnerability to a global recession) are already visible. Also, a number of adverse consequences have occurred (e.g., high unemployment, growing economic gaps between and within countries, and overwhelming domination of economic values over social values).

With the spread and diversity of international business and their involvement in global activities, it is generally felt that the levels of competition are increasing. Therefore, concerns have been expressed about standardised work practices of multinationals and also stakeholder pressure. Increased global competition not only has an impact on a firm's competitive position but also on issues such as business ethics and social responsibility of multinationals, and this needs the attention of HR managers. A contributing element of, and also response to global competition has been an increase in the number of mergers and acquisitions.

It has been recognised that as a consequence of growth and changes in their environment, firms constantly realign their operations and activities to support changes in strategic directions. The past decades have seen large-scale downsizing as firms outsource activities, sell underperforming units, engage in plant rationalisation, integrate acquired operations and merge businesses. Organisational restructuring is again an outcome or fall-out of global competition.

A striking example of advance in technology and telecommunication has been the rapid adoption of the internet. India is currently in the midst of an e-commerce revolution. As a consequence of the above forces of change, there is need for flexibility in terms of management approaches and action. Multinationals need to have: (a) flexibility of freedom of operations, (b) local responsiveness, (c) knowledge sharing, and (d) transfer of competence to manage people. We have to be alive to local situations and adapt ourselves to them so as to quickly respond to the same. That is why the mantra of the 1990s used to be 'think global, act local' – a slogan which makes managers in multinationals realise that subsidiaries require the freedom to act according to their local environment, and simultaneously have an overall view of the firm's global position.

In the context of multinationals, competition has to blossom into coordination and collaboration – even among competitors. Knowledge explosion has made everyone realise that all are not well versed in every aspect of technology and market. Therefore, today it is essential to share knowledge and information in order to survive and grow. Organisations need to provide proper communication networks that promote knowledge sharing. Along with this, employees are also to be trained and developed in the required competencies that are regarded as a source of competitive advantage. To achieve this goal, the management should identify what are the core competencies of the organisation to be nurtured in order to gain competitive advantage.

SUMMARY

- *The environment of international human resource management* traces the conceptual framework of IHRM.
- International human resource management may be defined as performing HRM and its related activities, and necessary immigration facilities for prospective and current expatriate employees by organisations operating in domestic and/or foreign countries.
- The forces which have an impact on IHRM are global competition; mergers, acquisitions and alliances; and organisational restructuring and advances in technology and telecommunication.
- The multinational management has to deal with the various forces through flexibility, local responsiveness, knowledge sharing and transfer of competence.
- The complexity involved in operating in different countries by employing different national categories of employees is a key variable differentiating domestic and international HR.
- International HRM differs from domestic HRM in six major dimensions like: (i) wider nationalities of employees, (ii) variety of functions to be performed, (iii) influence of international environment, (iv) broader and deeper relationships, (v) different approaches for the domestic functions, and (vi) enduring complexity of domestic HRM activities.
- There are four other variables that moderate differences between domestic and international HRM: the cultural environment, the industry (or industries) with which the multinational is primarily involved, the extent of reliance of the multinational on its home country domestic market, and the attitudes of senior management.
- There is a need for an expanded view of the role of HRM in an international operation.
- Global human resource manager formulates global human resource policies, oversees the human resource policies of various regions, and collaborates with the regional human resource managers.

REVIEW QUESTIONS

1. What are the factors that influence today's business environment?
2. Define the term 'international human resource management'.
3. What are the main similarities and differences between domestic and international HRM?

4. What are the different activities involved in international human resource management?
5. What are the different enduring complexities of international human resource management?
6. Global HR manager formulates global human resource policies, oversees the human resource policies of various regions, and collaborates with the regional human resource managers. Elucidate.

REFERENCES

1. P. Morgan, *"International Human Resource Management: Fact or Fiction"*, Personnel Administrator, Vol. 31, No. 9, 1986.
2. Paul Sparrow, *"Convergence or Divergence: Human Resource Practices and Policies for Competitive Advantage Worldwide"*, Readings and Cases in International Human Resource Management, South-Western College Publishing, Cincinnati, OH, 2000.
3. P.J. *"Dowling, International and Domestic Personnel/Human Resource Management: Similarities and Differences"*, Readings in Personnel and Human Resource Management, 3rd edition, West Publishing.
4. Peter J. *"Dowling, Completing the Puzzle: Issues in the Development of the Field of International Human Resource Management"*, Management International Review, Special Issue, No. 3, 1999.
5. M.E. Porter, *"Changing Patterns of International Competition"*, California Management Review, Vol. 28, No. 2, 1986.

2

Organisational Context of IHRM

Objectives

- To explain different approaches adopted by managers in building multinationa organisations.
- To describe organisational structures in MNCs.
- To understand the control and coordination mechanisms.
- To appreciate different modes of operation like contractual operation an cooperative operation.

INTRODUCTION

The international human resource management examines the way in whic international organisations manage their human resources in different national contexts. Tl human resource function does not operate in a vacuum. As with other areas of organisatio the shift from a domestic to a global focus affects the HR functions to a considerable exte HR activities are determined by various organisational factors such as stages internationalisation, organisational structure, mode of operation in the various forei markets, and methods of control and coordination. To a certain extent, how the firm co with HR demands of its various foreign subsidiaries determine its ability to execute chos expansion strategies. Organisations working across national boundaries, therefore, have to agree on HR policies and practices which maintain some coherence while still being sensitive to critical aspects of difference.

STAGES OF INTERNATIONALISATION

Many multinationals go through the evolution from a domestic to a truly global organisation. P.J. Dowling and D.E. Dowling[1] indicate the diverse stages involved in this evolution process. Not all firms go through these stages sequentially. Though a few companies skip some of the stages and become global faster, others may go through all the stages at a faster rate than others, depending upon their already available networks. Invariably, the number of steps or stages, along the path to multinational status varies from firm-to-firm, as does the timeframe involved. Linked to this evolutionary process are structural responses, control mechanisms, and HRM policies.

Exporting, one of the early stages of internationalisation involves manufacturing the products in a centralised location and exporting them to other national markets. Exporting avoids the cost of establishing manufacturing facilities in the host country, which is substantial. It takes advantage of experience curve effects and location economies. Exporting will not be a profitable proposition when there is a possibility of manufacturing the products in favourable, low cost location away from company's home base. Another limitation is the high transport expenditure involved in exporting bulky items. Hence, many multinational companies manufacture their products in various regions. Moreover, the threat of tariff barriers by governments of host countries will make exporting uneconomical.

Exporting is typically the initial stage for firms entering international operations. As such, it rarely involves much organisational response until the level of export sales reaches a critical point. Of course, simple exporting may be difficult for service companies (such as legal firms) so that they may be forced to make an early step into foreign direct investment operations (via a branch office, or joint venture[2]).

Alternately, some companies try out international licensing. This involves an arrangement by which a foreign licensee buys the rights to manufacture a company's product in the licensee's country for a negotiated fee. Licensing is pursued as a strategy by manufacturing companies. The licensee has to make arrangements for the resources required for overseas operations.

The marketing or sales manager of the firm typically is responsible for setting up export activities. As foreign sales increase, an export manager will be appointed and given the responsibility for developing and maintaining customers, interacting with the firm's intermediaries and planning for overall market expansion. A firm starting international operations will usually hire an export manager from outside rather than promote from within. The reason is that knowledge of the product or industry is less important than international experience. Promoting an export manager from within and who does not have knowledge of the export market or the technology means that the firm would incur a huge cost for him to acquire this knowledge and wait for a longer time until he acquires it.

As the firm progresses from exporting to foreign involvement, human resources planning activities will initially focus on the need *vis-a-vis* various markets and functions. Existing personnel can be assessed and plans made to recruit, select and train employees for positions that cannot be filled internally. The four major categories of employees for overseas assignments are: (a) CEO – to oversee and direct the entire operation; (b) functional head – to establish and maintain departments and ensure their proper function; (c) trouble shooters – who are utilised for their special expertise in analysing, and thereby preventing or solving particular problems; and (d) white or blue-collar workers.

One of the major sources of competitive advantage of global corporations is their ability to attract talent from around the world. The corporations need effective management development systems, with the objective of creating and carefully allocating management personnel.

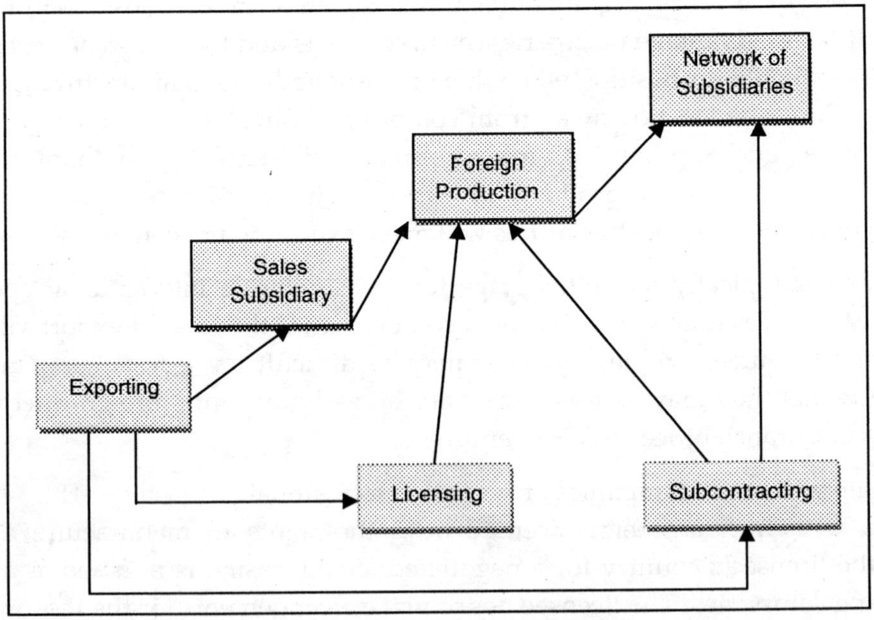

Fig. 2.1: Stages of Internationalisation

Source: Dowling *et. al.*, (2001), *International Resource Management*, p. 34.

ORGANISATIONAL STRUCTURE

Organisations are economic and social entities in which a number of persons perform multifarious tasks in order to attain common goals. Organisations are effective instrumen in that they help individuals accomplish personal objectives that they cannot achieve alone. According to Argyris, organisations are usually formed to satisfy objectives that can best be met collectively. Organisation is only a means to an end. It takes certain inputs from the environment and converts them into specified outputs desired by the society.

Organisational design deals with structural aspects of organisation. It aims at analysing roles and relationships so that collective effort can be explicitly organised to achieve specific ends. The design process leads to the development of an organisational structure consisting of units and positions.

As the organisation grows in foreign production/service/market size, it moves towards standardisation and diversification. This sheer magnitude of operations spread across the world makes the business unmanageable. A number of typologies of organisational firms that have been developed denote a move away from hierarchical structures towards hierarchical, transnational, and network structures.

Broadly, different forms of organisational structure that can be created to support business activity are:

Geographic divisional structure: It involves each country being a separate business activity in its own right within the overall corporate structure. Each division might have a full set of business functions (including HR) under the leadership of a divisional manager.

International divisional structure: All international activities of the business would be amalgamated within a single international division.

Product structure: Each type of product or service would form the basis of a division, for example, an automotive division; an aircraft division; and a general engineering division. Wherever they are based in the world, each local unit would report to its product division.

Functional structure: The organisational structure in which each function reports through its line managers to the functional director at the top of the organisation. For HR that would mean that each location would report to a regional HR manager and ultimately to the HR director.

Holding company structure: A number of separate companies within the group that are responsible for their own profitability and success. They have a high degree of autonomy over internal activity (including HR) with headquarters acting primarily as financier.

Matrix structure: In the matrix structure, horizontal differentiation process is across two dimensions: product division and geographic area. Its objective is that responsibility for operating decisions pertaining to a particular product should be shared by the product division and the various areas of the firm. In a classic metric structure, giving product divisions and geographical areas equal status within the organisation reinforces the idea of dual responsibility. Individual managers thus belong to two hierarchies (a divisional hierarchy and an area hierarchy) and have two bosses accordingly.

The reality of the global matrix structure is that it often does not work as the theory predicts. In practice, the metrics is often clumsy and bureaucratic. Normally, it requires so many meetings that it is difficult to get any work done. The need to get an area and a product division to reach a decision can slow down decision making and produce an inflexible organisation unable to respond quickly to market shifts or to innovate. The dual hierarchy structure can lead to conflict and perpetual power struggles between the area and the product divisions, catching many managers in the middle. In the light of these problems, many transnational firms are now trying to build flexible metric structures based more on firm-wide networks and a shared culture and vision than on a right hierarchical arrangement. Within such companies, informal structure plays a greater role than the formal structure.

Bartlett and Ghoshal[2] (1990) observe that, in practice, particularly in the international context, the matrix has proven to be all but unmanageable. They have forwarded four problems with matrix structure: (a) the dual reporting leading to conflict and confusion; (b) the increasing complexity of communication channel creating information overload; (c) overlapping responsibilities leading to ego conflicts and loss of accountability; and (d) the barriers such as distance, language, time and culture leading to more confusion in terms of decision making. They conclude that the most successful multinationals today focus less on searching for the ideal structure, and more on developing the abilities, behaviour, and performance of individual managers. In this process, individual capabilities are captured and the entire firm is motivated to respond cooperatively to a complicated and dynamic environment. If, however, the multinational opts for a matrix structure, particular care must be taken in its staffing function.

Mixed structure: In an attempt to manage the growth of diverse operations, some firms have opted for what can only be described as a mixed form. Although all structural forms are complex and difficult to manage effectively, given a firm's developing capabilities and experience at each new stage, mixed structures appear even more complex and harder to explain, implement, and control. However, it is important that all employees must understand the mixed structure and its supporting mechanisms, such as corporate identity, interpersonal relationships, management attitudes, and HR systems, particularly promotion and reward policies.

Heterarchy: The heterarchy is a structural form proposed by Hedlund[3] which recognises that a multinational may have a number of different kinds of centres apart from the traditional centre referred to as "headquarters". Hedlund argued that competitive advantage does not necessarily reside in any one country. Rather, it may be found in many countries; where each subsidiary centre may be simultaneously a centre and a global coordinator of discreet activities, thus performing a strategic role not just for itself, but for the MNE as a whole. From a HRM perspective, the heterarchy is interesting in that its success appears to rest solely on the ability of the multinational to formulate, implement, and reinforce the required human resource elements. Hedlund recognises that the heterarchy demands skilful and experienced personnel as well as sophisticated reward and punishment systems in order to develop the normative control mechanisms necessary for effective performance. Heterarchical structure of a MNC proposes lesser reliance on control mechanism from headquarter and increasing empowerment for decision making to its subsidiary units in the host country.

Joint venture: It refers to an agreement in which two or more partners own and control an overseas business. The business is located in the home country of one of the partners. The advantages of joint venture are improved efficiency, access to knowledge, and restriction in competition. In the context of strategic management, international joint ventures play a special role as a key form of strategic alliance, which is increasingly being used by MNCs.

Transnational: The term transnational has been coined to describe a new organisational form that is characterised by an interdependence of resources and responsibilities across all business units regardless of national boundaries. The transnational tries to cope with the large flows of components, products, resources, people, and information among its subsidiaries, while simultaneously recognising the distributed specialised resources and capabilities. As such, it demands a complex process of coordination and cooperation involving strong cross-unit integrating devices, a strong corporate identity, and a well-developed worldwide management perspective.

Transnational organisations aim to develop a truly global culture and mindset amongst their employees. As a matter of fact, the heterarchy and the transnational share a common factor with respect to the human resource spectrum. Hence, transnational managers should be developed to think and act across national and subsidiary boundaries. Staff transfers play a critical role in integration and coordination.

Network organisation: Some MNCs are linked formally via the organisational structure and standardised procedures, but they are informally so through interpersonal contact and socialisation which is otherwise known as networking. Apart from the intraorganisational network (comprising of headquarters and the numerous subsidiaries), each subsidiary also has a range of external relationships (involving local suppliers, customers, competitors, host governments, and alliance partners). Such a hierarchical structure has five dimensions, such as, delegation of decision making authority to appropriate units and levels; geographical dispersal of key functions across units in different countries; delayering of organisational levels; debureaucratisation of formal procedures; and differentiation of work, responsibility, and authority across the networked subsidiaries (P.J. Dowling and D.E. Welch).

Growth in the firm's international business activity does require structural responses, but the evolutionary process will differ across multinationals. Apart from the country of origin, other variables namely, size of organisation, pattern of internationalisation, and management policies also play a part in the evolution of the firm from a domestic-oriented into a global-oriented. Firms that classify themselves as global operators confront common coordination issues. Human resource management plays a key role in control and coordination processes particularly where less-hierarchical structures are concerned.

CHANGES IN ORGANISATIONAL STRUCTURES

To opposing trends consolidation and fragmentation have taken place at the same time in business organisations.

Consolidation is the result of a management philosophy that holds that companies need to expand in order to achieve efficiencies of scale, to operate globally, and to compete against multinational giants. Mergers of multinational companies and large corporations within countries that want to become multinationals are accomplished to reach the size needed for global-scale operations. Such large global companies often introduce corporate-wide policies and standards for all operation sites.

Fragmentation has been occurring at the same time because of a management philosophy that encourages decision making at the lowest practical level in the organisation in order to be able to adapt quickly to changing circumstances and to hold managers accountable for very specific well-defined operations. This trend has included management innovations known as decentralisation, delayering, and outsourcing.

In decentralisation, companies are fragmented into smaller units; managers of each unit make the important decisions rather than a central office; and each unit is held accountable for its own performance.

In delayering, organisations remove layers of management so that there are fewer positions in management or managers supervising the person actually doing the work. This management philosophy works both as a means of obtaining the greatest efficiency and to ensure that managers are in close touch with problems being faced in operating the organisation.

In outsourcing, any activity that is not directly relevant to the core business is contracted out to be done by another company or vendor. For example, a company that formally ran its own food services for employees and shipped its own products directly to customers may now contract with a food services company to run the cafeteria and a fulfilment company to ship out product orders.

IHRM APPROACHES

The IHRM literature uses four terms to describe MNE approaches to managing and staffing their subsidiaries: ethnocentric, polycentric, regiocentric, and geocentric. These terms are taken from the seminal work of Perlmutter,[4] who claimed that it was possible to identify among international executives three primary attitudes – ethnocentric, polycentric, and geocentric. To demonstrate these three attitudes, Perlmutter used various aspects of organisational design, such as decision making, evaluation and control, information flows, and complexities of organisation. A fourth attitude, namely regiocentric, was added at a later stage.

Ethnocentric: Few foreign subsidiaries have any autonomy; strategic decisions are made at headquarters. Key positions at the domestic and foreign operations are held by headquarters' management personnel. In other words, subsidiaries are managed by expatriates from the home country.

Polycentric: The MNE treats each subsidiary as a distinct national entity with some decision making autonomy. Subsidiaries are usually managed by local nationals (HCNs) who are seldom promoted to positions at headquarters. Likewise, PCNs are rarely transferred to foreign subsidiary operations.

Geocentric: In this, the MNE is taking a worldwide approach to its operations, recognising that each part (subsidiaries and headquarters) makes a unique contribution with its unique competence. It is accompanied by a worldwide integrated business, and nationality is ignored in favour of ability.

Regiocentric: It reflects the geographic strategy and structure of the multinational. Like the geocentric approach, it utilises a wider pool of managers but in a limited way. Personnel may move outside their countries but only within the particular geographic region. Regional managers may not be promoted to headquarter positions but enjoy a degree of regional autonomy in decision making.

IHRM STRATEGY AND MODEL

There cannot be any specific IHRM model which we can call a unique model. However, linking human resource practices with business strategy as propounded by Bird and Beechler[5] provides an approach to IHRM and helps evolve a model out of it.

The following model emerges out of their writings:

The Environment-business Strategy Match: One way of viewing the external environment of MNCs is to identify the nature of international competition in the industry in which a firm is involved. There are two types of industry competition – multidomestic and global. Firms strategic orientation can also be classified into two broad types cost-leadership and product differentiation. A cost-leadership strategy seeks to achieve competitive advantage by being the least-cost producer of a product, while a product differentiation strategy seeks competitive advantage by providing unique value to the product. Under a cost-leadership strategy, the internal operations of a firm command attention and the drive is for internal efficiency. On the other hand, a product differentiation strategy seeks competitive advantage through the ability to provide unique value to a product, one that will be more localised in terms of its appeal to a particular foreign market or segment. A differentiation strategy requires a firm to develop an external focus and be intimately aware of what its customer desire.

A Business Strategy – HRM Strategy Match: If an MNC's performance is based on its own capacity to internally align its operations in a way that allows it to match environmental constraints, then there must be a way to determine whether or not a firm is properly aligned with its environment. More than any other function within an MNC, the management of human resources is decentralised. With the exception of matters related to expatriates and international assignments, the vast majority of HRM affairs are handled at the level of the subsidiary. At the subsidiary level, the requirement for internal consistency and the degree of integration with the parent company is necessary for its success.

Human Resource Management Strategies: Business strategy determines how a firm competes in a given business. Firms select business strategies in accordance with: (a) the evaluations they make about the environment in which they wish to compete; and (b) the resources available within the firm. In order to develop and implement a business strategy, however, it is necessary to break it down into its various components or to develop functional strategies. These functional strategies are further broken down into policies which when implemented, become practice.

Consistency in Parent-subsidiary and HRM Strategy Alignment: Although HRM constitutes the most decentralised of all MNC functions, it is also true that the increasing globalisation of MNC has brought about an increased desire and need for greater coordination and consistency between parent and subsidiary. The need for a parent-subsidiary alignment of HRM activities may vary depending on the strategic orientation of the MNC and the nature of international competition for the industry in which it competes. There must be consistency between parent-level business strategy and subsidiary-level HRM strategy.

CONTROL MECHANISMS

In any social context, control mechanisms are both formal as well as informal. The formal mechanism embraces structure, reporting systems, budgets, performance targets, and formal communication. The informal mechanism has two major components, namely, (a) personal relationships and informal communication; and (b) corporate culture. Of the two, formal controlled mechanism is more of a bureaucratic nature which necessarily entails strict documentation.

Horizontal communication and networking of relationships with various internal and external groups of people or agencies in a personal capacity can be used for organisational advantage. It is during training programmes conducted for personnel from various parts of the world, either at the headquarters or any other common place, which usually enable international employees of the firm to come into contact with each other and develop personal rapport. What is most important for building relationships is a common language. Hence, language training for communication, both formal and informal, is a necessity.

Corporate culture is essentially a process of socialising people so that they come to share a common set of values and beliefs that shape their behaviour and perspectives. A strong corporate culture may inhibit the multinationals ability to introduce change and thus prevent the required level of local responsiveness and flexibility. In order to ensure that the corporate culture is productive, HR activities should point towards establishing corporate culture identity among the employees. Some of these activities are recruitment and selection practices, training and development programmes, reward systems, and promotion and placement of staff.

MODE OF OPERATION

According to Welch and Welch[6] internationalising organisations may adopt contractual (such as licensing, franchising, management contracts and projects and cooperative such as joint ventures) modes in order to enter and develop foreign markets. These modes are not mutually exclusive. They suggest that these forms of operation modes may demand different skills and place varying stresses on the resources of the company, particularly on its personnel.

Contractual mode: In the contractual mode, normally skills and talented staff will be needed. Knowledge transfer is an important component, involving the training of HCN staff. The overall success of the contract operation, including the training aspect, depends on the quality of staff transferred or appointed.

Cooperative mode: This means different things to different people: strategic alliance, cooperative venture, collaborative agreement, and so on. However, it is a formal and mutually agreed commercial collaboration between companies, wherein the partners pool, exchange, or integrate specified business resources for mutual gain; and yet continue with businesses. Regardless of the motive for entering into such an arrangement, the resultant partnership adds another dimension to a firm's structure.

The various forms of inter-firm linkages affect HRM in different ways depending upon the type of alliance involved. For example, in an international joint venture, a new entity that brings together managers from two or more firms, the managers must become accustomed to working with a foreign partner or partner(s). The most important task of human resource is staffing the joint venture with managers who are flexible in terms of different management styles and philosophies. Assigning managers to the joint venture, evaluating their performance, handling their career path, and compensation and benefits are some of the HR issues and activities that affect the successful conduct of international joint ventures.

SUMMARY

- *Organisational context of IHRM* focuses on the IHRM activities that take place globally.

- Organisations are economic and social entities in which a number of persons perform multifarious tasks in order to attain common goals.
- There are various stages of internationalisation, and different approaches to building up multinationals.
- There are different organisational structures and approaches of MNCs like matrix structure, mixed structure, the heterarchy, transnational, and approaches like ethnocentric, polycentric, geocentric, and regiocentric.
- Structuring the organisations become critical and rather difficult when the organisations grow to the stage of a transnational company and become truly global.
- The various modes used by multinationals for foreign market entry and expansion have considerable IHRM implications.
- A MNC may operate through contractual and cooperative mode.

  Both formal and informal control mechanisms are important HR systems in an international business organisation.

REVIEW QUESTIONS

1. Trace the early stages of internationalisation.
2. Enumerate different approaches to organisational structures in MNCs.
3. Elaborate on the control mechanism in international human resource management.
4. What are the contractual and cooperative modes of operation?

REFERENCES

1. Peter J. Dowling and Denice E. Welch, (2006). *International Human Resource Management: Managing People in a Multinational Context*, 4th edition, Thomson Learning, London.
2. C. Bartlett and S. Ghoshal, (1986). *Organising for Worldwide Effectiveness*, p. 66.
3. G. Hedlund, *The Hypermodern MNC – A Heterarchy?, Human Resource Management*, Vol. 25, No. 1, pp. 9-35.
4. H.V. Perlmutter, (1969). *The Tortuous Evolution of the Multinational Corporation*, Columbia Journal of World Business, Vol. 4, No. 1, pp. 9-18.
5. Bird, Allan and Schon Beechler, (2000). *The Link Between Business Strategy and International Human Resource Management Practices,* in Mark Mendenhall and Gary Oddou (eds.), Readings and Cases in International Human Resource Management, 3rd edition, South-Western College Publishing, Cincinnati, OH.
6. D. Welch and L. Welch, (1994). *Linking Operation Mode Diversity, and HRM* in The International Journal of Human Resource Management, Vol. 5, No. 4, pp. 911-26.

3

Strategic IHRM

Objectives

- To understand the meaning of strategy and strategic management.
- To analyse the process of international strategic management.
- To explain business strategies, organisational strategies, and relevant human resource strategies of MNCs.

INTRODUCTION

International human resource management policies and practices need to be aligned with the strategies of MNCs as well as domestic companies employing expatriates. Similarly, MNCs and domestic companies employing expatriates modify the organisational strategies in tune with the availability of human resources as well as human resource costs and other considerations. Thus, MNCs' domestic organisations' strategies should be formulated by considering the international labour market conditions and the human resource strategies are to be aligned with the MNCs and domestic company's strategies. Any strategy for a globalising firm needs to address the challenge between global policy and local approach in the context of different geographical locations.

FEATURES OF STRATEGIC PLANNING

Strategic planning is the process of determining an organisation's basic mission and long-term objectives, followed by implementing a plan of action for attaining those goals (Hodgetts and Luthans, 2003). The stages of strategic planning are: (a) defining the goals, (b) analysis of competitive advantage, (c) internal arrangements of an organisation, (d) designing and formulating competitive strategy, and (e) implementation of strategy.

The goals include both explicit (market, financial, political, and cultural), and implicit (corporate, business, and departmental). Competitive advantage involves analysis of existing and potential business, internal resources available, and the external environment. Internal arrangements refer to organisational culture, values, leadership and decision making. In designing and formulating competitive strategy an MNC may focus on economic imperative to do business globally; political imperative to protect country-centred local market needs; quality imperative to meet or exceed customer expectation and to improve products and services on a continuous basis; and administrative coordination to use strategic formulation and coordination. Implementation of strategy refers to the process of providing goods and services in accordance with the plan and action.

FEATURES OF GLOBAL STRATEGIC MANAGEMENT

Strategic management of the global companies has peculiar features as compared to those of a national company. These are:

- International strategic management is concerned with the flow of goods and services across the countries. It deals with the opportunities, threats, challenges, and risks in various markets in the world.
- Global strategic management is an integrated strategic management of a global company.
- Strategies of the global corporations are formulated by analysing the global environment. In some cases, strategies are formulated for the cluster of markets or countries.
- Global strategic management is concerned with the impact of the present decision on the future. Management has to assess the impact of strategic decisions on the future product path, future markets, and so on.
- Global strategic management is mostly action-oriented. All the managers are the active players in this process.
- Global strategic management is a continuous and dynamic management. The changing business environment across the globe influences and interacts with the global corporation.

- Global strategic management process takes into account the strategies and reaction of their global competitors.
- Global corporations operate in their home country as well as in various foreign countries. Hence, the global strategic management process integrates both domestic operations and operations in the foreign countries.
- Global strategic management designs the organisational structure based on the divisionalised geographical structure.
- Global strategic management mostly depends upon the cultural differences among the countries, differences in the laws of the land, policies of the government, and political environments in the various countries.
- Global strategic management is more critical on control front mainly due to unique factors influencing the international business.

INTERNATIONAL BUSINESS STRATEGIES

International business firms can use four basic strategies, *viz.*, international strategy, multidomestic strategy, global strategy, and transnational strategy.

International strategy: International business firms adopt this strategy in order to transfer the valuable skills and products developed in the home country to the foreign markets where such skills and products are not available.

Multidomestic strategy: International business firms adopting this strategy customise their products and marketing strategies to the host country requirements and environment. The international business firms establish their production, marketing, finance and R&D facilities in various host countries.

Global strategy: International business firms adopting this strategy concentrate on profit earning through cost minimisation. Therefore, these firms produce standard products, by locating the manufacturing and other facilities in certain locations where the cost of production/operations is the lowest.

Transnational strategy: International business firms adopting this strategy pursue low cost leadership-cum-local responsive or customisation strategy due to intensive global competition. Firms can achieve this strategy by exploiting experience-based economies and location-based economies.

Christopher Bartlett and Sumantra Ghoshal emphasise that the transfer of experience-based economies and skills should flow not only from home firm to foreign subsidiary, but also from foreign subsidiary to home company and from one foreign subsidiary to another foreign subsidiary. They referred this learning process as 'global learning'. This process of simultaneous value creation is called 'transnational strategy'.[1]

INTERNATIONAL STRATEGIC MANAGEMENT PROCESS

The international strategic management process starts with the organisational analysis of the international company in order to know its strengths and weaknesses. The next step is the analysis of international environmental factors in order to know the opportunities and threats provided by the environment. Goals of the international company along with the SWOT analysis leads to the formulation of alternative strategies. The strategist analyses the alternatives and selects the best strategy for implementation.

International strategic management process includes:

Analysis of existing mission and goals: Most of the companies initially start as domestic firms and transform into international companies at the later stage. Further, it goes on adding new products to its portfolio and/or adding new countries to the existing portfolio. The company finds that the existing mission statement would be redundant over a period of time. Then, the global company prefers to reformulate the existing mission statement. The global company also changes its goals depending upon the changes in the environment.

Organisational analysis of a global business firm: The organisational analysis requires a detailed study of the following aspects of the global company and its subsidiaries:

Organisational structure: The analysis of organisational structure includes flat or tall organisation, team structure or individual based structure, and geographical or strategic business unit structure. This analysis requires identification of strengths and weaknesses of the company with regard to the structure.

Marketing: The marketing analysis includes the analysis of four Ps, *viz.*, product, price, promotion, and place. The global company analyses each of these factors in detail and identifies strengths and weaknesses of each.

Production: The production analysis includes sourcing of materials, location of plants, logistics spread, plant layouts, sourcing the human resources, quality considerations, past experience, and inventory levels. The strategist has to analyse each factor and identify the strengths and weaknesses of each.

Finance: Important finance factors include sources of finance, capital structure, earning per share and the like. The strategist has to identify the strengths and weaknesses for each o the finance factors.

Human resources: The human resource factors include the sourcing of manpower, th skill of employees, cultural compatibility of the employees with the cultures of variou countries, cost of employees, and the like. The strategist of a global company analyses eac of the human resource areas and identifies its strengths and weaknesses.

After identifying the strengths and weaknesses of the global company, the strategist has to analyse the international environment in order to find out the opportunities provided and the threats posed by the international environment.

Analysis of international environment: Strategic management of a global organisation requires an understanding and analysis of international business environment in order to assess opportunities and threats. The strategist formulates alternative strategies to exploit the opportunities provided by the environment by using company strengths. For example, Sony formulated the strategy of low priced televisions to enter the expanding Indian middle class market.

International business environment factors include:

Political-legal factors: All countries have their own political systems and legal framework that affect business. Various statutory provisions may provide an opportunity or pose a threat to the businesses going abroad.

Economic factors: Growing economic activities, increasing gross national product and per capita income are indicators for opportunities for business. High inflation rates and devaluation of currencies pose threats to international business.

Technological factors: Technology plays a major role in global business. Technology is one of the main bases for joint-ventures particularly in the developing world. Manufacturing companies in technologically advanced countries locate their production plants in developing countries where cheap labour and raw materials are available.

Social factors: Every country has its own distinctive culture, i.e., generally accepted values, traditions, and patterns of behaviour. Different social and cultural factors of different countries will affect MNCs. Difference in language and social norms will affect the marketing mix for a particular country. Product presentation, packaging, distribution channels, pricing and advertising must be attuned to each culture. Religious belief may also make a significant impact on a country's business practice. Cross-cultural differences in norms and values require modifications in managerial behaviours. Social norms that are not well understood by outsiders often constrain business transactions. For instance, Japanese business executives expect their clients or suppliers to interact socially with them after working hours. In fact, these social settings are requirements for serious business relationships.

The companies should evaluate their strengths, weaknesses, opportunities, and threats to international environment before making a final decision about going global. The companies can use the following questions in evaluating their strengths and weaknesses (Exhibit 3.1).

Exhibit 3.1

International SWOT Analysis – Evaluation

1. Do the companies' have a strong market position in the respective countries in which they operate?
2. Do the companies' quality of products/services compare favourably with those of their respective world competitors?
3. Do the companies' have technological advantage in the world regions where they will operate their major businesses?
4. Do the companies' have a strong brand reputation in the countries in which they sell their products or services?
5. Do the companies' managers and employees have more talent than those of their world competitors?
6. Do the companies' financial profile compare favourably with that of the industry?
7. Are the companies' consistently more profitable than their world rivals?
8. Are the companies' product and process research and development efforts likely to produce better results than their competitors?
9. Are the companies' various world operations subject to unionisation?

Source: P. Wright, *Doing Business in Islamic Markets*, Harvard Business Review, Vol. 59, No. 1, Jan-Feb. 1981, pp. 34-40.

Formulation of alternative corporate level strategies: Formulation of corporate level alternative strategies of a global business is different from those of a domestic company. The global company first decides the country to enter and then formulates the corporate level strategies. The strategies which can be formulated are broadly classified as corporate level strategies and business unit level strategies. The companies, before deciding which markets to go, should know the risks involved in a nation's market. There are many risks involved in going international including shifting borders, unstable governments, foreign exchange problems, corruption, and technological pirating.

Formulation of alternative business unit level strategies: The global companies formulate business unit level strategies based on the corporate level strategies, organisational strengths and environmental opportunities. The important strategies at this level include:

(a) *Low cost strategy*: The global companies plan to reduce the cost of production, cost of marketing and so on by locating the firms close to the raw materials or close to the markets, by adopting latest technology. The strategy of low cost provides the global company two options, *viz.*, fix the price at a lower level compared to that of the competitors or to increase the profit margin or both.

(b) *Focus or niche strategy*: Transnational companies formulate specific strategies for specific markets, whereas international and multinational corporations apply the same strategy in a number of countries. The transnational companies are expected to think globally and act locally. Thus, they become global companies. They adopt the focus strategy for each local market in order to compete with the domestic companies.

(c) *Differentiation strategy*: Transnational companies mostly adopt the differentiation strategy. They differentiate the product policies, price policies, service policies from country-to-country, and from one customer group to other customer group.

Selection of the best among the alternative strategies: The global company after formulating the alternative strategies has to select the best among the alternative strategies. The strategists analyse the alternative strategies, rank them, and select the best among them.

Strategy implementation: After selecting the best strategy, the global company implements it in order to achieve its goals. The factors of strategy implementation include: (a) partner selection; (b) organisational structure; (c) behavioural implementation; (d) marketing implementation; (e) production implementation; (f) financial implementation; and (g) human resource implementation.

Strategy evaluation and control: The strategic management process may not be implemented as planned due to changes in environmental factors. Therefore, the global company has to evaluate its process and control measures. The activities in this regard include: (a) establishing the standards; (b) measuring the performance; (c) comparing the performance; (d) observing the deviations; and (e) taking corrective steps.

MNCs BUSINESS STRATEGIES

Some companies operate in a number of countries while some companies operate in fewer countries with a deeper commitment. The firms can choose to enter the market with high market attractiveness, high competitive advantage, and lower risk.

After deciding the country to enter, the company has to decide the best mode of entry. There are different modes of entry.

Indirect exporting: Indirect exporting means exporting through independent intermediaries to various countries. The various types of intermediaries include domestic based exporter and export agent; cooperative organisation; and export-management company. Indirect exports cost less to the producers and the producers can concentrate on manufacturing as the export arrangements are taken care of by the intermediaries.

Direct exporting: Companies depend on indirect marketing during the early stage of their exports. Eventually, they may decide to export directly in order to get more benefits and economies of scale. In this, the investment and risk will be greater as compared to the indirect exports.

The companies at this stage mostly follow ethnocentric approach for its human resource activities. They depute home/parent country nationals on short-term assignment to host country, and develop network and business relations with various market intermediaries in the host country.

Licensing: Under this approach, the licensor licenses a foreign company to use its production process, trademark, patent, trade secret or other item value for a fee or royalty. The manufacturer enters a foreign market with a little risk. The foreign company gains the advantage of production expertise or technology, or a well known product without having to start from scratch. Coca-Cola enters different foreign markets by licensing bottlers around the globe. It supplies them syrup, and train the personnel of the foreign companies in producing and selling the product.

International human resource management under this strategy would be the responsibility of the licensee company. MNCs under licensing strategy mostly follow geocentric approach. The licensee company in the foreign country formulate most of the human resource management strategies.

Franchising: Franchising is a form of licensing. The franchisor can exercise more control over the franchisee as compared to licensee. International franchising is growing at a fast rate. The franchisor provides to the franchisee certain services like trademarks; operating systems; product reputations; and continuous support systems such as advertising, employee training, reservation services, and quality assurance programmes.

International human resource management under this strategy would be joint responsibility of the franchisor company and the franchisee company. MNCs under franchising strategy mostly follow geocentric approach.

Direct investment: Direct investment is the ultimate way of going international. The direct investments include involvement of a company in ownership and control of foreign-based assembly or manufacturing or service facilities. The foreign company can: (a) buy part of the local manufacturing facilities; or (b) buy full interest in local company; or (c) build its own facilities on its own. The company after producing in a foreign country can meet the customer needs in that country and export to other countries. This strategy helps the company to widen the market and get distinct advantages.

International human resource management under this strategy takes a different mode as compared to that of other strategies. MNCs under this strategy follow ethnocentric approach during the initial period. At the later stage, MNCs slowly shift to regiocentric approach, polycentric, and geocentric approach.

Acquisitions: A foreign company rather than starting the business from scratch, may acquire an already established company in the host country. The foreign company may buy the established company in its entirety rather than on a piecemeal basis. International human resource management under this strategy is relatively a complex task due to the involvement of all alliance partners in the process of strategy formulation and implementation. Al partner companies jointly formulate and implement concerned strategies. However, the major partner plays a dominant role in crafting and implementing strategies.

Management contracts: Large MNCs may have a large amount of management talent at its disposal. Management contracts offer a means through which an MNC may use part of its profits and personnel to assist a firm in a host country for a specified fee and specified time. MNCs earn some income from their investment and continue operations until local management is trained and developed. In case of management contracting strategy, the contractor follows ethnocentric approach for selecting key managers and appoints the HCNs for other jobs. However, it can also be on the basis of agreement between the two companies.

Joint ventures: Foreign investor and local manufacturer join together to form a joint venture. The joint venture involves technological transfer, market sharing, and investment sharing. The foreign investor and local producer share ownership and control. Joint venture is an appropriate strategy for technological, economic, and political reasons. Some joint ventures are successful and run for many years.

Turnkey operations: Turnkey operations are typically contracts for the construction of operating facilities in exchange for a fee. The facilities are transferred to the host country or the firm concerned when they are complete. The foreign company supplies some of its own equipment for the project. In case of turnkey projects, MNCs mostly follow ethnocentric approach for all key positions including managerial positions.

COLLABORATIVE STRATEGIES

International business firms either perform their business operations on their own or collaborate with other companies. In fact, companies in some situations collaborate with their competitors also. Their collaboration choices are influenced by several factors including physical and economic factors, scale of operations, make and buy decisions, societal factors, and competitive environment. Motives for collaborative arrangements for international business include gain location, specific assets, diversity, and so on. Some of the motives for collaborative strategies are common for both domestic business and international business. These include:

Spread and reduced costs: It is economical to buy the products from other specialist companies when the quantity required is small and uneconomical to produce. Companies with fewer capacities can outsource the capacities from the companies with larger capacities. This arrangement helps both the companies to reduce and spread the costs and the start-up and waiting time. This facility also reduces the level of investment of small companies.

Specialise in core competencies: Companies have certain core competencies and as such they perform the activities concerning core competencies more efficiently as compared to other activities.

Vertical and horizontal integration: Vertical and horizontal linkages or integrations allow the companies to concentrate on the core competencies, operate on small-scale, and emphasise as a portion of the supply chain.

Learn from other companies: Collaborative strategies in the form of joint ventures enable the companies to learn about partner's technology, production methods, and systems and markets.

Sharing capacities: Companies can jointly share their production, service, marketing, human resource and other capacities in order to operate on optimum scale.

ORGANISATIONAL STRATEGIES

These strategies include:

Stability strategy: The stability strategies include maintenance of *status quo* and sustainable growth. Companies with stability strategy maintain the similar pattern of production, sales and profit. Appropriate HR strategies in this regard include motivation and retention of skilled employees. Job rotation, job enrichment and empowerment are appropriate HR practices to motivate the frustrated employees.

Growth strategy: Organisations select the growth strategies to increase their profits, sales and/or market share, reduce cost of production per unit. One of the growth strategies is internal growth. The appropriate HR strategies in this regard include training the existing employees and promote them to the higher levels; employee the new candidates at the lower level; and outsourcing some employees.

Concentration strategy: These strategies are achieved through concentrating the firm's efforts on a limited combination of customer groups, customer functions, and alternate technologies. Dabur India follows this strategy and concentrates on certain customer functions. Bata India follows the strategy of outsourcing in producing shoes targeted to rich income brackets. The relevant HR strategies in this regard are training and developing employees, and outsourcing specialised skills.

Mergers and acquisitions strategy: Firms prefer to go through mergers and acquisitions. A merger is a combination of two or more businesses in which one acquires the assets and liabilities of the other in exchange for stock or cash or both. Companies are dissolved and assets and liabilities are combined and a new stock is issued. Examples of merger include merger of Reliance Petroleum with Reliance Industries. Acquisition/takeover is defined as the attempt of one firm to acquire ownership over another firm against the wishes of the latter's management. But in practice, takeover can be hostile or friendly. Though there is conceptual difference between mergers and acquisitions, their effect regarding human resource strategies is the same.

HR managers play a significant role in mergers and acquisitions strategy. They help top management in assessing pension, provident fund, and other liabilities; labour contracts of the proposed target company; and skill, attitude and culture base of the target company. Other strategies are integrating the two wage structures, benefit programmes, seniority and so on.

Horizontal integration strategy: Horizontal integration strategy aims at related diversification. For example, Coca-Cola diversified to produce mineral water 'Kinley'. L&T constructions diversified to produce cement. Relevant human resource strategies are to train and develop the existing employees to provide the skills necessary in the area of new business. Other strategies consist of employing new candidates in the diversified business, formulation of performance appraisal systems, laying down compensation and industrial relations policies, which are slightly different from those of the existing business.

Conglomerate strategy: Conglomerate diversification is diversification into unrelated activity to the original business of the company. For example, Gujarat Gas Limited created another business unit, namely, Gujarat Finance Company Ltd. In such cases, the diversified HRM functions are altogether different from those of the existing company.

Joint venture strategy: Joint ventures are partnerships in which two or more firms carry-out a specific project. Joint ventures can be temporary, complete or partial, for example, Maruti and Suzuki, Modi and Xerox. As in case of mergers and acquisitions, this strategy also brings cultural diversity as a major HR issue.

Retrenchment strategy: The third major class of strategic alternatives available to a firm is retrenchment strategies. Retrenchment strategies include turnaround strategies, captive company strategy, disinvestment strategy, and liquidation strategy. For example, companies like HCL, Visakha Steel Plant of SAIL adopted turnaround strategies. They employed HR strategies like open communication, employee counselling, reduction in the labour cost by enhancing labour productivity, attitudinal change, and so on.

HR BUSINESS COMPETENCY

In today's global economy, HRM professionals must continuously realise that their function is creating value for the organisation; and in this context, the emphasis is on making human resources a strategic partner in business. A higher level of technical competence and an understanding of details of the business are required on the part of the HRM professionals to become strategic partners in organisations.

The four key HRM competencies are: (a) personal credibility (being a role model, leading and influencing others), (b) delivering results (achieving results by building strong relationships), (c) Knowledge of HRM (understanding and deciding which HRM processes could improve business performance), and (d) business knowledge (awareness of the external environment to enhance business performance). Being a "business allay" or having "business knowledge" means that HRM professionals understand all the parts of the business, what they must accomplish, and how they need to work together to make the organisation successful at what it does.

HRM competency business literacy questions should include the following:

1. What are the annual revenues of the business?
2. How does the business make money?
3. What is the company's market value?
4. What is the company's type of funding?
5. Who are the company's major customers?
6. What is the company's market share in its dominant product and service?
7. What is the company's brand or desired reputation among target customers?
8. Who are the primary competitors and what are their strengths?
9. What were the agenda items of a recent meeting of the company's board of directors?
10. What are the objectives and goals of the top executives of the company?

SUMMARY

- *Strategic IHRM* focuses on business and HR strategies that MNCs apply in their organisational development endeavours.
- Strategy is the unified, comprehensive, and integrated plan designed to ensure that the basic objectives of the enterprise are achieved.
- The development of an organisation's strategic plan requires careful analysis of: (a) the organisation's competitive situation; (b) the organisation's current position and destination; (c) the organisation's strategic goals; and (d) the organisation's plan of action, implementation, and allocation of resources.
- International human resource management policies and practices need to be aligned with the strategies of MNCs.
- The basic steps of strategic process include formulation of vision, mission and objectives of the MNC and also formulation of alternative strategies; selecting the best strategy; and strategy implementation, evaluation and control.
- The international business strategies include exporting, licensing, franchising, and foreign direct investment.
- Domestic companies enter international business through mergers and acquisitions.

- Two or more firms join together to create a new business entity that is legally separate and distinct from its parent company.
- These result in functional alliances which include production alliances, marketing alliances, finance alliances, human resource alliances, and research and development alliances.

REVIEW QUESTIONS

1. Define the term 'strategy'. What is strategic management?
2. What is strategic management process?
3. What are the human resource strategies of MNCs, when they opt for export strategies?
4. What type of human resource strategies do you formulate that opt for licensing and franchising strategies to enter foreign markets?
5. What type of human resource strategies do you formulate for an MNC that prefer business process outsourcing?
6. What type of human resource strategies do the MNCs use when they prefer contract manufacturing and management contracting?
7. Discuss various organisational human resource strategies.

REFERENCE

1. Bartlett and Ghoshal, *Managing Across Borders,* quoted in Charles W. L. Hill, *op. cit.,* p. 424.

4

Staffing for International Assignments

Objectives

- To explain the reasons for the failure of recruitment and selection process of expatriates.
- To understand the specific factors to be considered by the IHRM manager while recruiting and selecting expatriates.
- To appreciate various methods to be followed for recruiting and selecting expatriates.

INTRODUCTION

Recruitment and selection constitute the first step towards having the right manpower. Recruitment is the search and acquisition of potential job candidates of quality in the right numbers. It is here that the organisation selects the most appropriate people from among many candidates to fill its job needs. Selection, on the other hand, is the process of gathering information to gauge and decide who should be employed in a particular job.

According to ORC Worldwide Survey (2006) of International Assignment Policies and Practices, 56 per cent of companies have increased the number of expatriate recruitment. The types of assignments are also changing in line with the growing needs and challenges of today's global economy. Since recruitment and selection are the first steps towards building a committed workforce for any organisation, whether for domestic or international needs, great care must be taken by the HR department in this endeavour. In particular, for international operations, certain extra efforts are to be made.

INTERNATIONAL ASSIGNMENTS

When an organisation has staffing need and depending on the type of position and level involved, it will either employ someone locally or transfer a suitable candidate. In the process, it may so happen that the competence of the expatriates may decrease as they are not developing their own expatriates. To overcome this problem, the expatriates may be moved into the other parts of the organisation for training and development purposes and to assist in the development of common corporate values. For this reason, the staff of the headquarters is transferred to subsidiary operations, or subsidiary staff transferred to the parent operations or to other subsidiary operations for varied lengths of time.

The strategic objectives of the operation come into play in the development of organisations. International assignments allow staff to gain a broader perspective as they become familiar with more than one operation. Employees are transferred internationally for varying lengths of time depending on the purpose of the relocation and the nature of the task assigned to them. Hence, companies tend to classify international assignments into the following types depending on their length or duration.

Short-term: This is normally up to three months. These are usually for troubleshooting or project supervision or a stop gap arrangement until a more permanent one is found.

Extended: This is usually up to one year and may involve similar activities as those in short-term assignments.

Long-term: Such assignments vary from one to five years, involving a clearly defined role in the receiving operation.

Within these three broad categories, it is possible to identify what are termed as non-standard assignments namely, commuter assignments, rotational assignments, contractual assignments, and virtual assignments.

International sales staff travel abroad to attend trade fairs, to visit foreign agents and distributors or to demonstrate new products to potential clients and/or to negotiate sales contracts. Others visit foreign locations to deal with host-country government officials, alliance partners, subcontracting firms and foreign suppliers. Such international travel can make heavy demands on staff. There is a high level of stress involved for those whose job responsibilities include substantial international business travel.

MAJOR CONSIDERATIONS FOR SELECTING EXPATRIATES

An expatriate performance is highly influenced by his/her ability – and that of his family – to adjust well and at the earliest. Selecting the right people for the right job is a dictum in HRM. Organisations should never have any cause to regret their choice of personnel for their international operations, because an expatriate's failure to perform can be quite costly to his organisation. The failures are attributed more to adjustment problems. Hence, while selecting expatriates, the HR manager should first avoid such pitfalls.

A significant difference between domestic and foreign staffing relates to the family-oriented nature of the latter assignment. The importance in providing appropriate incentives for the expatriate's wife and other family members is well recorded. International companies are demonstrating a strong preference for staffing their foreign operations with local nationals in managerial and technical positions. Several factors contribute to this:

1. The local national has a native's understanding of the host country, especially its people and culture.
2. The ability of a local national to communicate effectively with his fellow nationals whether they may be customers, suppliers, government officials, other businessmen, or the general public.
3. The problems of environmental adaptation that be devil the expatriate manager and his family are irrelevant to the local national, enabling him to focus his energies on the management job.
4. The widespread use of local nationals leads to shortage of management resources in parent companies and hence maintaining them in foreign soil is extremely expensive.
5. The natural desire in the host nations to see their own citizens reap the benefits of employment in enterprises established on their own soil.

There are no specific guidelines, however, for hiring of foreign nationals. Much depends on the individual company, its business philosophy, its degree of internationalisation, the nature of its production, and its management resources. Much also depends on the particular countries in which the company carries on its business. Nonetheless, the broad movement towards the greater use of local managers is likely to accelerate in future and some companies are now moving beyond the traditional distinction between expatriate and local managers to create a corpus of multinational executives who are available to fill management positions at headquarters or in affiliates without regard to their national origin.

EXPATRIATE FAILURE

In the recruitment and selection of staff for international operations, the possibility of expatriate failure should be kept in mind. If one understands the issues related to why this takes place, then these issues can be taken care of well in advance instead of regretting one's decision later. Expatriate failure is defined as the premature return of an expatriate before the completion of the full tenure of the assignment. In such a case, an expatriate failure represents a selection error, often compounded by ineffective expatriate management policies. However, the premature return rate is not a perfect measure of success or failure, and may underestimate the problem. That is why the 1997-98 Price Waterhouse study added underperformance to its definition of assignment failure and found that, "the rates for employees currently underperforming on assignments as a result of difficulties in adapting to their cultural surroundings or even higher. 29 per cent of companies report a rate in excess of one in twenty, with 7 per cent reporting a rate over one in ten."

P.J. Dowling and D.E. Welch (2006) drew the following conclusions with respect to the magnitude of expatriate failure based on the different surveys done by GMAC Global Relocation Services and ORC Worldwide Survey in 2002.

The evidence on expatriate failure rates is somewhat inconclusive. Recent studies suggest that high failure rates reported in the 1980s have not persisted for all nationalities. Although recent reports do not break the result down into nationality groups, US firms form the largest group in these surveys. The European studies reported above were conducted at various intervals since Tung's original study did not include the same countries. Further, non-US researchers have been reporting from regional or single-country perspectives.

It may be that companies operating internationally have since become more aware of the problems associated with expatriate failure and have learned how to avoid them. In other words, multinationals have become more sophisticated in their approach to IHRM activities. Benchmarking against other firms may have assisted in the development of an awareness of international assignment issues.

There are several reasons for the failure of the expatriates in their foreign assignments:

- Inability of employees to adjust to organisational climate.
- Inability of employee's spouse to adjust to foreign environment.
- Inability to cope up with larger overseas responsibilities.
- Lack of technical and managerial competence.
- Unsafe living and working conditions in host countries.
- Absence of educational, medical, and recreational facilities in the host country.

The Cost of Failure: The visible or direct costs of the failure are airfares and associated relocation expenses, and salary and training. The precise amount varies according to the level of the position, country of destination, exchange rates, and whether the 'failed' manager is replaced by another expatriate. The 'invisible' or indirect costs are harder to quantify in monetary terms but can prove to be more expensive for the company. Failure at this level may result in loss of market share, difficulties with host government officials, and demands that expatriates be replaced with HCNs. Also, it has an effect on the expatriate concerned, who may lose self-esteem, self-confidence and prestige among peers. His future performance may be marked by decreased motivation, lack of promotional opportunities or even increased productivity to compensate for the failure. Finally, the expatriate's family relationship may be threatened. These are additional costs to organisations that are often overlooked.

ADJUSTMENT OF EXPATRIATES

A key issue concerning the ability of expatriates and their families is their ability to adjust to their new environment. Black *et. al.*,[2] provide a framework of international adjustment which consists of three dimensions – adjustment to the international workplace, adjustment to interacting with host nationals, and adjustment to the general international environment. Although these dimensions are not discreet and overlap, they do indicate some of the key areas of adjustment. Adjustment in each of these three domains is determined by a variety of factors. These domains fall into four main groups.

- Individual factors
- Non-work factors
- Organisational factors
- Job factors

Individual factors: Individual factors include self-efficacy, relations skills and logistical help. Hiltrop and Janssens[3], Coyle[4], and Collins[5] have identified additional factors in this category – flexibility, a desire to adjust, tolerance of ambiguity, leadership qualities, interpersonal skills and self-confidence, cultural empathy and emotional stability. Black and Stephens[6] and Black and Gregersen identified language ability and previous international experience also as additional factors.

Non-work factors: Particularly important among these factors is the family situation. The inability of the spouse and children to adapt to the cultural environment is a common source of difficulty. If a spouse or family member is undergoing severe cultural shock or experiencing difficulty in making the cross-cultural adjustment, the morale and performance of the expatriate may be adversely affected. Children also may be very resistant to moving due to the educational and social disruption it may cause. The older and larger the number of children, the greater is the likelihood of adjustment problems. A positive family situation is likely to enhance the expatriate's cross-cultural adjustment and increase the chances of a successful assignment. The degree of cultural difference between the home and host country can have a significant influence on the ability to adapt.

Organisational factors: These were classified by Black *et. al.*, as organisational culture novelty, social support and logistical help. If the organisational job is high in organisational culture novelty, the expatriate will have a difficult time adjusting to the work situation and in turn have a more difficult time in adjusting to the culture in general. Social support has an important impact on the expatriate's ability to adapt to the new environment. If the firm offers support for the expatriate and family in the form of housing, payment of school tuition, practical information about shopping, and so on, the expatriate will feel a part of the larger social group. Logistical support such as information on housing, education and travel should help to reduce the uncertainty, thereby facilitating adjustment.

Job factors: The job factors which affect adjustment include role novelty, role clarity, role discretion, role conflict, and role overload. Role novelty is the degree of difference between the expatriate's previous position and his or her new one. An expatriate, for example, who is working in a foreign subsidiary and managing its operations, is assigned the task of establishing a new unit in another foreign location. He now has a new role – that of a project manager. This is what we call "Role Novelty". Role clarity is the extent to which expatriates know what duties they are expected to perform in the overseas assignment. Role discretion will enable the expatriate to use past actions that proved effective in a previous role.

An example of role discretion is, suppose in the expatriate's previous assignment he had experienced certain effective methods in his role and he wants to make use of the same in another assignment, of course with some adjustment to the environment of the new locale, then he is making use of his discretion in deciding on the methods to be adopted. This is what we term as "Role Discretion". This should make adjustment easier because it reduces uncertainty and increases the expatriate's confidence in his or her ability to perform in the new environment. Role conflict and overload may negatively affect the adjustment of the expatriate.

In some cases, expatriates sent on foreign assignments return home earlier than planned because of job dissatisfaction or difficulties adjusting to a culture in another country. In Tung's (1987) early research on expatriate assignments, seven main reasons for expatriate failure were identified:

1. inability of the manager's spouse to adjust to a different physical or cultural environment;
2. inability of the manager to adapt to a different physical or cultural environment;
3. other family-related problems;
4. the manager's personality or emotional immaturity;
5. the manager's inability to cope with the responsibility posed by overseas work;
6. the manager's lack of technical competence; and
7. the manager's lack of motivation to work overseas.

Recruitment and selection process of an expatriate is very important for an IHRM manager and also for the company. Recruitment and selection activity is directed at getting the right people, in the right place, at the right time, and with the right skills to achieve the business objectives.

STAFFING POLICIES

Many countries have localisation policies requiring organisations to give precedence to local people in job appointment. There are three main influencing factors that determine the staffing policies of international businesses:

1. *Company characteristics:*
   - Form of ownership of the foreign operation.
   - Industry and technology factors.
   - Market tendencies.
   - Structural arrangements.
   - Operating procedures and systems.
   - HR policies of the parent group.
   - Cost.
2. *Personal characteristics of expatriates:*
   - Lifestyle and ambitions.
   - Career expectations.
   - Qualifications, experience and training.
   - Family circumstances.
3. *Host country characteristics:*
   - Level of economic development.
   - Political system, stability and requirements.
   - Immigration and investment policies.
   - Availability of appropriate labour.
   - Socio-cultural setting.
   - Location.

RECRUITMENT

Good recruitment is essential for effective HRM. The effectiveness of many other human resource activities, such as selection and training, depends largely on the quality of new employees attracted through the recruiting process. Recruitment is also essential to the society as a whole – it influences job-seekers opportunities of finding suitable employment and, because work is a central part of many people's lives, it has a substantial impact on the applicants' well-being. Recruitment should serve the following purposes:

- Determine present and future staffing needs in conjunction with job analysis and human resource planning.
- Increase the pool of applicants at minimum cost.
- Increase the success rate of the (subsequent) selection process; fewer will turnout to be over or underqualified.
- Increase the probability of subsequent retention.
- Encourage self-selection by means of a realistic job preview.
- Meet responsibilities and legal and social obligations.
- Increase organisational and individual effectiveness.
- Evaluate the effectiveness of different labour pools.

Recruitment practices differ between countries depending on the type and level of employment. Recruitment is an issue that is becoming more international. Not only has the growth of multinational enterprises meant that they now recruit in many countries, but has also been a growth in organisations that recruit for their domestic workforce. The Republic of Ireland, which used to export labour through emigration, now imports qualified workers.

Governments are also involved in the recruitment process. In the recruitment process, the government of a country has to follow certain mandatory provisions. This may result in discrimination against job seekers for reasons of race, gender, age, or because they belong to a disadvantaged group in society. Such a stand of the government may be viewed as undesirable from a moral, legal, and sometimes, organisational point of view. Monitoring staffing practices and outcomes in such cases is therefore relevant to many HR managers.

There are three specific areas of country difference that international HR managers must be aware of:

- The scope of labour legislation – it varies from one country to another.
- The type of labour market – which may be internal or external.
- The recruitment sources – informal and formal.

The Scope of Labour Legislation: The scope of labour legislation and associated collective agreements or customs and practices varies markedly. For example, certain constitutional provisions convey rights of the individual in relation to appointment. In Norway, the Employment Act, 1947 specifies that every citizen has the right to make a living. Article 1 of the Italian Constitution defines the country as a democratic republic based on labour, in which the employer is the provider of work and the employee the lender of labour.

In France, a range of collective agreements at national and industry level shape recruitment practices. In Germany, works councils can see personal information on all short-listed candidates and can veto an appointment within one week of offer. The motive is to ensure fairness and absence of nepotism.

Type of Labour Market: There are also marked differences across countries in terms of labour markets. Germany, Japan, France and Switzerland are noted for generally having internal labour markets where recruitment tends to be focused on specialised entry points at low levels of the hierarchy, and wherein promotion is through internal assessment. Internal labour markets are considered to have such benefits as improved morale, commitment and security among employees, and more opportunities to assess competencies.

Britain, the US, Denmark, the Netherlands and Hong Kong tend to be characterised as external labour markets where candidates can move in and out of the hierarchy at any level. The advantages of such labour markets can be the opportunity to bring in new blood as part of culture-change processes, insights into competitive capabilities, and the ability to respond to equal opportunities.

Recruitment Sources: Recruitment occurs through both informal and formal methods. Informal methods rely on the contacts of existing employees or on people just applying. Formal methods are invariably more expensive than informal ones. There are four methods of recruitment that are significant for international HR managers, namely, headhunting, cross-national advertising, the internet, and international graduate programme.

Headhunting: In developed countries, the use of 'headhunters' for managerial positions are most common. In this method, proper coordination between the international HR manager and the headhunters is important. Executive search is carried out for recruitment of the senior executives and specialists. This method is becoming popular in international recruitment.

Cross-national Advertising: Organisations are looking to Europe and beyond to attract professionals to work in the UK, or to work in locations around the globe. If the costs of getting a recruitment campaign wrong are high in the domestic market, then the potential costs of errors in global campaigns are very high. Trends in advertising vary across sectors. Many recruitment advertising service providers now operate as part of global networks in order to deliver the targeted global campaign. Advertising agencies gather a broad spectrum of international intelligence which focuses on the location of the target audience, the market they operate in, sample salaries, recruitment competitors and whether the job-seeking audience is passive or active. Knowledge about the best recruitment media for target audience is important. So is awareness of national custom and practice in order to ensure the 'cultural appropriateness' of a campaign. From an advertising perspective, the most important cross-cultural differences are: (a) the desired company qualities; and (b) softer cultural issues, such as what ideal employee should look like and the wording of advertisements. National differences in the use of advertising are large. Developed countries make more use of newspapers, specialist journals, and internet recruiting as compared to the less developed.

Internet Recruitment: Today, the internet recruitment has become one of the most popular and effective recruitment methods. The internet offers considerable potential as a source of recruitment for internationally mobile managers, small firms seeking specialist skills, or larger firms wishing to demonstrate their presence. It is proving most useful for international graduate recruitment, attracting MBAs and Ph.D. level candidates, and for specific roles such as marketing and IT staff. E-recruitment (electronic recruitment) has the potential to reduce the barriers to employment on a global scale. Using the internet allows firms to:

- widen recruitment sourcing at a relatively low cost
- attract applicants with a more specialised skills match
- target the specific group of applicants
- target the fresh graduates who are willing to work in a foreign country.

Internet technology has changed the way that organisations seek and attract applicants o apply for open positions and the way that applicants search for and pursue job pportunities. Now organisations can post job openings on their own web pages or post job penings on internet job boards and search globally for applicants meeting the selection riteria. Managers and professionals are more likely to use the internet for job hunting when ne geographical scope of the job hunt is wide, when a major salary increase is desired, and vhen both small and large organisations are being considered as potential employers ·eldman and Klaas, 2002).

There are significant advantages in making use of internet technology to do recruiting. b listings can be created in a shorter period of time for an online posting than for a ewspaper advertisement, and it provides immediate access to a large number of potential b applicants.

Internet recruitment is essential in a global marketplace. To attract more qualified ndidates, recruitment cannot be limited to one country; organisations must search globally aabs, 1998). Global recruiting means searching worldwide for qualified applicants gardless of their current location. Using the internet to recruit makes geography important because contacts between organisations and applicants are made by electronic mmunication; it doesn't matter where the organisation or the applicant is (Wyld, 1997).

Using the internet for international recruitment has received mixed reactions but is wly emerging as a useful tool. Firms have faced a number of problems with web ruitment; many existing service providers do not as yet have truly global coverage, and web is currently not appropriate for all countries.

Some of the disadvantages of e-recruitment are:

- Targeting a particular segment becomes difficult. For example, in running web pages in Singapore, applications are received from unexpected sources like Malaysia.
- Generating a larger number of applicants from more diverse social groups may lead to the need for extensive screening activities.
- Company image or brand may not be well known in a foreign country.
- Quality becomes more variable and needs managing.
- Equal opportunity issues might exist in that most applicants still tend to be male and from a small range of countries.

Nonetheless, the internet has become the primary port of call for most international talent, and so developing this as a viable recruitment channel is important. It is one of the fastest growing methods of recruitment. Obviously, its use is restricted to those countries and organisations where the internet is widely used.

International Graduate Programme: Another form of international sourcing is the external recruitment of graduates into international roles. Infosys, for instance, is recruiting large number of management trainees from foreign universities. However, a number of significant problems with international graduate programmes must be taken care of. These are as follows:

- This form of internationalisation has only a slow impact on the level of internationalisation, acting as a slow-burning fuse.
- Retention rates may prove to be low.
- Visa issues mean that the cadres have to be managed for a significant period of time.
- Many organisations note that graduates are becoming more reluctant to move.
- This reluctance to move is also responsible for changing attitudes to compensation forcing organisations to be more responsive to individual needs and circumstances.

SELECTION

Selection involves the identification of the most suitable person from a pool applicants. The main purposes of selection are:

- To obtain appropriate information about jobs, individuals and organisations order to enable high-quality decisions.
- To transform information into a prediction about future behaviour.

- To contribute to the bottom line through the most efficient and effective way to produce service/production.
- To ensure cost-benefit for the financial investment made in an employee.
- To evaluate, hire and place job applicants in their best interests and in the interest of the organisation.

Selection Criteria

The international selection of employees is based on certain considerations. The following are the important factors which determine the success or failure of an expatriate selection process.

Technical Competency: This is a very significant criterion for selecting a manager for foreign assignment. MNCs rely heavily on the relevant technical skills during expatriate selection (Hixon, 1986). Assessing technical skill is relatively easy because the MNCs may assess the potential candidates skills based on past performance, both internally and from his earlier organisation.

Personal Attributes: This refers to the individual's ability to deal and communicate effectively with superiors, peers, subordinates, customers, and other stakeholders in cross-cultural settings.

Environmental Variables: Ability to cope with environmental factors is a criterion while selecting expatriates for international posting. Some of the environmental factors include government policies, unions' participation, competitors profile and *modus operandi*, and consumer behaviour.

Family Situation: The success of an expatriate manager in a foreign country largely depends on the formal and informal support from his/her spouse and family, both at home country and foreign country.

Cross-cultural Suitability: The cultural environment in which the expatriate operates is an important factor in determining successful performance. In addition to the obvious technical competency and managerial skills, expatriates require cross-cultural skill that enable the person to operate in a new environment. These include cultural empathy, adaptability, diplomacy, and emotional stability and maturity.

MNC Requirements: While making selection decisions, as a matter of policy, the multinational may consider the proportion of expatriates to local staff. Further, it may consider other situational factors such as: (a) the mode of operation involved; (b) the duration of the assignment; and (c) the amount of knowledge transfer inherent in the expatriate's job in the foreign operation.

Language: Language skills may be regarded as of critical importance for some expatriate positions. Obviously, some knowledge of the host country's language is an important aspect of expatriate performance, regardless of the level of position.

Selection Methods

The most common forms of selection tests are:

- interviews
- the monitoring and targeting of disadvantaged groups
- assessment centres
- psychological testing

Interviews: In the US, interviews generally follow a structural format so that each applicant is asked the same questions. Elsewhere, this is not the case, even though unstructured interviews have low predictive validity. There are also national differences in the number of people involved in the interviews and who they are. Thus, an HR specialist would often be one of the interviewers in Northern Europe; less commonly elsewhere. In a simple face-to-face interview, the assessors may be confronted by significant problems. For example, one US multinational, while recruiting managers in Korea, found that interviewers had to be trained in cross-cultural differences. It is the cultural norm in Korea, when asked a 'good' question, to keep silent as a sign of respect. The better the question, the longer the period of silence the candidate maintains. In the US, if you ask a good question and receive silence, you do not attribute the behaviour to respect but to ignorance. This is probably the same in many other cultures as well. Face-to-face interviews can create quite distorted judgements.

The monitoring and targeting of disadvantaged groups: HR policy and practices, including staffing practices, are influenced by national and transnational (for example, the European Union) employment loss restrict the direct and sometimes indirect discriminations based on factors such as gender, race, colour, disability, religion and marital status. These laws, and their effects, vary considerably by country, not only in what they outlaw but also in how they interpret discrimination.

Assessment centres: Because assessment centres are regarded as one of the most robust and valid selection techniques in general, it should be expected that they would be used to assess competence for international managers. This is rarely the case, however. Even where assessment centres are used to select managers in international settings, the concerned cross-cultural assessment centres design the assessment process in accordance with the local environment in which they operate.

Psychological testing: The validity of some psychometric testing methods is also disputed. Psychologists claim that the variability of validity across settings for the same type of job and across different kinds of jobs is small. Nevertheless, some variation is observed and, in particular, there are concerns for organisations operating internationally about the cross-cultural transferability of many psychometric tests. Of course, only a small minority of organisations in any country uses psychometric testing, and the proportion of organisations that use assessment centres is even smaller. International HRM managers are increasingly becoming aware of cross-cultural assessment issues.

The use of psychological tests is increasingly becoming a problem in the international selection field. In the pursuit of the global manager, organisations have to look outside their normal recruitment territory in order to benchmark interviews. Behaviourally-based work simulations are subject to culturally different behaviours of both the candidates and the assessor and, hence, international HR managers might be tempted to use more testing.

There is also the problem of fairness. Candidates find that poor knowledge of English in the work situation hampers their test performance and may find it difficult to progress well even through internal selection systems. Such discrimination is inappropriate. Countries also differ greatly in terms of the practices related to user qualification, legal constraints on test used and the consequences for those tested, and the controls exercised over the use of tests.

Organisations can choose from a wide range of selection methods, including references, interviews and tests. Many organisations use not just one but a combination of selection practices. If there is one area in HRM where national differences are very apparent, it is in the area of selection. Some selection methods are common in some countries but may not be used at all in others. Such differences reflect different assumptions about the nature of selection. If a selection method has low validity or reliability, then it is considered inappropriate.

Expatriate selection: Making successful selection decisions is critical for multinational organisations, and especially so because of the substantial expense of sending employees on expatriate assignments. The three key factors that lead to job success are: (a) technical competence on the job; (b) relational abilities or personality traits; and (c) environmental variables.

Black and Gregerson (1999) identified five characteristics that multinational organisations tend to look for in potential expatriates:

(a) drive to communicate with local people in their own country;

(b) broad-based sociability and willingness to establish social ties with local residents;

(c) cultural flexibility and a willingness to experiment with different customs;

(d) cosmopolitan orientation and a respect for diverse viewpoints; and

(e) collaborative negotiation style.

RETAINING, DEVELOPING AND RETRENCHING STAFF

Despite the shortage of international managers, failure to effectively recruit, retain, and develop HCN managers remain a major problem to many international firms. Many multinationals open up their subsidiary units in foreign locations for the sake of cost advantage due to cheap labour. Cost considerations produce what has been referred to as mobile factories since multinationals move in and out of countries as the changing circumstances dictate. The IT industry in India has been regarded as attractive owing to its workforce composition. To capitalise on cost advantage, US firms such as IBM, Hewlett-Packard and Electronic Data Systems have outsourced software development to Indian suppliers.

Hiring of HCNs to take care of the networking operations, and the opportunities available to all nationals to move around globally these days, makes it all the more necessary for HRM professionals to concentrate on retaining talent. Talent management is not only in the realm of domestic HRM, but also in IHRM.

In call centres, employees become disillusioned sooner or later, because of shift duties, strict supervision, abuse by supervisors, and lack of opportunity to socialise with the outer world. This kind of pressure soon drives them out of job. Also, poaching of trained personnel by competitors also contributes to turnover. Today's employees have become more mobile. No one considers loyalty to the organisation which gave him/her the first job, to be of any importance. Hence, multinationals should be careful in designing schemes and incentives to retain rare talents.

Many MNCs have focused most of their management development efforts on their PCN managers and have tended to neglect the development of other HCN managers. In this context, there are three things for the MNCs to keep in mind when they seek to develop HCN managers. First, the need to avoid the mistake of simply exporting parent country training and development programmes to other countries. Second, the management development programmes need to be contextualised for each country as well as the overall strategy of the firm. Third, and most important, is the need to utilise much more the practice of inpatriation, which has been defined as the selective process of transferring HCNs and/or TCNs into the domestic organisation headquarters of the MNC on a permanent or semi-permanent basis.

The golden handshake or voluntary retirement scheme is also resorted to in some companies. This is easier than retrenchment from the legal angle, but there is a danger of skilled and talented workforce leaving the organisation. Retrenchment or downsizing is not a problem only with the host country; even the parent country operations may be shifted lock, stock and barrel to some other country for various considerations like cost effectiveness or closeness to the market. Consequently, HR has to face situations involving strikes, boycotts, and political pressure.

DUAL-CAREER COUPLES

The increase in the dual-career couples is a worldwide trend. It is becoming an increasing source of concern to companies when they send individuals on international assignments. Assumptions about the problems associated with sending a woman abroad if she is in a dual-career couple have caused organisations to use this as a reason for not selecting potential female expatriates.

How organisations handle dual-career issues is currently the focus of much attention. Recent surveys of practice indicate a wide divergence of practice amongst organisations in this area. Many MNCs are sending large number of international managers on short-term assignments which are up to twelve months. Many allow them to remain at home and commute to the place of work. These are helpful when the international manager is unwilling or unable to go on a long assignment because the spouse is working or because of other family problems, like children's education or having older parents in poor health.

The spouse/partner may decide to remain in the home country and the couple workout ways to maintain the relationship with the help of the firm. One multinational firm supports this kind of arrangement through subsidised telephone bills and three return airline tickets. Alternatively, the couples may move to jobs in adjoining countries, or within the same geographical region. For instance, one may work in Indonesia (the original posting), the other in Philippines. This makes commuting and relationship maintenance easier than from the USA. Multinationals adjust the compensation and benefits to fit with the agreed arrangements.

Some multinationals are endeavouring to come up with solutions to the dual-career challenge. According to Reynolds and Bennett (1991) most companies still use informal or *ad hoc* approaches to addressing the problems of their expatriate career couples. Companies are beginning to generate innovative programmes and interventions to assist the dual-career couples.

WOMEN AS INTERNATIONAL MANAGERS

Discrimination against women in selection is discouraged in many countries. Keeping this in view, the IHRM should address the issue of women managers being selected for international assignments. The number of women undertaking international assignments is relatively low. Some firms show hesitant to ask women to go to overseas because of the potential hardships associated with some locations. However, there is growing evidence to show that women make good expatriate managers. This suggests that firms will appoint more women in foreign locations. Many international organisations are concerned about assigning women to countries like Japan where there is likelihood that they would not be well accepted by male counterparts. Jelinek and Adler report that this is not true. They have found that North American women managers in Japan were viewed as foreigners rather than as women and that their sex was not an impediment to competent management.

While the information currently available suggests that women make effective managers internationally, they clearly face certain difficulties. Earlier reports of women's effectiveness are based on the small number of women who were offered, and who had accepted, international assignments. Given the general bias against female candidates, it is likely that these women were particularly good candidates. It is to be expected, therefore, that their performance would also be good. It is only practical for firms, and for women seeking expatriate assignments, to investigate the reality of the foreign work environment for a woman manager. A realistic assessment of the environment means that the expatriate can be appropriately prepared and the firm can provide the needed support to allow for high performance. From the perspective of the firm, the important outcome is the effective use of women managers. From the women's perspective, the important outcome is her ability to perform at an appropriate level.

Harris examined the impact of an organisation's selection system for international assignments on the participation rates of women. She drew on the wider research into discrimination in selection to assess the extent to which differing types of selection systems would influence ideas about what is 'fit'. From a sociological perspective, selection is perceived as a social process, to be used by those in power within the organisation as a means of determining the continuing form of the organisation by recruiting and promoting only those individuals who most closely conform to organisational norms. Individuals would, therefore, be judged more on the basis of their acceptability than their suitability.

There are four typologies of selection systems for international manager positions. These are divided into two dimensions. The first dimension is related to the extent to which organisations used open or closed selection systems for international management assignments. An 'open' system is one in which all vacancies are advertised, anyone with appropriate qualifications and experience may apply, and candidates are interviewed with greater or lesser degrees of formalised testing. In contrast, a 'closed' system is one in which selectors at corporate headquarters nominate 'suitable' candidates to line managers who then have the option of accepting or rejecting the offer. The second dimension is related to the extent to which the process is 'formal' or 'informal'. In a 'formal' system, the selection criteria are made explicit and an objective debate takes place amongst selectors to decide which candidate most closely matches the criteria. An 'informal' system consists of selectors using subjective and often unstated criteria for assessment with minimal systematic evaluation. Four possible variations of selection systems could be open/formal, closed/formal, open/informal and closed/informal.

CASE

Failed Expatriate

Mr. Gafoor, a Malaysian national and an MBA from international Islamic University Malaysia was unable to fulfil the long awaited desire of his wife for working and living in a foreign country. Finally, situation has set-in as Ghana Telikom, Accra, Ghana selected Mr. Gafoor as its marketing manager on a contract basis for a three-year period. Mrs. Gafoor was excited and planned for the departure of the entire family including two children, and her old parents. In fact, Mr. Gafoor tried to convince his wife that he does not know anything of Ghana. In addition, he informed his wife that the culture, climate, living cost, social security, and political situation of Ghana are quite different from that of Malaysia and he has no clear idea of all these aspects. But Mrs. Gafoor did not listen to him and ultimately she herself decided the date for their travel.

The Ghana Telikom could not arrange for their work permit, visa and air tickets before the date fixed by Mrs. Gafoor. Then she asked her husband to arrange for visitors visa for all of them and buy the tickets from their savings as Ghana Telikom any how reimburses the cost of travel. Mr. Gafoor could not displease his wife and ultimately they landed in Accra as planned by his wife.

The housing and schooling facilities in Accra are quite inferior to the expectations of Mr. and Mrs. Gafoor. However, she initially did not complain as everything was done as per her wishes. But the two children started complaining of the facilities in the school everyday. Sooner or the later, her mother fell sick and Mr. Gafoor had to spend 50 per cent of his savings for her medical expenses, as Ghana Telikom's pay package does not include medical allowances for other family members, except the employee, spouse and children. Sooner or the later, Mrs. Gafoor's father-in-law also fell sick and Mr. Gafoor started experiencing financial crisis.

Mrs. Gafoor's honeymoon stage was over within three months and her desire of living in a foreign country was also fulfilled. Sooner, she developed a negative picture of Ghana and started feeling that they could not live properly as the food stuff they desire is not available in Ghana as well as the entertainment facilities are not according to their taste. She started murmuring and pressurising Mr. Gafoor that we should go back to Malaysia as the homeland is far better than any other country including Ghana. All the family members could muster the strength and support from Mrs. Gafoor that we should leave Ghana within 15 days.

Mr. Gafoor could not do anything except tendering his resignation and Ghana Telikom did not pay for their return fare as he did not honour the contract of working for three years. His superior expressed his unhappiness over the resignation, as the Ghana Telikom has to restart the selection process for the job of a marketing manager. Mr. Gafoor requested his friends in Malaysia to send money for their return ticket fares as his savings were just dismal. Finally, the whole family landed in Malaysia.

Discussion Questions

1. Discuss the major reasons for the failure of Mr. Gafoor.
2. To what extent Mrs. Gafoor is responsibile for the failure of her husband?
3. To what extent Ghana Telikom is responsible for the failure of Mr. Gafoor.
4. What strategies do you suggest for the prevention of such expatriate failures?

SUMMARY

- *Staffing for international assignments* deals with various considerations of HR professionals in recruiting and selecting personnel for their multinational operations.
- There are three major considerations that HR professionals need to take note of at the time of selection of personnel for their international operations.
- The first consideration is expatriate failure, which was defined more in terms of non-performance rather than in terms of failure to adjust.
- The second area of consideration is in cases where international employee can become a liability in the field of adjustment.
- The third consideration is the employee relationship which is affected through relational contract, transactional contract, and psychological contract.
- Some MNCs follow centralised recruitment while some others follow decentralised recruitment.
- The selection methods consist of interviews, monitoring and targeting of disadvantaged groups, assessment centres, and psychological testing.
- Most of the expatriate employees fail in the first foreign assignment due to various reasons including job factors, cultural factors, and family factors.
- For dual-career couples in the context of international assignments, alternative arrangements exist such as short-term assignment and commuter assignment.
- There are several issues related to women as international managers.

REVIEW QUESTIONS

1. Why expatriate failure is an important concern for an international organisation?
2. What are the factors that an HR manager should keep in mind while selecting expatriates? Explain.

3. For recruiting and selecting expatriates for international operations, what methods are to be followed?
4. Critically examine the various issues and difficulties involved in selecting and assigning roles to women as international managers.

REFERENCES

1. Price Waterhouse 1997. *International Assignments: European Policy and Practice,* 1997-98.
2. J.S. Black, M. Mendenhall and G. Oddou 1991. *'Toward a Comprehensive Model of International Adjustment: An Integration of Multiple Theoretical Perspectives',* Academy of Management Review, Vol. 16, pp. 291-317.
3. J.M. Hiltrop and M. Janssens (1999), *'Expatriation: Challenges and Recommendations',* European Management Journal, March, pp. 19-27.
4. W. Coyle (1992). *International Relocation,* Oxford: Butterworth-Heinemann.
5. S. Collins (1995). *Expatriation: A Moving Experience,* Dublin: Michael Smurfitt Graduate School of Business.
6. J.S. Black and G.K. Stephens (1989). *'The Influence of the Spouse on American Expatriate Adjustment in Overseas Assignments',* Journal of Management, Vol. 15, (1991), pp. 529-544.

5

Training and Development in International Context

Objectives

- To appreciate training of expatriates for foreign assignments abroad.
- To understand the importance of pre-departure training programmes like relocation assistance and language skills.
- To explain international career paths emanating from developmental aspects of international assignments.

INTRODUCTION

Training and development have received considerable attention in recent years. The question for the multinational firm is how to maintain and leverage its human resources so that suitably trained, internationally-oriented personnel are available to support its strategic responses and contribute to its core competencies. In India, some of the reputed software companies have their own learning centres both at the corporate level and at the unit level. Many other professionally-oriented companies, both in private and public sectors, have also established their own learning and management development centres. This only goes to prove the importance given to the training of human resources in India. Multinational companies are also providing suitable training for international assignees at different venues. In any training, identification of training needs assumes great significance.

Generally, training needs identification consists of organisational analysis, task analysis, and individual analysis.

TRAINING CYCLE

Training and development of the international staff should be viewed as a complete deployment cycle and should be directly linked with career development plans. The components of training and career development cycle consist of:

- Selection of the candidates/employees for international assignments.
- Identification of training needs in general.
- Identification of country-specific training needs and training of expatriates accordingly.
- Orientation programmes for the new host country employees.
- Provision of complete support during the re-entry process after completion of the assignment.
- Resumption of original position in the parent/home country.

The five training levels that ensure success of the training and development cycle of the international staff are:

1. Learning about the host country.
2. Understanding the requirements of the assignment.
3. Preparing for the new job at the new location.
4. Providing assistance to adjust and adapt to the new environment.
5. Contacting family and visit to home during vacation.

TRAINING OF EXPATRIATES

Most expatriates – whether PCNs or TCNs – are selected from within the multinational's existing operations, although some expatriates may be hired externally. Once an employee has been selected for an expatriate position, pre-departure training is considered to be the next critical step in attempting to ensure the expatriate's effectiveness and success. Effective cultural training enables individuals to adjust more quickly to the new culture.

There are significant country-level differences in the way training and development is managed. These differences show themselves in:[1]

- Training expenditure and budgeting
- Recipients of training
- Key areas of training

- Training delivery mechanism
- Monitoring of training effectiveness
- Management development

Training expenditure: The training expenditures generally vary by sector, with financial services and similar sectors spending more and the public sector tending to spend less. But there are also clear country-specific differences. For example, French organisations in all sectors are likely to spend more than organisations in other countries. This is partly because French legislation requires organisations to spend a minimum proportion of their labour costs on training (or pay equivalent sums to the government to help them provide training). In practice, French organisations tend to spend around double of what the law requires – the clear evidence of positive effect of the legislation.

Recipients of training: The recipients of training also show country-specific differences. Scandinavian countries are more likely to spread their training across a wide range of their employees. In every country, however, it tends to be the better-educated managers and professional staff who receive most training. Many countries in the Pacific region and in Africa tend to provide training for a more limited group – usually, again, the managerial and professional staff. There are also specific differences related to recent history. Thus, the provision of training in South Africa is supposed to emphasise training for the black population to overcome the earlier discrimination.

Key areas of training: The key areas of training tend not to change very much. Despite changes in technology, the main areas generally covered stay constant in each country – although there were changes in, for example, the central and eastern European countries when, following the collapse of the Communist governments there, a need for training in such areas as marketing became apparent. Generally, however, across Europe for example, the top four subjects are the management of people (supervising), information technology, the management of change, and customer service skills. In Asia, IT training appears to be more common; customer service skills do not figure so highly.

The process of formal identification of training needs is also widespread in Europe and the US, but less common elsewhere. However, the form of training needs analysis varies considerably. In North America and Europe, training needs are often identified through a performance appraisal system. Indeed, the use of performance appraisal has, over the last decade, consistently been the favourite method of identifying training needs in North America, the Republic of Ireland and the UK. It requires a culture where employees and managers are comfortable discussing such issues in a more or less informal way.[2] Elsewhere, it is often line management requests that are the main means of identifying training needs. This is the case in the southern countries of Europe and in many South American countries.

Training delivery: There is a growing interest in training being delivered through computer-based packages. This is obviously more likely to happen in those countries where organisations use the internet and intranet more extensively. Training is also an area of HR activity that is most likely to be outsourced to an external agency. Many organisations bring in outside experts or send their staff to universities, college or other organisations for particular areas of expertise either because internal resources are too bogged down to offer them or because they simply do not exist internally.

Monitoring of training effectiveness: Monitoring of training effectiveness is done assiduously in, for example, French, Italian and British organisations. However, other countries, including the Scandinavian and perhaps most non-European countries, pay much less attention to monitoring the effectiveness of training. This may be because they do not know how to do so, or it may be because they are prepared to accept that there are likely benefits from the training, and believe that trying to justify it is not worthwhile.

Management development: This is one area that is growing substantially around the world because of the notion that managers are the key people in an organisation. However, the approaches to management development vary from country-to-country. In most of North America and Europe, the objective is to identify high-flyers and then facilitate their development. Other countries and, of course, some organisations in those countries do not accept that the process of identification of future leaders is sufficiently advanced, and tend to 'leave the door open' for developmental activities for a wider pool of managers. The processes of management development also tend to exhibit country differences. Thus, in Japan and France rotation through different functions is in practice, whereas in the USA specialist training from business school experts for the particular function is more common.

International companies are developing local managers through informal on-the-job training within the subsidiary. Expatriate managers play the dominant role in this training, supplemented by visits of headquarters managers. Top level local nationals are also frequently invited to corporate headquarters to give them an understanding of corporate policies and a feel of the company as a whole. Periodic international management conferences at home or abroad are also organised to bring about face-to-face contacts between local managers and the headquarters staff. Some of the sophisticated international firms have integrated local management training programmes.

Expatriates tend to view their international assignment as an opportunity for personal and professional development and career advancement. Management development programmes to prepare expatriates for their international assignment often include environmental briefings about the geography, climate, housing, and schools; cultural orientation about the cultural institutions and value systems; language training; and sensitivity training to develop attitudinal flexibility.

AREAS OF GLOBAL TRAINING AND DEVELOPMENT

The areas of global training and development include:

- Technical training
- Functional training

- Strategic management skills training
- Human relations/soft-skills training
- Cross-cultural training
- Language training
- Expatriate training
- On-the-job training assignments
- Global mindset training
- Team training
- Pre-departure training.

Technical Training

Most of the MNCs select the expatriates mostly based on the technical skill background to perform the new job successfully. Most of the host country nationals need technical training as many of them join various MNCs without required technical skill. Hence, MNCs provide such training to the host country nationals as well as the expatriates who take up long-run assignments.

Functional Training

Expatriates are employed in functional jobs in the areas of accountancy, law, production, sales, teaching, and so on. Expatriates normally possess required functional skills before joining the MNCs but such skills may not exactly suit to their functional job requirements. MNCs need to train the expatriates in such skills in order to plug the gaps. Moreover, MNCs should train host country nationals in functional skills on a continuous basis.

Strategic Management Skills Training

MNCs prefer expatriates for strategic level positions in view of their exceptional skills initially. However, MNCs aim at developing the host country nationals even for strategic management positions. Strategic managers are core and critical managers of MNCs and viewed as critical strategic assets of the organisation. Therefore, MNCs train and develop these employees on priority basis in internationally reputed institutions.

Human Relations/Soft Skills Training

These skills refer mostly to interpersonal skills like interpersonal communication, leadership skills, motivational skills, commitment skills, team building skills, emotional balance skills, social skills, and the like. MNCs train both expatriates as well as host country employees in all kinds of soft skills in order to enhance the human relations skills of managers under multi-cultural environment.

Cross-cultural Training

Cross-cultural training is most significant and critical one among the areas of global training. Hence, most of the MNCs follow the training procedure systematically to conduct such training. MNCs follow different approaches to train expatriates, nationals of the subsidiaries, and employees of joint venture partners. Cross-cultural training include: (a) parent country nationals, (b) host country nationals of subsidiaries, (c) third country nationals, (d) other kinds of expatriates, and (e) employees of joint venture partners.

Language Training

Language plays a predominant role in international business. English language is widely used in international business transactions, but most of the stakeholders like customers, marketing intermediaries may not communicate in this language. In addition, there are some countries in which even business transactions take place in languages like French, Arabic, and German. Many MNCs employ expatriates who cannot speak the language used for business transactions in the host country. This situation forces MNCs to provide appropriate language training.

Expatriate Training

One of the reasons for the failure of expatriate, spouse, and other family members is lack of adjustment to physical and cultural environment of the foreign country. Other reasons include: (a) employee's immature personality and less emotional intelligence; (b) employee's inability to cope-up with the responsibilities and challenges of foreign assignment; (c) employee's lack of technical competence; and (d) employee's lack of motivation to work in foreign countries. Hence, training is needed to help the expatriates and their family members to overcome these barriers and behave in a particular way in the foreign social culture and work setup.

On-the-Job Training Assignments

MNCs provide specific cultural skills, interpersonal skills and technical skills relating to the workplace and the job through on-the-job assignments. These assignments provide employees an opportunity of interacting with colleagues, superiors, subordinates, and other stakeholders.

Global Mindset Training

Global mindset is the ability to scan the world from a broad perspective, always looking for unexpected trends and opportunities that may constitute a threat or an opportunity to achieve personal, professional, and organisational objectives. Employees of MNCs, in order to interact effectively with managers, customers, market intermediaries and suppliers and colleagues in other countries, should have the ability and willingness to interact from others' point of view and approach. Further, to acquire global mindset, they should: (a) cope up with globally competing priorities, (b) sustain a holistic global outlook, (c) imbibe tolerance, flexibility, curiosity, and ability to deal under different situations, (d) learn global awareness of behaviours and cultures, and (e) develop adaptability to live and work across different cultures and practices.

Team Training

Team work is regarded as a distinctive characteristic of Japanese companies, where employees view themselves as members of team community rather than just employees. Working in team is rather difficult than that of individual as the former requires proper understanding and adaptation to culture, values, norms, and other behavioural aspects of the team members.

International team training offers the following advantages to the MNCs:

- Sharing and exchanging of technical skills, functional knowledge, and cultures across nations.
- Developing global mindset and preparing the employees for effective international assignments.
- Providing an opportunity to realise highest potential of international employees by creating challenge and competition among them.
- Developing problem solving skills, crisis management skills, conflict management skills, and so on.
- Inculcating organisational learning, global culture, and global human resources.

Pre-departure Training

Pre-departure training is provided to the selected new employees as well as the existing employees who are assigned jobs in other countries. This training is imparted at the country where the candidate currently lives or in other nearby country other than the future place of work. For instance, some MNCs provide training either in New Delhi for the candidates selected from India, Pakistan and Nepal for jobs in European countries. This training is usually in four major areas, *viz.*, (a) culture, (b) language, (c) preliminary aspects of the job and (d) business environment in the destination countries.

COMPONENTS OF PRE-DEPARTURE TRAINING

Studies indicate that the essential components of pre-departure training programmes that contribute to a smooth transition to a foreign post include cultural awareness programmes, preliminary visits, language instruction, and assistance with practical day-to-day matters:

Cultural Awareness Programmes: As is well known, habits and practices relating to work motivation, profit motivation, negotiating skills, gift-giving customs, eating and dressing, body gestures, time-consciousness, interpretation of colour and numbers vary across countries. It is essential that employees are trained to handle these nuances before posted overseas. This thought is devoted to expatriate pre-departure training activities that are mainly concerned with developing cultural awareness.

It is generally accepted that in order to be effective, the expatriate employee must adapt to the host country and not feel isolated. A well-designed cultural awareness training programme can be extremely beneficial as it seeks to foster an appreciation of the host country's culture so that expatriates can behave accordingly or at least develop appropriate coping patterns. The components of cultural awareness programmes vary according to the country of assignment, duration, purpose of the transfer and the provider of such programmes. As part of her study of expatriate management, Tung[3] identified five categories of pre-departure training, based on different learning processes, the type of job, the country of assignment, and the time available:

- Area studies programmes that include environmental briefing and cultural orientation
- Cultural assimilators
- Language training
- Sensitivity training
- Field experiences

To understand the possible variations in expatriate training, Tung proposed a contingency framework for deciding the nature and rigour of training. Two determining factors were the degree of interaction required in the host culture and the similarity between the individual's native culture and the new culture. The related training elements in her framework involved the content of the training and the rigour of the training. Essentially, Tung argued that if the expected interaction between the individual and the members of the host culture was low, and the degree of dissimilarity between the individual's native culture and the host culture was low, then training should focus on task and job-related issues rather than culture-related issues. The level of rigour necessary for effective training should be relatively low.

Tung's model specifies the criteria for making training method decisions, such as the degree of expected interaction and cultural similarity. One of its limitation is that it does not assist the user to determine which specific training methods to use or what might constitute more or less rigorous training. For example, let us consider an Indian expatriate assigned to work in Pakistan, the dissimilarity between these two cultures is low and further if the assignment is only on planning and design which does not require any interaction between the individual and the members of the host country, then training should focus on task and job-related issues rather than culture-related issues. That is why in the pre-departure training of expatriate there cannot be a uniform pattern of training; it has to be tailormade.

Mendenhall *et. al.*, propose the three dimensional training methods – low, medium and high levels of training rigour, and the duration of the training relative to the degree of interaction and culture novelty – as useful guidelines for determining an appropriate programme. For example, if the expected level of interaction is low and the degree of similarity between the individual's native culture and the host culture is high, the length of the training should probably be less than a week. Methods such as area or cultural briefings via lectures, movies or books would provide the appropriate level of training rigour. On the other hand, if the individual is going overseas for a period of two – twelve months and is expected to have some interaction with members of the host culture, the level of training rigour should be higher and its duration longer. In addition to the information giving approaches, training methods such as culture assimilators and role plays may be appropriate. In addition to the less rigorous methods, sensitivity training, field experiences, and inter-cultural experiential workshops may be appropriate training methods in this situation.

Preliminary Visits: One useful technique in orienting international employees is to send them on a preliminary trip to the host country. A well-planned overseas trip for the candidate and spouse provides a preview that allows them to assess their suitability for an interest in the assignment. Such a trip also serves to introduce expatriate candidates to the business context in the host location and helps encourage more informed pre-departure preparation. When used as part of a pre-departure training programme, visits to the host nation can assist in the initial adjustment process.

The aim of the preliminary visit is often too-fold – partly the selection decision and partly the pre-departure training. The multinational could send mixed signals if it offers the preliminary visit as part of the selection process.

Somehow, if they do not like the assignment and are forced into it, the expatriate failure which is very costly would occur. Even in India, for senior positions preliminary family visits are arranged, particularly in non-metro locations. The visiting family often declines the position on grounds of unsuitability.

However, if an expatriate community exists in the country of prospective posting, the preliminary visit may pave the way for interaction with the community and allay the misgivings the expatriates may have about the location. This is one of the positive points of such visits.

Language Instruction: Language training is a seemingly obvious, desirable component of a pre-departure programme. However, there are three inter-related aspects related to a language ability that needs to be recognised:

The role of English in the business world is very well known. It is generally accepted that English is the language of world business, though the form of English is more 'international English' than that spoken by native speakers of English. Multinationals from English-speaking countries such as the United States, United Kingdom, and Australia often use this fact as a reason for not considering language ability in the selection process and for not stressing language training as part of pre-departure programmes.

Host country language skills and adjustment: Clearly, the ability to speak a foreign language can improve the effectiveness of the expatriates and their negotiating ability. It can improve a manager's access to information regarding the host country's economy, government and market. Of course, the degree of fluency required may depend on the level and nature of the position that the expatriate holds in the foreign operation, the amount of interaction with external stakeholders, such as government officials, clients, trade officials, as well as with host country nationals. Also, language skills are important in terms of task performance and cultural adjustment.

Knowledge of the corporate language: *Marschan et. al.*, highlight what appears to be a somewhat neglected issue – the impact that the adoption of a common corporate language has upon HRM activities within the multinational. They argue that for multinationals from non-English-speaking countries, the standardisation of information and reporting systems tends to be handled in the language of the (parent) country of origin until geographical dispersal makes that problematic. The multinational then adopts (either deliberately or by default) a common language to facilitate reporting, standardising, and other control mechanisms.

A PCN fluent in the parent-country language and the language of the host subsidiary can perform a gate-keeping role, whichever formal position the expatriate may hold. What this line of research suggests is that for multinationals that have adopted a corporate language, pre-departure training programmes may need to include both the language of the host country and the corporate language.

Practical Assistance: Instead of throwing the expatriate and his/her family to fend for themselves in the new environment in the host country, which may sometimes become a harrowing experience causing them to panic and return, it would be a good move to provide practical assistance to them until they overcome all the hurdles they may face with respect to customs, language, and so on. The local subsidiary may arrange some kind of orientation programme not only for the expatriate but also for his/her family members.

It makes good sense to help them settle down in terms of housing, schooling, medical facilities, shopping centres, and so on. The sooner the expatriate and his family settle down, the faster will be his ability to perform at his peak level. It is, therefore, important that the corporate HR department liase with the line managers in addition to the HR department in the foreign location to ensure that practical assistance is provided.[4]

HCN Training

When the expatriate is posted to a subsidiary in a foreign location, he/she desires to get back once a replacement is made available from amongst the HCNs. Therefore, it becomes a necessity for the expatriate to impart or transfer knowledge to the HCN. Towards this, he/she needs to be trained even before he/she leaves the shores of the parent country. The training cannot be done after the expatriate takes on the job in the host country, because the subsidiary then suffers without the needed expertise to run its operations. The ability to transfer knowledge and skills in a culturally-sensitive manner should perhaps be an integral part of pre-departure training programmes. In fact, all staff members should be provided with the necessary level of pre-departure training, given the demands of the international assignment.

Owing to the availability of cheap labour, many multinationals have set-up training facilities in host countries with a view to imparting the needed skills, both technical as well as managerial, to the HCNs. The cost involved in training all the HCNs at times becomes huge and the 'cheap labour' factor does not workout. Yet, after all the effort of training the HCNs, the competitors may also set-up such facilities in the same host country and offer a slightly better compensation package to the already trained HCNs and lure them away. This kind of poaching costs the original multinational that had spent money and energy on training.

The mode of operation is another issue related to HCN training. For instance, entering a joint venture arrangement can lead to unexpected training costs if the local partner regards the joint venture operation as a convenient way of redeploying surplus employees who may not have the skills required. The multinational may have to invest heavily in the training of the joint venture. These costs may, however, be offset by the benefits that airse out of training such as improvement in the ability to adjust to the new environment, perceiving support from the employer, establishing rapport with the HCNs, and the local government officials.

When it comes to HCN training programmes, given our understanding of cultural differences, it could be assumed that this is an area that the multinational would automatically delegate to the local operation. To a certain extent, training programmes are localised, but there are many cases where multinationals have successfully replicated work practices in their foreign subsidiaries through intensive-training programmes designed and implemented by the headquarters. This is particularly true regarding technical training for operating employees in areas where certain skills and work practices are regarded as strategically essential. To save on costs, some multinationals are now using satellite technology to deliver custom-designed training courses from home country locations.[5]

DEVELOPING INTERNATIONAL STAFF

It has been already seen that international exposure for any individual offers a lot of learning to him/her which can be channelised towards management development, organisational development, and individual development.

Individuals gain international experience, which assists in career progression, while the multinational gains because it has a pool of experienced international individual operators on which it can bank for its future international assignments. Expatriates assist in the transfer of knowledge and competence and they also act as agents of direct control and socialisation. A global mindset is a by-product of these assignments because of which the organisation is poised for future growth through its knowledge and skill base.

International job assignments for employees from different countries on a single project provide an opportunity to work together and share and exchange their skills, culture and behaviours. Once this storming stage is over, they learn from each other technical and managerial skills which lead to significant human resource development. Further, it also results in global mindset of employees, creates distinctive competency to the MNC, and ultimately leads to organisational development.

Individuals accept international assignments because they perceive in them financial gain and career advancement apart from opportunities to enhance their abilities by exposing them to a range of jobs, tasks and challenges. Therefore, it is not wrong to assume that international assignment *per se* has management development potential.

Surveys consistently report that expatriates consider career progression as a primary motive for accepting international assignments. Such a consistency of response – that is, career development as a reason for accepting an overseas assignment – has masked the issue of whether these career expectations are indeed met. Career development occurs only when both organisational and individual expectations are met. But in international assignments, we do not have enough evidence on whether this actually happens.

Establishing truly global operations means having a team of international managers (PCNs, HCNs and TCNs) who are available to go anywhere in the world and can think globally. To develop such teams, many multinationals are conscious that they need to provide international experience to many levels of managers (regardless of nationality) and not just to a small number of PCNs. One technique used to develop larger pools of employees with international experience is through short-term development assignments ranging from a few months to several years.

International job rotation is one well-established technique for developing multinational teams and international operators. It may be supported by PCN, TCN and HCN attendance at common training and development programmes held either in the parent country or regional centres or both. The global leadership programmes at the University of Michigan is an example of externally provided training programmes. For a period of five weeks, teams of

American, Japanese and European executives learn global business skills through action learning. To build cross-cultural teams, the programme utilises seminars and lectures, adventure-based exercises and field trips to investigate business opportunities in countries such as Brazil, China and India. The overall objective of the global leadership programmes is to produce individuals with a global perspective. The success of such programmes depends on participants being able to apply these skills in their home location and assist in the development of multinational, cross-border, and cross-functional teams.

International meetings in various locations have also become important forums for fostering interaction and personal networks that may be used later to build global teams.[6] In line with a general trend towards an emphasis on work teams, there is a suggestion that multinationals would benefit from building on their inherent diversity to foster innovation, and organisational learning and transfer of knowledge. Fostering a sense of corporate identity and teamwork seems an important aspect of leveraging resources and ideas from all parts of the multinational.

CROSS-CULTURAL AND ETHICS TRAINING

Cross-cultural Training

Traditionally, communication training mainly focussed programmes for special target groups, preparing for assignments outside the trainees' home country. However, there is a growing awareness that in a world that is becoming a global village and in multi-cultural societies, education on cultural matters should be part of the school curriculum.

The inability of an expatriate to adjust to the host country's social and business environment is costly in terms of management performance, client relations, and operations efficiency. Under the circumstances, cross-cultural training of expatriation will be more effective in their adjustment and development during the pre-departure, expatriation, and repatriation stages of international assignments.

A key component of preparing employees for expatriate assignments is cross-cultural training, to prepare them (and their families) for the cultural adjustments they will need to make. Typical components of cross-cultural training are attribution training, cultural awareness training, interaction training, language training, didactic training, and experiential training.

Cross-cultural orientation and training programmes train individuals belonging to one culture ways of interacting effectively with minimal interpersonal misunderstanding in another culture. Training is a worthwhile investment in terms of public relations and goodwill for the company.

There is some consensus among cross-cultural trainers that certain basic areas need to be dealt with:

1. Self-awareness
2. Awareness of one's culture
3. Belief and values
4. Host country area information
5. Culture and the natives' expectations
6. The expatriate's purpose for going abroad
7. The extent of responsibility and risk in performance.

Many of the goals of training and education are the same, i.e., increased awareness of cultural differences, increased knowledge, movement beyond stereotypes, introduction to emotional confrontations, coverage of different behaviours, and so forth. It can be argued that much of this education should be part of foreign languages. A weak point of intercultural training programmes is the lack of evaluation of their effects. Often, a brief questionnaire is administered at the end of a training programme, but this indicates whether the trainees liked the programme, rather than its effectiveness.

Training in Cultural Diversity: Diversity training is basically done due to the following reasons:

- For legislative compliance, for the purposes of equal opportunity and the prevention of race discrimination and disability discrimination. Diversity policies frequently cover gender, ethnic status and disability under the various laws of the country. Sometimes, diversity laws cover age and sexual harassment.
- For providing diversity training to employees with the ability to handle the increased heterogeneity of their markets and customers, thereby giving the organisation a competitive edge.
- For providing an opportunity to bring together a mix of people where differences are valued – an environment where people grow with innovative ideas and help in improving productivity and solving problems of the organisation.

Box 5.1

Cross-cultural Training at Procter and Gamble

The company organised a training programme to train all the far flung managers of different countries on the P&G way, and to reduce cultural and linguistic barriers. The training programme had three elements; (a) grammar and vocabulary of business English and basics of written and oral communication; (b) the subtleties of cross-cultural communication – eye contact gesturing, verbal feedback during conversation; and (c) exploring the P&G culture and understanding broad values that transcend geographic boundaries.

The programme's participants began with a preparatory course in Brazil, followed by a three-to-five month intensive programme conducted by outside consultants.

Ethics Training

Teaching ethical behaviour is more than supplying a list of do's and dont's. No adult likes to be told what to do in an authoritarian manner. In many cultures, especially those that value the independence of the individual, such an approach is likely to encourage potentially disastrous resistance to the ethics effort. It is a matter of not what you teach, but how you teach it.

Many large multinational corporations have shifted the emphasis of their training programmes away from passive employee compliance toward a focus on accountability and active employee commitment to living out corporate core values. The reason for this shift is simple. In the past, ethics training took on a dictatorial tone that alienated employees. Now in vogue is a more positive approach, one that stresses individual responsibility, gives employees the tools to understand corporate standards and values, and make sound ethical decisions that put those values into action. Ultimately, the role of ethics training has become the empowerment of each and every employee to make ethical decisions.

Before designing a training course on ethics, management needs to consider three basic facts of life:

1. Employees should be held accountable for their actions.
2. They cannot be held accountable for rules that are vague or unclear.
3. Employees are basically trustworthy, but may not be able to make good decisions in circumstances that are confusing.

Employees need to be armed with the knowledge to analyse and resolve ethical dilemmas so that they aren't paralysed. In fact, the word "training" can be misleading when applied to corporate ethics programmes. No company, regardless of its geographic location or home culture, can train employees to act ethically in the same way that it can provide training in specific job skill courses like computer software or accounting methods. After all, employees come to a job with a personal set of moral standards and values already in place.

With this perspective in mind, the role of ethics training should be to raise awareness about business ethics issues and educate employees about proper business conduct standards and the core values of the organisation. The goal should be to provide employees with the guidance and tools they need to apply these standards and values in the workplace and make sound ethical business decisions.

The goals of a corporate ethics training programme can be summarised as follows:

- Enhance staff knowledge on legal requirements.
- Enable staff to understand and realise ethical standards set by their company.
- Equip staff with skills to handle ethical dilemmas.

- Equip management with skills to detect early warning signs of corruption, fraud and malpractice.
- Enable staff to abide by the company's code of conduct.

As for benefits, an ethics training programme can:

- Improve performance by linking corporate values to individual success.
- Enhance overall organisational effectiveness by encouraging mutual respect and trust.

SUMMARY

- *Training and development in international context* lays emphasis on different training programmes for developing international staff.
- The differences in the management of training between countries are in: (a) training expenditure and budgeting; (b) the recipients of training; (c) the key areas of training; (d) the training delivery mechanism; (e) the monitoring of training effectiveness; and (f) management development and appraisal.
- The areas of global training and development include: (a) technical training; (b) functional training; (c) strategic management skills training; (d) soft-skills training; (e) cross-cultural training; (f) ethics training; (g) language training; (h) pre-departure training; (i) expatriate training; (j) on-the-job training assignments; (k) global mindset training; and (l) team training.
- The analysis of cross-cultural training needs helps to identify cultural skill and knowledge gap, and assist in designing the content of the training programme accordingly.
- The components of effective pre-departure training programmes are: (a) cultural awareness programmes; (b) preliminary visits; (c) language training; (d) practical assistance; (e) training to train; and (f) HCN training.
- Diversity training is done for: (a) legislative compliance; (b) providing employees with the ability to handle the increased heterogeneity of their markets and customers, thereby giving the organisation a competitive edge; and (c) providing the opportunity to bring together a mix of people where differences are valued.
- The three important elements of language training are: (a) the role of English as the language of world business; (b) host country language skills and adjustment; and (c) knowledge of the corporate language.
- Exposure to the international work environment leads to development at many levels, such as: (a) management development; (b) organisational development; (c) individual development; and (d) development of international staff and multinational teams.

- Ethics and communication training should receive due importance in a global context.

REVIEW QUESTIONS

1. What are the country-level differences in training? Explain.
2. Elaborate on the various components of pre-departure training programme for expatriates and on their importance.
3. How does an international assignment assist in developing a team of international specialists? Why is it necessary to develop such a team?
4. Discuss the various components of pre-departure training programme for expatriates and their importance.
5. What is the significance of ethics training?
6. Workout a management development programme to prepare managers for expatriate assignments. The programme should include technical, business, language, cross-cultural training, and on-going expatriate support.

REFERENCES

1. H. Harris, C. Brewster and P. Sparrow (2003), *International Human Resource Management*, Chartered Institute of Personnel Development, London.
2. P. Lawrence and V. Edwards (2000), *Management in Western Europe*, Macmmillan, London.
3. R. Tung (1981), *Selecting and Training of Personnel for Overseas Assignments*, Columbia Journal of World Business, Vol. 16, pp. 68-78.
4. M. Marschan, D. Welch and L. Welch (1997), *Language: The Forgotten Factor in Multinational Management*, European Management Journal, Vol. 15, No. 5, pp. 591-97.
5. J.P. Giusti, D.R. Baker and P.J. Graybash (1997), *Satellites Dish Out Global Training*, Personnel Journal, June, pp. 80-84.
6. Edstrom and J. Galbraith (1977), *Transfer of Managers as a Coordination and Control Strategy in Multinational Organisations*, Administrative Science Quarterly, Vol. 322, pp. 248-63.

6

International Compensation System

Objectives

- To understand the general objectives and complexities of international compensation from different perspectives.
- To find out what components go into the making of the compensation package.
- To discuss the existing approaches or systems in the field of international compensation.

INTRODUCTION

The main problem facing any organisation is the laying down a fair and equitable compensation system. For multinational firms, successful management of compensation and benefits requires knowledge of employment and taxation laws, customs, environment, and employment practices of many foreign countries. Also needed are familiarity with currency fluctuations and the effect of inflation on compensation, and an understanding of why and when special allowances must be given and which allowances are necessary in what countries. All of these needs must be fulfilled within the context of shifting political, economic, and social conditions. Because of their high-cost, HR managers spend a great deal of time developing effective compensation and benefit programmes for international employees.

OBJECTIVES

While developing international compensation policies, a firm seeks to satisfy several objectives. It also tries to achieve its compensation goals by specifying certain sound policy decisions. *First,* the policy should be consistent with the overall strategy, structure, and business needs of the multinational. *Second,* the policy should work to attract and retain staff in the areas where the multinational has the greatest needs and opportunities. *Third,* the policy should facilitate the transfer of international employees in the most cost-effective manner for the firm. *Fourth,* the policy should give due consideration to equity and fairness. *Fifth,* the policy should be properly administered and cost-effective as far as practicable.

The international employee will also try to fulfil his/her expectations from the firm's compensation policy. *First,* the employee will expect that the policy offers financial protection in terms of benefits, social security, and cost of living in the foreign location. *Second,* the employee will expect that the foreign assignment offers opportunities for financial advancement through income and/or savings. *Third,* the employee will expect that issues such as housing, education of children and recreation will be addressed in the policy.

If we compare the objectives of the multinational and the employee we see the potential for many complexities and possible problems since some of these objectives cannot be maximised on both sides. The firms must rethink the traditional view of international compensation and accept that local conditions dominate compensation strategy.[1]

Cherrington (1991) suggests that the compensation decisions should achieve the following six critical objectives:

1. *Be legal*: Compensation should be consistent with federal, state, and local laws and regulations.
2. *Be adequate*: Compensation should be sufficient to attract qualified job applicants and retain them.
3. *Be motivating*: Compensation should be adequate to provide necessary incentives for motivating employees to high performance levels.
4. *Be equitable*: Compensation should make a person feel that the system is equitable.
5. *Be secure*: Compensation should make the employees feel that their income is secure and predictable.
6. *Be cost-effective*: Compensation system should be administered effectively and result in cost-effectiveness.

COMPLEXITIES

Compensation management function is more critical and complex over other functions. The factors responsible for these are:

- Varying salary and benefit levels from country-to-country.
- Varying cost of living among countries.
- Varying requirements of housing, schooling, medical and health facilities for employee family members in different countries.
- Varying salary levels of expatriates in their respective home countries.
- Varying and fluctuating foreign exchange rates in different countries.
- Varying tax rates.
- Varying rates of inflation and deflation among the developed and developing countries.

The major differential factors in compensation between countries are:

1. Prosperity and capacity of the company to pay differs from country-to-country.
2. The institutional frameworks within which wage bargaining takes place are quite different in different countries.
3. Cultural differences between countries.
4. Considerable differences between organisations and industries.

COMPENSATION PLAN

Any international compensation plan must be well thoughtout; thoroughly understood by employees at all levels; properly executed by management; and remain flexible to demands of the personnel involved. International compensation plan must be up to date, sensitive, and responsive to changing overseas conditions relating to all important components of compensation package. The plan once devised should be simple to understand and operate, and achieve due recognition and support from all those covered by it. Compensation of overseas personnel for the multinational organisation concerns itself with three categories of staff namely, expatriates, third-country nationals, and local nationals. Some considerations which should be kept in mind while developing the expatriate compensation plan are: (a) consistency, (b) competitiveness, (c) motivation, (d) control of costs, and (e) affordability. Further, the plan should consider not only the professional expertise of the expatriate manager but also certain other factors like his ability to adjust to the local culture, adaptability and flexibility, diplomatic skills, and language aptitude.

INFLUENCING FACTORS

The goals of MNCs include profit earning, expansion of markets, increasing market share and the like. There are a number of variables that affect international compensation.

The factors that affect international compensation in MNCs are both internal, environmental factors, and external environmental factors.

The internal environmental factors which are related to the company's strategic management and functional areas of management are:

Capacity to pay: An MNC's capacity to pay is based on its long run profitability.

Competitive strategy: MNCs adopting aggressive and offensive business strategies would like to be competitive. For example, Coca-Cola adapts competitive strategies over Pepsi-Cola and Xerox over Canon. Such companies also adopt competitive strategy in designing a pay package over that of their competitors.

Organisational culture: Organisational culture is embodied by the quality of work life. Quality of work life in its turn is influenced by the benefits and facilities provided by the MNCs. Therefore, MNCs provide various benefits like car allowance, health insurance, stock options, and so on.

Role of subsidiaries: Subsidiaries play a vital role in designing the compensation package in view of their specific requirements in terms of job skills, operational requirements, culture, stakeholder demands and the system.

Human resource structure: It includes age, gender, educational qualifications, skill level and attitudes of employees which influence the compensation packages. Thus, HR policies and programmes as such affect the compensation structure and package.

Employee-employer relations: Employee-employer relations are determined by their attitude towards each other and the existence of trade unions. Trade unions influence wage bargaining and wage structure of a firm to a great extent.

Level of technology: Level of technology determines the level of skill and knowledge requirements, demand for and supply of specific skills, level of difficulty in adjusting to the new technology. All these factors influence the structure and level of compensation and benefits.

The external environmental factors which influence the compensation package and benefits are:

Parent country: Country of the MNCs headquarters, its culture, cost of living, values and attitudes towards compensation influence the initial compensation structure. The compensation package levels and patterns and types of benefits in the parent country influence in designing the pay package.

Labour market characteristics: Labour market characteristics that influence compensation include demand for and supply of different categories of employees and their skills and knowledge. Labour market characteristics like demand and supply play pivotal role in designing compensation package. Other factors that influence compensation package in this context are the availability of training and educational institutions; the location of organisations competing for the same kind of skills; the influence of cultural factors on equity or differentials in the compensation package; and the beliefs, attitudes and tolerance levels towards compensation inequities between expatriates and nationals.

Local conditions: Local conditions of the country where MNC or subsidiary is located include the security conditions, availability of housing, medical, educational, telecommunication, hospitality, transportation and recreational facilities and their cost. These conditions determine the cost of living in that country along with general price trends. Level of cost of living influence the cost of living package.

Host and home country government roles: Governments through their labour policies, enactment of compensation laws and guidelines issued to various companies influence the compensation levels as well as benefits package.

Industry type: Compensation package and structure mostly depend on the type of industry. For example, the salary levels of employees working in software industry are higher than that of cement industry. International compensation strategies also vary according to industry type.

Competitor's strategies: Competitors' strategies in business, human resource management as well as compensation package influence the compensation package of foreign companies.

KEY COMPONENTS

The key components include base salary, foreign service inducement/hardship programme, and various allowances and benefits.

Base salary: The term 'base salary' acquires a somewhat different meaning when employees go abroad. In a domestic context, base salary denotes the amount of each compensation that serves as a benchmark for other compensation elements. For expatriates, it is the primary component of a package of allowances, many of which are directly related to base salary. It may be paid in home or local-country currency. The base salary is the foundation block for international compensation whether the employee is a PCN or TCN. Major differences can occur in the employee's package depending on whether the base salary is linked to the home currency of the PCN or TCN or whether an international rate is paid.

Allowances: Issues concerning allowances can be very challenging to a firm establishing an overall compensation policy, partly because of the various forms of allowances that exist.

The cost of living allowance which typically receives the most attention, involves a payment to compensate for differences in expenditures between the home country and the foreign country. It varies from one city to another city of the same country and from one country to another country. In addition, it varies from one period of time and the other period of time in the same city and country and year.

The provision of a housing allowance implies that employees should be entitled to maintain their home country living standards (or, in some cases, receive accommodation that is equivalent to that provided for similar foreign employees and peers). Such allowances are often paid on either an assessed or actual basis. Other alternatives include company provided housing, either mandatory or optional; a fixed housing allowance; or assessment of a portion of income, out of which actual housing costs are paid. Housing issues are often addressed on a case-by-case basis.

There is also a provision for home leave allowance. Many employers cover the expense of one or more trips back to the home country each year. The purpose of paying for such trips is to give expatriates the opportunity to renew family and business ties, thereby helping them to avoid adjustment problems when they are repatriated.

Educational allowances for expatriates' children are also an integral part of any international compensation policy. Allowances for education can cover items such as tuition, language class tuition, enrolment fees, books and stationery, transportation, room and board, and uniforms.

Relocation allowances usually cover moving, shipping, and storage charges, temporary living expenses, subsidies for appliance or car purchases (or sales), and down payments or lease-related charges. Allowances regarding perquisites may also need to be considered. These allowances are often contingent upon tax-equalisation policies and practices in both the home and the host countries.

Hardship allowance is designed to induce expatriates to work in hazardous areas or in an area with a poor quality of life. These payments may be in the form of a lump sum or a percentage of the expatriates' base salary. It is again a case of relativity. For instance, Americans posted even in Indian metros are given a hardship allowance.

Parent country nationals often receive a salary premium as an inducement to accept a foreign assignment or as compensation for any hardship caused by the transfer. Under such circumstances, the definition of hardship, eligibility for the premium, and amount and timing of payment must be addressed.

Most MNCs are lean organisations and would not offer a job unless there is a vacant position. Many have policies of not employing spouses in the same company/location. Some do, however, have a separate arrangement with other companies.

Benefits: Company policy must be defined prior to adopting an employee benefit programme for expatriates. Decisions about: (a) centralisation or decentralisation of the plan, (b) installing one international plan or separate plans in each country, (c) eligibility requirements for coverage, and (d) selection of a funding method.

After a company policy is approved, the basic parameters of the plan should be developed to meet certain objectives, such as: (a) making it cost competitive, (b) meeting operating costs, (c) ensuring equitable treatment, (d) promoting employee understanding, (e) simplifying administration, (f) attracting and retaining high calibre employees, and (g) meeting the requirements of varied income levels.

The complexity inherent in international benefits often brings more difficulties than when dealing with compensation. Pension plans are very difficult to deal with country-to-country because national practices vary considerably. Firms need to address many issues when considering benefits, including:

- Whether to maintain expatriates in home country programmes particularly if the firm does not receive a tax deduction.
- Whether firms have the option of enrolling expatriates in host country benefit programmes and/or making up any difference in coverage.
- Whether expatriates should receive home country or host country social security benefits.

In addition to the already discussed benefits, multinationals also provide vacations and special leave. As part of the employee's regular vacation, annual home leave usually provides airfares for families to return to their home countries. Rest and rehabilitation leave, based on the conditions of the host country, also provides the employee's family with free airfares to a more comfortable location near the host country. Apart from rest and rehabilitation leave, emergency provisions are available in case of a death or illness in the family.

MANAGING PAY VARIATIONS

Five factors make variations in international pay packages. These are: (a) social contract, (b) national culture, (c) trade unions and employee involvement, (d) ownership and capital markets, and (e) managerial autonomy.

Social contract: Different people in different countries hold differing beliefs about the role of government, employees, unions, and employers in determining compensation system. Understanding how to manage employee compensation in any country requires knowledge of the social contract in that country. For example, United Kingdom, United States, Canada, and Brazil use highly decentralised approaches with little government involvement. On the other hand, Denmark, Sweden, and Austria use highly centralised approaches that create a national pay system.

National culture: The assumption that pay systems must be designed to fit different national cultures is based on the belief that a country's inhabitants mostly share a national character. Therefore, the job of a global manager is to define the national characteristics that influence payment systems. Advocates of national culture believe that the companies should adjust their compensation practices to the cultural specifics of a particular host country.

Trade unions and employee involvement: Trade union density varies across the globe. For instance, Europe remains highly unionised. In Sweden 91 per cent of the workforce belongs to unions, in the United Kingdom 33 per cent, and in Italy 44 per cent. Asia is less heavily unionised, Japan's unionisation rate is 24 per cent, and South Korea's is almost 13 per cent (all approximate figures). In some countries, workers' payments are determined by collective agreements even for non-unionised members, for example India and France. In addition to having higher rates of unionisation, Germany, Belgium, and the European Union (EU) require the involvement of works councils in any changes to a pay plan.

Ownership and capital markets: Social legislation laying down statutory payment of wages, working hours, and employee participation varies among European countries. Ownership and financing of business enterprises differ widely around the world. These variations are important in knowing and managing international pay.

Managerial autonomy: Managerial autonomy refers to the degree of discretion managers enjoy in the organisation. It is mainly related to the organisational structure – centralised or decentralised. For example, most UK and US based organisations have greater freedom to alter employee pay practices as compared to most European companies. The centralised pay-setting prevalent in European Union countries is a limiting factor in an organisations' autonomy to align pay to business strategies and changing market conditions. Trade unions, government agencies, and corporate policies of some companies are also responsible for limiting managerial autonomy.

VARIED APPROACHES

There are mainly four approaches in the area of international compensation – the going rate approach (also referred to as the market rate approach), the balance sheet approach (sometimes known as the build-up approach), the budget approach, and the hybrid approach. Of these, the two main approaches are the going rate approach and the balance sheet approach.

The going rate approach: The key characteristics of this approach are: (a) it is based on local market rates; (b) it relies on survey comparisons; (c) the compensation is based on the selected survey comparison; and (d) the base pay and benefits may be supplemented by additional payments for low-pay countries. Under this approach, the base salary for international transfer is linked to the salary structure in the host country. For instance, an Indian bank operating in London would need to decide whether its reference point would be local UK salaries, other Indian competitors in London, or all foreign banks operating in London. There are advantages and disadvantages of the going rate approach. The advantages are: (a) equality with local nationals; (b) simplicity; (c) identification with host country; and (d) equity amongst different nationalities. The disadvantages are: (a) variation between assignments for same employee; (b) variation between expatriates of same nationality in different countries; and (c) potential re-entry problems.

The balance sheet approach: This is a method by which the multiple factors of total compensation are broken down into component parts. In this manner, the plus and minus factors of the compensation package are combined to ensure that there will be no losses or gains for the expatriate. A savings made by the expatriate in a low cost of living area might be offset by higher taxes in the same foreign location. The basic objective of this approach is to maintain home country living standard, plus financial investment. Home country pay and benefits are the foundations of this approach. The balance sheet approach to international compensation is a system designed to equalise the purchasing power of employees at comparable position levels living abroad and in the home country.

There are four major categories of outlays incurred by expatriates that are incorporated in the balance sheet approach. These are: (a) goods and services – home country outlays for items such as food, personal care, and clothing; (b) housing – major costs associated with housing in the host country; (c) income taxes – parent country and host country income taxes; and (d) reserve – contributions to savings, payments for benefits, investments, education expenses, social security taxes, and so on. The advantages of this approach are: (a) equity between assignments and between expatriates of the same nationality; (b) facilitates expatriate re-entry; and (c) easy to communicate to employees. Its disadvantages are: (a) it can result in great disparities between expatriates of different nationalities and between expatriates and local nationals; and (b) it can be quite complex to administer.

While the balance sheet ties salary to the home country, the modified balance sheet ties salary to a region (for instance, Asia-Pacific, Europe, and North America). Another common modification is to decrease allowances over time. One more approach is lump sum cafeteria which sets salaries according to the home country system and simply offers employees lump sum of money to offset differences in standards of living. Cost of living, tax equalisation, and housing are most frequently included in the balance sheet approach. Reimbursement for education costs is also included by some employers.

The budget approach: This system takes into account all costs incurred by the employee at both the home and host country. These costs and the effects of the local tax system form the basis on which employees' income is calculated. This system is extremely expensive to keep up because of the many adjustments which need to be made, notably in the high inflation countries (Harzing and Ruysseveldt, 1995).

The hybrid approach: This method is usually a compromise between a home-based balance sheet and the local market rate. A typically hybrid approach might be a variation of the greater of home or host system where a balance sheet is compared to the local market rate equivalent. Another approach is pay the expatriate an amount in the host country that equates to the spendable income of his or her peers, but continue to pay an amount in the home country that allows the employee to maintain home country expenditure on housing and savings.

Variable Pay – A Global Scenario

"Variable pay" is that segment of performance pay that is required to be re-earned year-after-year based on a defined measure of corporate, team or individual performance. The payout in a variable pay plan is not guaranteed and not added on to the fixed pay component.

Variable pay comes in a multitude of different forms. The classic examples are piece-work wages, wages based on commission and productivity bonuses of all kinds. An example of a collective form of variable pay is profit-sharing, whereby all or some employees receive a proportion of the company's profits. Recently, the focus in many countries has been on remuneration in the form of share options or shares to employees. Schemes linking variable pay to employability have become more popular in the information and communication technology (ICT) as well as financial sectors. Where the labour market is very tight, "labour market bonuses" to attract or retain employees are flourishing.

In some countries, however, specific types of variable pay schemes can be found. France, for example, has its own mandatory and voluntary profit-sharing systems. Mandatory profit-sharing (participation) is a statutory requirement in companies with a workforce of over 50. Under this mechanism, companies set aside a statutory defined percentage of their profits or a higher proportion where special mandatory profit-sharing agreements exist, for distribution to employees. Voluntary profit-sharing which was introduced in 1959, ties a percentage of workers' pay to company performance in the form of profits or productivity. This type of bonus system is not a statutory requirement.

Austria, for instance, has its own system known as the "distribution option" (Verteilungsoption). This system splits pay increases into two components: (a) a general percentage increase in actual pay to be applied to all employees; and (b) a percentage increase which can be distributed flexibly among a company's employees on the basis of a agreement between the management and the works council. The distribution option was first introduced in the metal working industry, for both blue-collar and white-collar workers. A few other sectors of manufacturing industry then imitated this arrangement. The decision as to whether to apply a standard option of a flat-rate percentage pay increase, or to use the distribution option, is left to the individual company. Under the distribution option, the flexible component may be used to reward specific groups of employees. Also it may be applied to both low-income groups and high-performance groups, thus meeting the system of variable pay.

In Germany, there is a specific form of downward pay flexibility related to company performance. Many sector-wide agreements contain opening clauses that allow downward variation of collectively agreed pay rates, mainly in the event of economic difficulties. However, the use of these clauses has been rather limited.

In Asian countries also, increasingly companies are opting for new incentive and compensation mechanisms. In the past, salary and bonuses were more a reflection of an expanding market than actual improvements in business performance and productivity. This shift was an outcome of the realisation that to survive and maintain competitiveness, the compensation package needs to change. For compensation to be a driver of change, it has to be more closely linked to business performance and have less of a fixed and more of a variable component.

GLOBAL REWARD STRATEGY

The effective management of human resources can be a source of competitive advantage, but to achieve that advantage, the organisation's reward systems must be aligned with the organisation's mission, vision, values, and goals (Chen and Hsich, 2006). Determining how much employees in specific jobs should be paid and differentiating and rewarding performance are important.

Global organisations are faced with a two pronged HRM challenges: to appropriately compensate employees in local markets and facilitate the mobility of skills and expertise to the places worldwide where they are most needed (Dwyer, 1999). It is a significant HRM challenge to find ways to effectively use pay to motivate employees in multiple countries and multiple cultures who are all networked together and can talk in real time about pay issues with each other (Gross and Wingerup 1999). Also, a reward strategy that works in one country may not work as well in another. For example, stock options are a part of compensation plans in the United States and in the United Kingdom, but not in Eastern Europe.

Schuler and Ragovsky (1998) have examined the relationship between compensation practices and national cultures and found that the tendency to use seniority-based and skill-based compensation systems was positively related to Hofstede and Bards (1988) cultural dimension of "uncertainty avoidance". Similarly, in high-powered distance cultures, wages and salaries are based on the subjective evaluation of managers who reserve the right to assign differential salaries to employees recruited for the same job. Although pay-for-performance and a focus on individual performance are common in individualistic cultures, there is greater emphasis on group-based rewards in collectivist cultures (Aycan, 2005).

Monitoring a global reward strategy is clearly a challenge. Companies are reviewing and revising their strategies regularly due to an increased need for cost control governance and consistence. The key factors influencing pay include individual and business performance and position against market. Designing incentive and benefit programmes to attract, motivate, and retain top talent presents unique challenges. Depending on the type and form of organisation, various tags, legal and accounting considerations affect ideal compensation and benefit programmes for companies. Companies must compete on a global scale and therefore offer creative, flexible, and transparent global executive benefit plans. Corporations hope to retain native talent in their countries of operation and also reward executives in multinational positions.

INTERNATIONAL TAXATION

Taxation is probably of greatest concern to HR practitioners and expatriates (both PCNs and TCNs) since it generally evokes emotional responses. No one enjoys paying taxes and this issue can be very time-consuming for both the firm and the expatriate. To illustrate the potential problems, for the US expatriate an assignment abroad can mean double-taxation, both in the country of assignment and in the United States.

Personal income tax makes wide variations in the salary of employees among different countries. The jobs in United Arab Emirates, Oman, and Brunei Darussalam are more attractive than that of Sweden as the tax rate is zero per cent in the former group of countries and 54.02 per cent in Sweden. The tax rates are also high in Netherlands, Japan, Australia and South Africa. MNCs consider the varying tax rates in different places, while designing the compensation package for expatriates.

Multinationals generally select one of the following approaches to handle international taxation:

- *Tax protection* – When an expatriate is paid a gross salary and working in a location where the tax rates are low, the employer need make no adjustment, but when the host country tax rates are higher than in the employee's home country, the difference is reimbursed, usually in the home country. The employee pays up the amount of taxes he or she would pay on compensation in the home country.
- *Tax equalisation* – Firms withhold an amount equal to the home country tax obligation of the PCN, and pay all taxes in the host country. This system is more equitable than that of tax protection and therefore favoured by multinationals with large numbers of overseas employees. The tax equalisation system offers a fairer global policy in that it reimburses tax excesses to those in high tax areas but makes a deduction from the total remuneration of those in low/zero rated countries. Thus, all staff members are maintained on a tax standard that reflects the home country.

Tax equalisation is by far the more common taxation policy used by multinationals. The firm typically pays any additional premiums or allowances, tax-free to the employee. As multinationals operate in more and more countries, they are subject to widely discrepant income tax rates. However, it is important to note that by just focusing on income tax can be misleading. We have to take into consideration various other factors such as cost of living, political system of the country, level of economic, political and social development, and social security contributions. MNCs of various countries follow different approaches in managing international compensation. The major income tax can be misleading because the shares of both social security contributions and consumption taxes are rising in the OECD countries.

In her review of global compensation, Stuart[2] adds to other approaches, namely, (a) *ad hoc* (each expatriate is handled differently, depending on the individual package agreed with the firm), and (b) *laissez-faire* (employees are 'on their own' in conforming to host country and home country taxation laws and practices).

COMPENSATION PRACTICES

MNCs of various countries follow different approaches in managing their compensation system. A brief review of compensation practices in selected countries is as follows:

United States of America

Compensation package of American executives include base salary, bonus, long-term incentives, and other benefits and perks. The base salary is a small part of the total package. Some of the companies are also following the system of linking significant portion of the compensation package to employee performance. Stock options are an important source of earning long-term and deferred income for the American executives. The compensation package depends upon the size of the company, company's annual revenue, job clusters and job level of the executives, and the city where the company operates in the country.

Germany

Traditional German pay systems are embedded in a social partnership between business, labour, and government that creates a generous *vater staat* or *nanny state. Vergutung* is the most common German word for compensation. Base pay accounts for 70 to 80 per cent of German employee's total compensation depending on their job level. Base pay depends on job descriptions, job evaluations, and employee age. While there is a trend towards performance-based bonuses, they have not been part of a national German pay system for unionised workers.

Germany's social contract includes generous social benefits. These nationally mandated benefits, paid by taxes levied on employers and employees. It includes unemployment protection, health care, nursing care, and other programmes. Employer and employee contributions to the social security system can add up to more than one-third of wages. In addition, companies generally provide other benefits and services such as pension plans, savings plans, housing loans, company cars, life insurance, and so on.

Japan

Traditionally, Japan's employment relationships were supported by "three pillars": (a) lifetime security within the company; (b) seniority based pay and promotion systems; and (c) enterprise unions.

Japanese pay systems tend to emphasise the person-based factors rather than the job; seniority and skills possessed rather than job or work performed. Promotion is based on supervisory evaluation of trainability, skill/ability levels. Japanese pay systems can be described in terms of three basic components: base pay, bonuses, and allowances/benefits. The base pay accounts for 60 to 80 per cent of an employee's monthly pay, depending on the individual's rank in the organisation. Job pay is purely based on a combination of career category, years of service, and skill performance level.

There are five career categories in Japan: (a) general administration, (b) engineering/ scientific, (c) secretarial/office administration, (d) technical/blue-collar jobs, and (e) miscellaneous. Bonuses account for between 20 and 40 per cent of annual salary, depending on the level in the organisation. Generally higher the position is, the larger the percentage of annual bonus. Typically, Japanese companies declare bonuses twice a year in July and December. They are not necessarily related to performance.

Benefits and allowances in Japan come in a variety of forms: family allowances, travelling allowances, housing allowances, and so on. Legally mandated benefits include: social security, unemployment, and employee compensation for disability, health insurance, and employment of the handicap.

China

The compensation system in China, before the reforms, was characterised by egalitarianism at both enterprise and individual levels, regardless of performance. A nationally unified wage system was structured by the country in 1956 for both blue and white-collar employees. Under the then grade system, the highest pay received in the company was only three times more than one in the lowest, and the entry level wage was very low. Wage increases were infrequent and occurring at long intervals.

In China, reform of the compensation system began at the enterprise level from 1984 in which compensation was linked to performance. Subsequent legal measures aimed at separating the ownership of an enterprise from its controlling authority, so that each enterprise had autonomy and incentives. The state-regulated compensation schemes have now been replaced by diversified pay packages with more emphasis on enterprise profitability and individual performance. Bonus constitutes an important component of the pay structure and is more closely linked to individual performance. Performance-based compensation has become the trend today.

European Union

Generally, European executives are paid less compensation than that of American executives. However, the compensation disparity between the two is gradually narrowing down with the increasing phase of globalisation. Among the large companies, the American chief executives get compensation package twice to that of European executives. Moreover, American executives get more take home pay, due to lower tax rates as compared to European countries. However, of late many European companies have been changing their compensation package by including various tax free fringe benefits, stock options, performance-based bonus, and so on.

SUMMARY

- *International compensation system* throws light on the balancing role of HR professionals in determining international compensation.
- Managing compensation in international context is a very complex and crucial activity of multinational corporations.
- International compensation package vary from country-to-country based on the economic and social systems, and also on an organisation's policies, procedures, and rules determining the compensation system.
- Usually, companies competing in the same product market adopt uniform pay structure.
- The key components of international compensation include base salary; foreign service inducement; allowances such as cost of living allowance, housing, home leave, education, relocation and hardship allowance; and benefits.
- The MNCs of various countries follow different approaches in managing their compensation.
- The main expatriate compensation strategies currently in use are: (a) the going rate approach, (b) the balance sheet approach, (c) the budget approach, and (c) the hybrid approach.
- Any reward system of an organisation must be aligned with its mission, vision, values, and goals.

REVIEW QUESTIONS

1. What are the objectives of international compensation?
2. What are the different approaches to international compensation?

3. What are the different components that go into formulating international compensation?
4. Should the organisation have a common compensation strategy to be applied across all countries, or should there be local variations?

REFERENCES

1. Peter J. Dowling, Denice E. Welch and Randall S. Schuler (1999), *International Human Resource Management: Managing People in a Multinational Context,* 3rd Edition, South Western College Publishing.
2. Stuart (1991), *Global Payroll – A Taxing Problem,* Personnel Journal, October, pp. 80-90.

7

International Performance Management

Objectives

- To understand the challenges of international performance management.
- To analyse the role of multiple appraisers in international performance appraisal.
- To discuss the system of international performance appraisal and the problems associated with it.
- To suggest various measures to make the international performance appraisal more effective.

INTRODUCTION

Performance can be viewed as a combination of several variables, such as motivation, ability, working conditions, and expectations. Performance management is an exercise in observation and judgement; it is a feedback process and is an organisational intervention. It is a measurement process as well as an emotional process. It is a system of estimating or judging the value, excellent qualities or status of a person or thing. The ideal performance management cycle is a five-phase process which includes planning, execution, assessment, review, development and audit. When attempting to determine expatriate performance, it is important to consider the impact of certain variables and their inter-relationship that influence success or failure in a foreign assignment. These are compensation package, task, headquarters' support, environment in which performance occurs (subsidiary or foreign facility), and cultural adjustment of the individual and the accompanying family members. HR management needs to recognise that technical competence is necessary but not sufficient condition for successful performance in international management positions.

OBJECTIVES

Objectives, or performance indicators, can be defined at business, team, or individual levels. At business unit level they are closely aligned to organisational goals. At team or individual level the objectives need to relate specifically to their role in the team or individual and the contribution that they are expected to make to the achievement of business unit objectives. Management normally determine objectives and setting such objectives requires familiarity on the part of the managers about the skills and competencies of the employees. Managers should be able to describe the objectives in terms of tasks and behaviours and to allocate these tasks to the most appropriate individuals or teams. In order to maximise the business impact of the performance management process the description and allocation of objectives should be done within a framework of equity and fairness and aim to provide motivating jobs which utilise skills and competencies while offering personal development opportunity. Further, the objectives should be specific, measurable, attainable, realistic, and time-bound (SMART).

CHALLENGES

Managing employee performance based on the organisational needs, strategic requirements, and customer preferences is crucial aspect of international human resource management. MNCs incur high cost on human resources due to employment of different kinds of foreigners. Therefore, they expect the foreigners to perform distinctly and create, contribute, and add significant value to the organisational activities. MNCs expectations from foreign employees are diversified and varied widely as compared to domestic or national employees. Measurement of employee performance in MNCs is comparatively more complicated than that in domestic company. MNCs encounter critical challenges in the process of performance appraisal and management of foreign employees.

International human resource managers as well as the managements of MNCs face a variety of challenges and difficulties in managing the performance of different types of employees. These challenges include:

Total company versus parts of it: MNC consists of headquarters, subsidiaries, and its various alliance companies. Making different types of appraisals using different performance appraisal techniques is critical and conflicting in MNC as the decision affects various organs of the MNC differently. In addition, even the implementation process of the decision results in contrasting outcomes. For example, alliance between Coca-Cola Ltd., and Pepsi Cola Ltd., would be a viable proposition in small countries from the cost as well as operational points of view; but this alliance would negatively affect both the companies in other countries. MNCs too face dichotomy situations in its pricing policy. The autonomous subsidiaries fix the price for their products taking into account the purchasing power of the people of the country concerned. The subsidiaries in low income countries fix lower price while the subsidiaries of higher income countries fix higher price. For example, Johnson & Johnson (India) Ltd., fixes lower prices for its products compared to its counterparts in USA and Japan.

Now, the core issue is how to measure the performance of employees working in headquarters and subsidiaries when they follow different strategies and implement varied actions. These aspects of dichotomy in decision making and implementation of decisions also result in dichotomy in measuring the performance of employees. Another difficulty of performance appraisal is the time span of the impact of the decision or action. Employee makes decision/acts in a particular year, but the impact may be in other years.

Standard format versus customised format: Generally, common performance criteria/ performance factors are applied for a group of employees belonging to the same level and kind. Some companies apply quantitative factors like profits, return on investment, cash flows, and productivity, and some MNCs apply qualitative factors like innovation, leadership, value creation, and value addition. Environmental factors of the country concerned, also affect the performance criteria. Therefore, MNCs prefer to use different criteria for different subsidiaries. However, this would affect the uniformity of performance rating within the company.

Another challenge is that most of the environmental factors in foreign countries would be beyond the control of expatriate employees. Sometimes, the favourable environmental factors result in boost-up of the sales and thereby profits. For example, increase in sales of Whirlpool washing machines in India is mostly due to the enlargement of middle income group in the country. Similarly, increase in the sales of Hewlett-Packard's computer sales in India was mostly due to the increased use of computers in offices and educational institutions. An additional challenge is whether the performance of parent country national be evaluated based on the format adopted by the headquarters or by the subsidiary where the employee is actually working? If the performance of parent country national is evaluated against the headquarters format, what additional factors from the point of environment of subsidiary should be included? These additional factors may include the relationships with trade unions, customers, local government, local community, local market share, negotiation skills, cultural adaptation skills, community involvement, and relationship with local workers.[1]

Uniformity of data: MNCs and their subsidiaries operate in several countries under varying environmental influence. In addition, they carry-out different kinds of business including manufacturing, trading, dealing in services, construction projects, and the like. Even in manufacturing sector, they manufacture a variety of products. Therefore, providing uniform data in physical units would not be possible. However, variations in measurement of scale pose a problem, though it is minor. Therefore, measurement of employee performance of different subsidiaries in terms of physical productivity on a uniform scale is rather difficult.

Differences in accounting standards among countries pose challenges in measuring employee performance on a uniform scale. Factors responsible for difference in accounting standards among various countries include:

- Cultural differences among world nations.
- Relationship between business and capital providers.
- Political and economic ties with other countries.
- Historic cost and inflation accounting.
- Level of development of various countries.

Environmental variations: Environmental factors became more vibrant particularly after the recent phase of globalisation. The significant vibrations include:

- Trends towards the erosion of national cultures and formation of global culture.
- Establishment of World Trade Organisation.
- Increase in global business by five-fold after 1990.
- Increased mobility of human resources.
- Revolution in information technology and the emergence of global as well as customised manufacturing.
- Widespread use of outsourcing practice.
- Adopting global strategy, i.e., think globally, but act locally.
- Shift in political ideology.

In view of the variations in environmental influences among subsidiaries as well as different growth rates of environments, employees' performance across the subsidiaries cannot be measured using uniform performance appraisal criteria and scale. However, one should view that the managers in various subsidiaries should adjust/modify the strategies from time-to-time based on environmental influences of the country concerned rather than implementing a fixed strategy crafted by the headquarters.[2] As such, performance of subsidiary managers depends on how well they localise the global strategies and implement them efficiently. Therefore, appraising employee performance in MNCs is a challenging task.

Validity of performance criteria: Companies use different performance criteria – some based on end-contribution to the company and some based on employee traits. The criteria concerning the end-contribution to the company includes: profits, return on investment cash-flow, sales and productivity/input-output ratios.[3] Employee traits that can be used for evaluating performance include: dynamism, decisiveness, aggressiveness, initiative, judgement, adaptability, negotiation skills, social relations orientation, productivity, ability to work in odd hours and punctuality. These criteria would be valid for local settings. But they may be quite inappropriate for foreign settings.

Time and distance variations: Performance of business activities in MNCs are complicated by the distance between parent company and subsidiaries. Added to this, time variations from one country to another country where headquarters and subsidiaries operate complicate the task further, in spite of the information technology. However, devices like videoconferencing, e-mail, fax and telephone[4] reduce the complexities to some extent. But they do not fully substitute for face-to-face contacts between subsidiary managers and corporate staff. Meeting personally is often necessary to fully understand each person's situation. Measurement of performance of employees working in MNCs is challenging compared to those working in a domestic company as the employees in domestic companies can meet the colleagues face-to-face, while the employees of MNCs have a limited choice to do so.

The following example reveals the enormity of this difficulty in IHRM. The head of the HR Systems at British Airways faces the challenging task of handling 50,000 employees in eighty-three countries, many of them in a different location every day of the week. When HR needs to notify employees of a change in benefits or policy, many of the workers are 40,000 feet above the earth. When it needs to track head count or up date employee records, it has to deal with 24 time zones and dozens of languages and cultures. Yet, British Airways' automated system handles recruiting benefits, head count, basic record keeping and an array of other functions cutting across technology platforms and breaking language barriers.

Varied levels of maturity and skills: People of different countries are generally strong in different skills, have different levels of maturity, and are strong in different disciplines. MNCs, therefore, should not adopt the same performance appraisal format and scale to measure the performance of employees of home country nationals and different host country nationals as well as third country nationals.

Rater competence: The one who appraises the performance of employees of MNCs, i.e., those who work in headquarters as well as in subsidiaries are called the raters. Mostly, the raters are either the executives in headquarters or in subsidiaries and are the nationals of either parent country or host country. Most of the MNC's executives without living and working in a foreign country cannot have the knowledge and experience of a foreign employee or an expatriate employee. They do not know the social, business and work challenges that the foreign employees face. It is doubtful that such raters possess required competence to appraise the performance of foreign employees or expatriates.

Evaluation of Expatriate Performance

The evaluation of performance of expatriates is very much linked with the performance of subsidiaries which they are required to manage. How a subsidiary performs depends to a large extent on how well the multinational as a whole supports it and how much autonomy is granted in making its own strategy and implementation. Many multinationals assess performance using result-oriented measures.

Some MNC's headquarters officers/managers evaluate the performance of foreign employees/expatriates working in subsidiaries from an "out of sight, and out of mind" perspective without understanding the problems and the challenges the latter face in foreign social and work environment. The raters have no idea of the areas to be rated of the foreign employees. In fact, foreign employees are left alone from strategic activities of the parent company and from their home office superiors.[5] MNCs measure the inappropriate work areas of the foreign employees and often ignore the social, cultural, and security challenges that the foreign employees face due to the incompetence and inexperience of the raters. Added to this, the performance appraisal systems in some cases are designed poorly as the designers may not have the adequate knowledge of the foreign working and living environment. In addition, absence of top management's commitment and understanding of overseas business realities further reduces the validity of performance appraisal ratings.

Rater bias: The rater biases include:

- *Halo effect*: The raters fail to understand all the traits and behavioural aspects of the foreign employees due to lack of understanding of foreign employees' activities and the challenges they face. Therefore, the raters appraise the performance of foreign employees based on one factor with which they are familiar with.
- *Error of central tendency*: Some raters follow safe policy in rating, by rating all the employees around the mid-point of the rating scale and avoid rating the people at both the extremes of the scale whatever they deserve.
- *Leniency and strictness*: Depending upon the appraiser's own value system which acts as a standard, an employee may be rated leniently or strictly. The leniency bias crops up when some raters have a tendency to be liberal in their rating by assigning higher rates consistently and such ratings do not serve any purpose Equally damaging one is assigning consistently low rates.
- *Personal bias*: Perhaps the most important error of all arises from the fact that very few people are capable of objective judgements entirely independent of thei values and prejudices.
- *The recency effect*: The raters generally remember the recent actions of the employe at the time of rating and rate on the basis of these recent actions – favourable o unfavourable – rather than the whole range of activities.

Host environment: Environment in the host country makes significant difference over the performance of foreign employees. The environment that affects the performance of expatriates includes both internal and external aspects of environment. The internal aspects of environment include organisational structure and nature of ownership. Flat structures and simple structures enable the expatriates to perform efficiently. The external aspects of the environment like social and cultural issues, and political and economic issues affect the employee performance. In addition, availability of school and other educational facilities, medical and hospital facilities, recreational facilities, and transportation facilities in the host country have their bearing on foreign employee's performance.

Adjustment of the employee to the organisational culture and country's culture, and adjustment of employee's family members to the country's culture significantly influence the employee's performance. Though the employee is technically competent and possesses all kinds of job skills and knowledge, he may still fail to perform as he may be unable to deal with superiors, subordinates and colleagues, as well as external customers and other stakeholders. In addition, employees may encounter cultural problems in the society. Therefore, adjustment of employee and his/her family members with cultural aspects should be considered while evaluating his/her performance.

Areas to be appraised: Areas to be appraised vary from one type of employee to other type of employee like parent country national, host country national and third country national. In addition, it also varies based on the purpose/assignment for which an expatriate is sent to the host country.

Organisational role expectations: Parent companies predetermine the roles and expectations of the parent country nationals before departure for the subsidiary. The critical aspect of the role is the task performance. However, task performance does not take place on its own. Infact, the host country environment, and the parent company's expectations influence the task performance. For example, the employee who is successful in performing a task in parent company need not be successful in doing the same/similar job in the subsidiary. The *vice-versa* is also true. This is because the aspects of the role other than the task impose complications in task performance. In contrast, certain employees perform their jobs better in the host country than in the parent company. This is mostly due to the best fit of the employee to the host country environment compared with that in the parent country. For example, the task performance of most of the Indian employees working in foreign environment is superior to that in the home environment. This is because some employees may not be comfortable to the political and cultural environment of India, but they feel more comfortable with the foreign environment. This is true with most of the developing countries, thus contributing to the braindrain from developing countries to the advanced countries.

Thus, performance appraisal of the foreign employees should consider the role rather than just task. Role is broader than the task. Role includes task and various other factors like leadership skill, inter-personal relations, team-building skills, understanding and adapting towards organisational culture and culture of the host country at workplace, unlearning the parent country and other countries' culture that is unacceptable in the host country, motivational skills, emotional balance and stability skills, managing environmental influences, maintenance of integrity, and meeting the conflicting interest of parent company and subsidiary.

The family of the employee like spouse and parent also influence employee's job performance. Employee's performance, to some extent, depends upon the degree of adjustment of his/her spouse to the host country's culture, facilities and the institutions. The process of adjustment of the spouse can be smoothened and fastened, if the employee takes initiative and interest in his/her spouse's adjustment. Similarly, the adjustment of employee's children to the various institutions like schools and facilities also influences the employee's job performance. Thus, a number of aspects are to be included in the areas of performance appraisal of foreign employees.

Measuring performance of host country nationals is relatively difficult as compared to that of employees of a domestic company as the host country nationals work with employees of varied cultures like parent country nationals' cultures and third country nationals' cultures. Host country nationals have to understand the culture and behaviour of parent country nationals and the third country nationals, and accordingly adjust their interpersonal behaviour. The areas to be appraised of the host country nationals include skills of understanding varied cultures and behaviours, cultural adaptability and behaviour modification based on others' cultures, and adapting to local situations in addition to job tasks. The areas to be appraised vary from one employee to the other due to the variations in expectations of parent company and subsidiary, cultural issues, and other varying roles of employees. However, they include cultural adaptations, adjustment/initiating to the institutions and facilities of parent country as well as host country; in addition to the conflicting task requirements of the parent company, host company and client company in some situations.

The evaluation of the expatriate by his/her local management is very necessary because the local management possesses a better knowledge of the work of the employee and can, therefore, assess more or less correctly. However, such a process is sometimes problematic because local management evaluates the expatriate's performance from its own cultural frame of reference and set of expectations. Further, each country values different performance dimensions, for e.g., deference vs. self-assertiveness, formality vs. informality, group vs. individual work, impersonal vs. personal interactions, and efficiency vs. productivity. These values determine what constitutes performance. Cultural values also come into play in the rater's interpretation of performance behaviour.

A performance appraisal has come to stay in all companies irrespective of whether they are multinationals or not. In that case, a subsidiary in a host country should have such a system in place. But what is important to mention here is that the practice of performance appraisal itself confronts the issue of cultural applicability. In Japan, for example, it is important to avoid direct confrontation to 'save face' and this custom affects the way in which performance appraisal is conducted. A Japanese manager cannot directly point out a work-related problem or error committed by a subordinate.

EVALUATION CRITERIA

The variables that influence performance of expatriates are: (a) compensation package, (b) nature of assignment, (c) support from headquarters, (d) environment in which performance takes place, and (e) cultural adjustment of the individual and the accompanying family members.

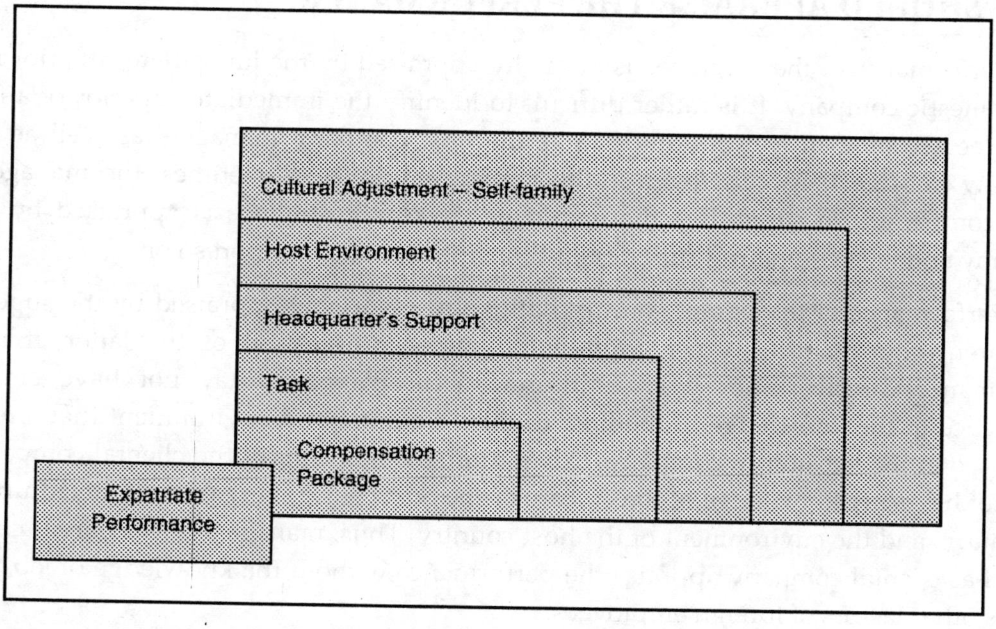

Fig. 7.1: Variables Affecting Expatriate Performance

Three types of criteria such as hard, soft, and contextual are often used as the basis for performance evaluation.

Hard criteria are objective, quantifiable, and can be directly measured such as return on investment, market share, and so on. However, using hard criteria to compare the performance of the expatriates against domestic performance standards may be inappropriate because expatriates face more external influencing factors in a more complex business environment, whereas domestic managers may be insulated from these conditions.

Soft criteria tend to be relationship or trait-based, such as leadership style or interpersonal skills. Because of the subjective nature of soft criteria factors such as rater errors, biases and cultural differences, care should be taken while evaluating such criteria.

Contextual criteria are situation-specific criteria. These are dependent on the expatriate's specific assignment and represent a variety of external conditions that may affect both hard and soft criteria.

Home office management may not have access to relevant information and tend to use a different set of criteria than host country raters. Without direct on-site experience, awareness of appropriate criteria for overseas success is limited and may make accurate and valid appraisals difficult.

WHO SHOULD APPRAISE THE PERFORMANCE?

Performance of the employee is normally appraised by the immediate superior in case of a domestic company. It is rather difficult to identify the immediate superior of a foreign employee working in a host company as the host company managers as well as parent company manager supervise/oversee the foreign employee. Sometimes, the manager of a client company also supervises the employee. Also, performance is appraised by parent company and host company's superiors, subordinate, customers, and so on.

Performance of the parent country national is invariably appraised by the superior in the parent country, the former oversee the career progression of the latter, if not the performance directly. The superior in the parent company may not have either the experience or the knowledge of the host country's culture and environment that affects the employee in the subsidiary company. In addition, the manager of the cliental company also may not have any knowledge of the culture of the host country, organisational culture of the subsidiary, and the environment of the host country. Thus, managers of the parent company as well as cliental company appraise the performance without the knowledge of job tasks as well as other factors of foreign employees.

In addition to this practice of appraising the performance by multiple reviewers, MNCs also adopt 360 degree appraisal process, which further complicates the practice of appraising the performance. Various stakeholders like customers, bankers, governments, suppliers, market intermediaries, trade unions, subordinates, colleagues, human resource professionals, superior in the parent company, superior in the subsidiary company, and certifying officer of the client company appraise the performance of employee under 360 degree appraisal system.

PROCESS OF PERFORMANCE APPRAISAL

Performance appraisal for international employee is a twelve-step process:

1. *Establish performance standard*: Performance standards should be based on job description, job specifications, cultural requirements, and adaptability to foreign environment. Separate performance standards should be established for each category of employees of MNCs like PCNs, TCNs, immigrants and returnees.
2. *Communicate standards/expectations*: Communicate standards/expectations to employees as well as evaluators.
3. *Decide upon the performance appraisal format*: Different appraisal formats are based on various appraisal techniques. MNCs may use either standard format or customised formats for each subsidiary.
4. *Measure actual performance*: Measure actual performance by following instructions by the evaluators through observation, interviews, records and reports.
5. *Decide frequency of appraisal*: Normally, appraisals are conducted once in a year or in a six months interval. But, the problem of once in a year appraisal is the recency effect. The raters generally remember the recent actions of appraisee and rate on the basis of recent action/performance – favourable or unfavourable – rather than on the total activities.
6. *Adjust actual performance*: Environmental factors, particularly cultural factors affect the actual performance. Therefore, the rater has to adjust the performance considering the nature and degree of environmental influences.
7. *Compare the adjusted performance with that of others*: Comparing the adjusted performance with that of others as well as previous performance ratings gives an idea of where the employee stands. If performance of all employees is ranked either too high or too low, there would be something wrong with the standards or job tasks or the rater.
8. *Compare the actual performance with standards and find out deviations, if any*: Deviations may be positive or negative. If the actual performance is more than the standards, it is positive deviation and *vice versa* is negative deviation. This exercise helps for adjustment of standards, if necessary.
9. *Feedback to the appraisee*: The appraiser has to communicate the actual performance to the employee concerned. Mutual discussion of the appraiser and appraisee makes the appraisal effective.
10. *Suggest changes in job analysis and standards, if any*: Based on the employee's feedback and explanation to the rating, as well as considering other factors, the evaluator should suggest changes in job description, job specification, and standards of appraisal.

11. *Consider the appraisal results for contract renewal and promotion*: MNCs should consider performance appraisal ratings for contract renewal of employment and also for promotion. In addition, MNCs can also plan career planning and development, and promotion based on performance ratings.
12. *Plan for employee training and development*: MNCs should consider the performance appraisal information for employee training and development. MNCs, in doing so, should analyse the information very carefully as the performance ratings, sometimes, keep the cultural and other issues outside the purview of ratings.

HOW TO MAKE PERFORMANCE APPRAISAL EFFECTIVE?

International performance management is not that effective as it should be owing to the challenges as well as the problems of appraisal as discussed earlier. However, it can be made effective by the following measures:

1. Performance appraisal system should provide reliable and valid data and information. The techniques/methods of appraisal should satisfy the conditions of inter-reliability.
2. The appraisal technique should measure the performance and provide information for which it is designed or planned. The techniques should be designed covering the areas and content of the job based on the purpose of the appraisal.
3. Different factors influence the performance of different types of MNCs like PCNs, TCNs, and HCNs. In addition, performance appraisal requirements of parent company as well as various subsidiaries vary significantly. Therefore, MNCs should design different appraisal forms based on the factors that affect the performance of different kinds of employees in different organisations.
4. International performance appraisal should consider several issues that cannot be known by the appraiser as well as the designer of the appraisal form. The appraiser and appraisee in consultation with each other, should design the form, content, and consider the nature and degree of influence of various factors.
5. Most foreign employees want to know continuously how well they are performing on the job. A result-oriented appraisal system should provide needed feedback on a continuous basis.
6. Performance appraisal forms, appraisal procedure, and evaluators should be sensitive to the changing and varying ground realities relating to cultural factors, language, semantics, trade unions, and government policies and functions.
7. Appraisee should know the rules of the game. They should receive information and adequate feedback about the performance results on continuous basis in order to correct the performance deficiency, if any.

8. Performance appraisal forms as well as procedure should be easy to operate on the part of the appraiser as well as the appraisee. It should not be complex and time-consuming.
9. The rater should have the knowledge of the appraisee, appraisee's work, behaviour, culture, environmental factors, and so on and so forth. In other words, the appraiser should be in direct and close observation of the appraisee and his/her work.
10. The successful performance of managers abroad should be based on the following criteria:
    (i) Flexibility – the ability to change structures to implement changed strategies.
    (ii) Inter-personal understanding and respect.
    (iii) Empowerment – to share information, delegate responsibilities and motivate employees to feel more capable.
    (iv) Team support to help employees cooperate
    (v) Versatility – the capacity to adjust in a new environment.

The criteria for top management personnel evaluation of performance should be:

- *Strategic thinking* – the capacity to grasp changing environments and market possibilities, responses to competitive threats.
- *Initiating change* – the capacity to convey strategic vision and make people feel involved and motivated.
- *Managing relationship* – the capacity to influence and seek the cooperation of customers, trade unions, government institutions and lobby activities.[6]

An effective performance management system has to deal with the challenges of comparing subsidiary managers in different countries. For example, it is difficult to compare the performance of an American subsidiary manager with that of an Indian subsidiary manager because each manager works under quite different environmental conditions. It is equally challenging to evaluate the performance of the various subsidiary employees. However, performance management with its emphasis on mutual goal-setting between managers and employees may assist in overcoming these difficulties.

CASE 1

Misconceived Appraisal System

A corporate president put a senior executive of his firm in charge of a failing operation. He directed him to do whatever necessary to get back the operation in right track. Within two years of his instruction, the new executive moved the operation from a deficit position to one that showed a profit of several million. Far from his success, the executive applied for a higher level position, in which he indicated that he was already receiving better offers from other companies.

The corporate president, however, did not share the executive's positive opinions about his behaviour. Indeed, the president was not at all pleased with the way the executive had handled things. Naturally, the executive was dismayed and when he asked what he had done wrong, the corporate president told him that he had indeed accomplished what he had been asked to do, but he had done it single handedly, by the sheer force of his own personality. Furthermore, the executive was told that he had replaced people whom the company thought to be good employees with those regarded as compliant. In effect, by demonstrating his own strength, he had made the organisation weaker. Until the executive changed his authoritarian manner, his boss said, it was unlikely that he would be promoted further.

Discussion Questions

1. What is the misconception in performance appraisal, particularly in MBO?
2. How to convey appraisal to subordinates and convey the same more effectively?

CASE 2

Performance Appraisal at Pepsi-Cola International

Pepsi-Cola International (PCI), with operations in over 150 countries has devised a common performance appraisal system that focuses on motivating managers to achieve and maintain high standards of performance. Administrative consistency is achieved through the use of a performance appraisal system of five feedback mechanisms – instant feedback, coaching, accountability-based performance appraisals, development feedback, and a human resource plan.

The common system provides guidelines for performance appraisal allowing for modification to suit cultural differences. For example, the first step namely instant feedback is based on the principle that any idea about any aspect of the business or about an individual's performance is raised appropriately and discussed in a sensitive manner. The instant feedback message can be delivered in any culture; the important thing is not how it is done but that it is done.

In practice, in PCI the successful delivery of instant feedback requires some adjustment to local cultures. Americans use it because it fits the fast-paced way of doing business. In most Asian cultures, feedback may be tough and direct but is never given in public. In some cases, head nodding either signifies agreement, or simply that the message has been heard. Some Latinos will argue very strongly if they do not agree with the feedback, and some employees, Indian nationals for example will insist on a great deal of specificity. The purpose of instant feedback is always to improve business performance, not to criticise cultural styles. Using this system, PCI tries to balance the cultural and administrative imperatives for successfully managing the performance of a diverse workforce.

Discussion Questions

1. How did Pepsi-Cola achieve administrative consistency through the use of performance appraisal system?
2. How did PCI deliver feedback by adjusting itself to local cultures?
3. "The purpose of feedback is to improve business performance, not to criticise cultural styles." Comment.

SUMMARY

- *International performance management* mainly dwells on different issues and challenges confronting performance management.
- International human resource managers as well as the managements of MNCs face a variety of challenges and difficulties in managing the performance of different types of employees.
- These challenges to performance appraisal includes total company versus parts of it, standard format versus customised format, uniformity of data of performance, environmental variations, validity of performance criteria, time and distance variations, varied levels of maturity, rater's competence, rater bias, and host environment and cultural adjustments.
- Areas to be appraised vary from one type of employee to the other type of employee like parent country national, host country national and third country national; and it also varies based on the purpose/assignment for which an expatriate is sent to the host country.
- The process of cultural adjustment may be a critical determinant of expatriate job performance.
- International performance management is not that effective as it should be, owing to the challenges as well as the problems of performance appraisal.
- Some of the rater's biases include halo effect, error of central tendency; leniency and strictness; personal prejudice; and recency effect.
- The two main reasons for management's inability to understand and value an expatriate employee's performance are: (a) communication gap, and (b) lack of international experience.

- The vital criteria for evaluating the performance of expatriate managers include: (a) his/her technical job know-how, (b) personal adjustment to the culture, and (c) various other environmental factors.
- Some criteria for performance evaluation of top management personnel include: (a) strategic thinking, (b) initiating change, and (c) relationship management.
- A suitable performance appraisal system has to be designed keeping in view cultural and organisational requirements.
- An important aspect of an effective performance management system is the provision of timely feedback of the evaluation process.

REVIEW QUESTIONS

1. What are the challenges in international performance appraisal?
2. Why should international employees need to be appraised in the areas different from those in pure domestic organisations?
3. Explain the role expectations of an employee. How the role expectations of a foreign employee influence international performance management?
4. Discuss the system of performance management in MNCs.
5. What are the problems of performance management in MNCs?
6. How do you make the performance management in MNCs more effective?

REFERENCES

1. Black *et. al.*, (1999), *"Internationalisation of Business"*, New York, Dryden Press.
2. V. Pucik, *"Management of Multinational Corporations"*, Wiley, New York, 1985, pp. 429-430.
3. Dennis R. Briscoe, and Randall S. Schuler, *op. cit.*, p. 355.
4. Peter J. Dowling, and Denice E. Welch, *op.cit*, p. 234.
5. Gregersen *et.al.*, (1995), *op.cit.*, p. 739.
6. S.K. Bhatia, (2005). *International Human Resource Management: A Global Perspective – Practices and Strategies for Competitive Success*, New Delhi: Deep and Deep Publications Pvt. Ltd.

8

Expatriation and Repatriation

Objectives

- To understand the factors involved in expatriate selection.
- To study the process of repatriation and factors which contribute to its success or failure.
- To appreciate the responsibilities of IHRM towards the repatriates.

INTRODUCTION

The process of expatriation and repatriation constitute two important components in managing international human resources. An expatriate is a home country or third country national who is assigned to a host country operation location for a particular term. Repatriation, on the other hand is an activity of bringing the expatriate back to the home country. Back in the home organisation, repatriated employees should get themselves adjusted to a closer working and reporting relationship with other corporate employees. Often, expatriates have a greater degree of flexibility, autonomy and independent decision making authority than their counterparts in the home country. In many cases, no sufficient care is taken in repatriating the expatriates. To counter these concerns, a great deal of effort is required to provide career planning, mentoring programmes and even an employment guarantee after completion of foreign assignments.

SELECTION CRITERIA

It should be noted that selection is a two-way process between the individual and the organisation. A prospective candidate may reject the expatriate assignment, either for personal reasons, such as family considerations, or for situational factors such as the perceived rigidity of a particular culture. The factors involved in selection, under both the situations, are as follows:

Technical ability: Technical and managerial skills are an essential criteria in selection. It seems that the US companies lay greater emphasis on technical competence despite the importance of all other criteria. It is rather easy to evaluate the technical skills of an expatriate on the basis of past performance.

Cross-cultural suitability: The cultural environment in which expatriates operate is an important factor in assessing successful performance. Apart from the obvious technical ability and managerial skills, expatriates require cross-cultural competencies that enable the person to operate in a new environment. These include cultural empathy, adaptability, diplomacy, language ability, positive attitude, emotional stability, and maturity (Harvey, 1985).

Family requirements: The contribution that the family makes, particularly the spouse, to the success of the international assignment is highly significant. This is so because the adjustment of the spouse is highly correlated to the adjustment of the expatriate manager.

Country/cultural requirements: Some regions and countries are considered 'hardship postings' – remote areas away from major cities or modern facilities, or war-torn regions with high physical risk. Accompanying family members may be an additional responsibility that the MNC does not want to bear. There may be a reluctance to select females for certain Middle East or South East Asian regions. Indeed, some countries will not issue a work permit for a female. These are some of the considerations in the selection of HCNs rather than expatriates.

MNC requirements: The multinational may consider the proportion of expatriates to local staff while making selection decisions, mainly as an outcome of its staffing policy. Other situation factors include the mode of operation involved, the duration of the assignment, and the amount of knowledge transfer inherent in the expatriate's job in the foreign operation.

Language: The ability to speak a second language is an aspect often linked with cross-cultural competency. Language skills are of critical importance for some expatriate positions. Some would argue that knowledge of the host country's language is an important aspect of expatriate performance, regardless of the position.

FEMALE EXPATRIATES

Traditionally, three reasons have been put forth for the low number of female expatriates, namely: (a) women are not interested in international careers; (b) fear of poor job performance; (c) foreign cultures discrimination against women. However, researchers in this context have found that women are very much interested in international assignments and indicate that they would like to accept expatriate positions. Nearly 70 per cent of MNC court prejudice against women as one of the main reasons for not selecting and sending women expatriates on foreign assignments (Adler, 1987). It is true that in many countries and societies gender biases exist. Anyhow, the evidence today shows that women can and do succeed at working abroad even in presumably hostile environments.

Women expatriates, particularly managers face the following work-related problems which play a vital role in their performance:

- Overseas expatriate women managers face a variety of environmental and job-related uncertainties that may affect their work status and work outcomes, both positively and negatively.
- Expatriate women managers who are adaptable and proficient in foreign language can prove to be an asset to overseas organisation as compared to women who are devoid of this particular skill. Marital status, number of children, level of education, technical skills, communication skills, and professional experiences can also have a role to play in their performance.
- One of the most restricting factors limiting the number of female business expatriates seems to be the unfavourable perceptions at headquarters regarding their potential to succeed on foreign assignments (Harris, 1995; Linchan, 2001). Adler (1993) has pointed out the reason for preferring males over females which is based on the fear of possible failure, and low viability of business operations abroad.
- The cultural differences between the host and the parent country are also important for the expatriate women managers. Women accepting overseas positions may face different reactions from the people with varying local culture.
- Also, there are certain barriers confronted by women who attempt or aspire to attain senior positions in corporations, government, educational or non-profit organisations.

Human resource professionals have to play a significant role in developing domestic and international women managers by adopting various workplace policies and practices, and organisational changes. Recruitment, selection, and promotional policies should be amended wherever necessary. Equal opportunity policy should be implemented strictly in all the spheres of HR activities.

STAFFING THE LOCAL SUBSIDIARY

The multinational should observe the host country's legal requirements while hiring staff. Mode of entry is an important consideration in selection. If the multinational establishes its own facility, it may have more discretion in its hiring practices. Entry through acquisition generally means a ready-made workforce initially. In the recruitment and selection process, multinationals must address the issue of equal employment opportunity for employee in all locations. These laws are expressions of social values with regard to employment and reflect the values of a society or country. In parts of the Middle East, Africa, Asia, and Latin America, women have a lower social status and are not universally employed. Multinationals should be aware of legislation and must ensure compliance where appropriate. The selection procedure must be defended against any illegal practices resorted to by any multinational.

Expatriate selection and training: There can be little doubt that a great contributor to the problems and failure rates of expatriates is the selection and training of expatriates by the MNCs. Hixon (1986) reports that US expatriates fail because of three critical factors: (a) they are selected solely on their domestic and track record; (b) they lack adequate cross-cultural training; and (c) their family situation is misjudged and are not even considered in the selection process. Overall, US selection and training practices continue to lag behind those of Japan and Germany. In Japan, for example, expatriates are selected a year or more prior to their posting so that they and their families can undergo extensive training programmes. As a result, the overseas success rate for the Japanese is significantly higher than that for Americans (Naisbitt, 1984).

Expatriate role: An expatriate is mainly a bridge between the home and foreign location operations. He is:

- an agent of direct control
- an agent of socialisation
- an agent of knowledge-competency transfer
- a network builder
- a boundary scanner
- a language node.

Managing expatriates: An expatriate is a home country or third country national who is assigned to a country of operational location. Most expatriate managers are highly-trained technical experts. Studies by Gross and Kujawa (1992) have identified major advantages and disadvantages of using expatriates.

The advantages of using expatriates include:

- Expatriates usually have the necessary technical and managerial skills.
- Expatriates enhance communication between the parent company and the foreign subsidiary.

- Expatriates are more familiar with corporate culture, thereby enhancing parent-subsidiary relations.
- Assigning expatriates to foreign positions is an essential ingredient of progress toward becoming an international manager.

The disadvantages of using expatriates include:

- The total compensation paid to the expatriate is usually much higher than that paid to a host country national.
- Host country nationals do not require special training in adaptation to the local culture.
- The use of host country nationals is consistent with promotion from within policies espoused by many MNCs.
- Host country nationals do not require work permits.
- Using expatriates with special employment contracts may block promotional opportunities for locals and be in violation of local equal employment regulations.

The expatriate should meet the following conditions for their successful assignment:

- They must be willing and motivated to go overseas.
- They must be technically able to do the job.
- They must be adaptable.
- They must have good interpersonal skills and be able to form relationships.
- They must have good communication ability.
- They must have supportive families.

Success in an expatriate assignment is dependent on a combination of corporate and individual variables, as well as the dynamics of the expatriation/management development process. The following are the six most significant competencies for expatriate managers:

- Leadership skills
- Initiative
- Emotional stability
- Motivation
- Ability to handle relationships
- Cultural sensitivity

Typically, on completion of the foreign assignment, the multinational brings the expatriate back to the home country. Home transfer may not always be the case to the expatriate and he can be reassigned to another international position.

PROCESS OF REPATRIATION

The process of repatriation can be divided into four phases:

- *Preparation* involves developing plans for the future and gathering information about the new position.
- *Physical relocation* refers to removing personal bonds, breaking ties with colleagues and friends, and travelling to the next posting, usually the homecountry.
- *Transition* means settling into temporary accommodation, where necessary, making arrangements for housing and schooling, and carrying out other administrative tasks such as renewing a driving licence and opening a bank account.
- *Readjustment* involves coping with a reverse culture shock and career demands. Of all the steps in the repatriation process, readjustment is the most difficult one. The re-entry adjustment is a tough task because of multiple factors, such as: (a) anxiety is experienced by the expatriate when he or she returns home; (b) the apprehension being accentuated by uncertainty about placement in the firm, career prospects, and a sense of isolation; (c) a feeling of 'devaluing' the international experience; (d) coping with new role demands; and (e) probable loss of status and pay.[1] The entry process is a complex interaction of several factors and can be grouped under two categories – job-related factors and social factors.

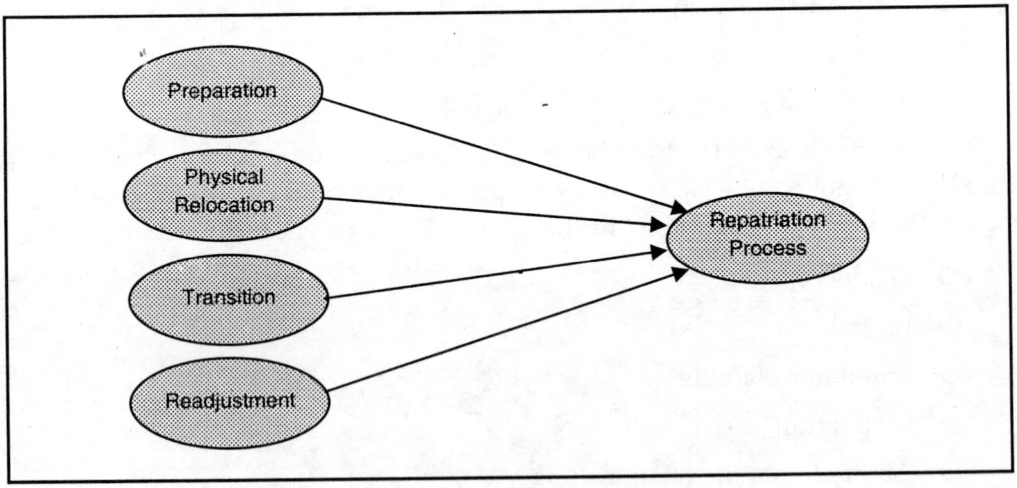

Fig. 8.1: The Repatriation Process

Source: P.J. Dowling, *International HRM,* (2001), p. 206.

The following are the job-related factors:

- If a suitable position for the manager is not available back home, the MNC may not provide post-assignment guarantee of employment.

- Managers suffer from the fear that the period overseas has caused a loss of visibility and isolation both at workplace and social relationships. If there is no post-assignment job guarantee, the anxiety level will be understandably high.
- It becomes difficult for managers to accept changes in the home workplace if it has undergone major changes in the organisational structure.
- If an expatriate expects a promotion after returning back home and if it is not possible for the firm at that point of time, then the manager feels frustrated.
- Expatriate managers feel that the international exposure will be devalued and underestimated back home.
- If the perception of the manager about his/her role back home does not match with the top management's expectation, the manager feels frustrated.
- International managers are afraid of losing status and monetary reward.

The following are the social factors:

- The family needs to be readjusted with the home culture, social values and norms.
- Children face difficulty in adjusting to different educational system.
- The spouse may face problems in getting a job.

Black *et. al.*, (1991) argued that work adjustment has an important impact on a person's intent to stay with the organisation. Career anxiety is one moderating factor, but others may also lead to readjustment problems.

Expatriates tend to view their international assignment as an opportunity for personal and professional development and career advancement. Management development programmes to prepare expatriates for their international assignment often include environmental briefings about the geography, climate, housing and schools; cultural orientation about the cultural institutions and value systems; and language training and sensitivity training to develop attitudinal flexibility.

Exhibit 8.1

Repatriation Check List

For employees returning from an overseas assignment, there are guidelines to help make their homecoming easier. Planning for repatriation begins even before a person leaves to go overseas. Then there are things to take care of during their stint abroad, and finally there are some important things to be considered when they come home.

Before they go

- Make sure you have clearly identified a need for international assignment. Don't send somebody abroad unnecessarily. Develop a clear set of objectives and expectations.

→

- Make sure that your selection procedures are valid. Select the employee and also look at the family situation. Provide language and cultural training for the employee and the employee's family.
- Offer counselling and career assistance for the spouse.
- Establish career planning systems that reward international assignments.

While they are away

- Jointly establish a developmental plan that focuses on competency development.
- Tie performance objectives to the developmental plan.
- Mentors keep the expatriates in the headquarters information loop so that they are better prepared for the changes that are occurring at home and also have a continuing sense of belonging.
- Keep communication open so that the expatriate is aware of job openings and opportunities.
- Arrange for frequent visits back home for the employee and the family. Make certain they do not lose touch with friends and relatives.

When they come back home

- Throw a 'welcome home' party.
- Offer counselling to ease the transition.
- Arrange conferences and presentations to make certain that knowledge and skills acquired away from home are identified and disseminated.
- The MNCs should have a policy of fully valuing and utilising expatriates' experience and understanding.
- Get feedback from the employee and the family about how well the organisation handled the repatriation process.

Source: Adapted from Bennet & Associates, Price Waterhouse and Charlene Marmer Solomon (1995), *'Repatriation Planning Check List'*, Personnel Journal, Vol. 14, No. 1, p. 32.

MAKING REPATRIATION SUCCEED

Infact, a successful repatriation programme starts before the assignment. The company's culture must convey the message that the organisation has international assignments as an integral part of continuing career development and advancement, and that it values the skills of the repatriates. The company's objectives should be reflected in the long range plans and commitment on behalf of the expatriate.

The high level of dissatisfaction with repatriation can pose problems for the multinationals, which may lead to high turnover. Since multinationals are increasingly using international assignments for overall career development purposes as opposed to merely filling a position abroad, they can lose out on such investments. A principal reason for the high level of dissatisfaction with repatriation is job insecurity or inadequate advancement opportunities after their return.

CAREER PERSPECTIVE

International career perspective is relevant not only to the organisation but also to the individual. Career planning strategies involves:

- Career goals (where you want to go)
- Career path planning (how you want to get there)
- Training and job experience (need to acquire knowledge and skills)
- Ongoing assessment (how far you have come, how far to go)

A company can derive many potential benefits by carefully managing the career of its expatriates. By helping managers make the right moves in their careers, the company will be able to retain people with increasing global experience and skills. In the international assignment, both the manager and the company benefit from enhanced skills and experience. Some of these acquired skills, reported by Adler, include the following:

- *Managerial skills, not technical skills*: Learning how to deal with a wide range of people, to adapt to their cultures through compromise, and not to be a dictator.
- *Tolerance for ambiguity*: Making decisions with less information and more uncertainty about the process and the outcome.
- *Multiple perspectives*: Learning to understand situations from the perspective of local employees and business people.
- *Ability to work with and manage others*: Learning patience and tolerance – realising that managers abroad are in the minority among the local people, learning to communicate more with others and empathise with them.

Expatriates acquire cross-cultural and managerial skills in their overseas assignment. The MNC benefits from the knowledge and experience of these managers as to how to do business overseas, and about new technology, local marketing and competitive information. If the company wants to develop a global competitiveness, it should be ready to make use of the knowledge and expertise gained by the expatriates. Towards this, there must be a high degree of shared learning among the organisation's global managers. If the company cannot retain efficient expatriate managers, then their hidden knowledge is not only lost, but also transferred to another organisation that hires the person concerned. This can be to the disadvantage of the company's competitive edge. The company should realise that the knowledge of the expatriates is an asset in which the company has invested.

RESPONSIBILITIES OF IHRM IN REPATRIATION

It is obvious that the expatriates need much more attention than an employee based in the home country. Once they are recruited, selected and placed in a foreign location after necessary expatriate training, the job of HRM does not stop with their compensation alone.

Designing a repatriation programme for the expatriates and adhering to the design are of paramount importance in as much as there is a need for training expatriates to cope with the new culture of the host country for better adjustment, so also they need to be prepared for their re-entry. A formal repatriation programme is shown in Table 8.1.

Table 8.1

Components of a Repatriation Programme

- Preparation, physical relocation and transition information
- Financial and tax assistance
- Re-entry position and career path assistance
- Reverse culture shock
- School systems and children's education and adaptation
- Workplace changes
- Stress management and communication-related training
- Establishing networking opportunities
- Assistance in establishing new social contacts

The concept of mentoring has been introduced in some companies. A mentor is assigned to an expatriate. The mentor is normally from a more senior position in the sending unit and who knows the expatriate personally. HR should make use of this option to prevent the 'out-of-sight', 'out-of-mind' feeling by providing the employee with information on who is who and up dates on these on a regular basis. This kind of constant updates will enable the expatriate not to feel as a stranger on his re-entry. The mentor should also ensure that the expatriate is not forgotten when important decisions are made regarding training and promotion opportunities.

HR should not stop with the mentoring of expatriates alone. Rehabilitating them is crucial once they get back to the headquarters or home country. Career planning and development commensurate with the position and experience of expatriates which should be evolved much before the actual repatriation takes place. Efforts should be made by HR professionals to show that they are 'welcome home'.

SUMMARY

- *Expatriation and repatriation* covers two important segments of international human resource management.
- The process of repatriation comprises preparation, physical relocation, transition, and readjustment.
- Of all the steps in the repatriation process, readjustment is the most difficult one because of multiple factors.

- The success of an expatriate assignment is dependent on a combination of corporate and individual variables.
- For repatriation to succeed there should be continued career development.
- The role of repatriation in developing a global management cadre involves managerial skills, tolerance for ambiguity, multiple perspectives, and the ability to work with and manage others.
- The task of IHRM is mainly to ensure that value addition happens through the expatriates even after their repatriation.
- It is the duty of HR to link up the expatriate to a mentor who will be of great help in giving proper perspective to his ultimate re-entry.
- HR must also see that the repatriate is on the proper career path and adds value to the organisation.

REVIEW QUESTIONS

1. What factors are to be taken into consideration while selecting expatriates?
2. Explain the process of repatriation in detail.
3. "A well-designed repatriation programme is important for achieving maximum benefit of international assignment." Comment.
4. What are the elements that go into a repatriate's satisfaction and what would be the career progression he/she should be put into?

REFERENCE

1. Peter J. Dowling, Denice E. Welch, and Randall S.S. (1999), *International Human Resource Management, Managing People in a Multinational Context,* 3rd Edition, South Western College Publishing.

9

International Industrial Relations

Objectives

- To discuss the key issues in employment relations.
- To explain the role of trade unions and the approaches of MNCs towards them.
- To describe labour relations practices in selected countries and of MNCs.
- To give a comparative analysis of participative arrangements in different countries.

INTRODUCTION

An understanding of the field of industrial relations (or labour relations or employment relations as the subject may be titled) remains an important one for those concerned with the management of people at work. Industrial relations often raise concerns in international situations for several reasons. Employers must comply with a wide range of employment and labour laws. With the shift from domestic to global business, new challenges are to be faced by international managers of multinational corporations (MNCs) operating in different countries. Corporations are required to develop a global attitude of understanding of market, people, culture, external influences, and government laws and regulations. It is all the more essential because HRM and IR practices have become the basis of success in an organisation. These practices are influenced by several factors such as trade unions, participative bodies, government authorities, and cultural traditions and beliefs. No MNC can afford to ignore the influence of the local culture on industrial relations or human resource management at its various subsidiaries.

CONCEPT AND SCOPE

The term "industrial relations" refers to the competitive and cooperative relationships that arise out of the employment of labour by an enterprise.

According to Dale Yoder, industrial relations is a collective relationship between the employees (trade) union and the employer which grows out of employment. The subject of industrial relations includes:

- Individual relations and joint consultation between employers and workers at the workplace.
- Collective relations between employers and their organisations and the trade unions, and
- The part played by the State (Government) in regulating these relationships.

In the words of John T. Dunlop an industrial relations system at any one time in its development is regarded as comprised of certain actors, certain contexts, an ideology which binds the industrial relations system together, and a body of rules created to govern the actors at the workplace and work community.

International industrial relations deals with the complex relationships among employers employing foreign employees, employees of different nationalities, home and host country governments, and trade unions of the organisations operating in various countries and their national and international federations. It does not exist in a vacuum but is affected by, and in turn affects, the political, economic, and social context within which it operates.

Blyton and Turnbull (2004) maintain that its relevance is four-fold. *First,* the world of work remains central to the lives of most people, provoking interest in the settlement of terms and conditions of employment and the way in which people are treated at work. *Second,* employees are vital to an organisation's ability to achieve its business strategy, whether in the manufacturing or service sectors of the economy or in the public and voluntary sectors. Unless employees deliver the required skills and attention to their work, an organisation's potential for success will not be realised. *Third,* while managers and employees may share a common interest in ensuring a continuing successful enterprise, a tension exists between an employer's need for profit and the workers' needs for wages and employment security. *Fourth,* the decline in the collective dimension to employment and the emergence of the individualism associated with contemporary HRM practices do not signal the end of the need to study collective employment relationships.

The human resource management policies and practices of different country nationals create a type of employment relationships among the management of MNCs and different kinds of employees. Such relations are called international industrial relations. They are influenced by various factors, namely, institutional factors, economic factors, and governmental factors. Industrial relations does not exist in a vacuum but is affected by, and in turn affects, the political, economic, and social context within which it operates.

KEY ISSUES AND CONCERNS

The following are some of the key issues and concerns in international industrial relations:

IR Policies and Practices of Multinational Firms: As there are different industrial relations systems across countries, multinationals generally delegate the IR functions to their foreign subsidiaries. However, a policy of decentralisation does not keep corporate headquarters from exercising some coordination over IR strategy. According to Hamill (1983), a high degree of integration was found to be the most important factor leading to the industrial relations function within the firms studied.

There is evidence of differences between European and US firms in terms of headquarters involvement in industrial relations (Roberts and May, 1974). US firms tend to exercise greater centralised control over industrial relations than do British or other European firms (LaPalombara and Blank, 1976). European firms have a tendency to deal with labour unions at industry level rather than at firm level. The opposite is more typical for US firms. In US, employer associations have not played a key role in industrial relations system, and firm-based industrial relations policies are the norm (Bean, 1971). An additional important factor is that of management attitudes or ideology concerning unions. Knowledge of management attitudes concerning unions may provide a more complete explanation of multinational industrial relations behaviour. This is of particular relevance to US firms, since union avoidance appears to be deeply rooted in the value systems of American managers (Kochan *et. al.*, 1984).

Another key issue in international industrial relations is industrial dispute. Hamil[1] (1983) examined strike-proneness of multinational subsidiaries and indigenous firms in Britain across three industries. Strike-proneness was measured by three variables, namely strike frequency, strike size, and strike duration. There was no difference across the two groups of firms with regard to strike frequency, but multinational subsidiaries did experience larger and longer strikes than local firms.

International Integration: This is defined as the generation of inter-unit linkage across borders. A number of recent developments have created scope for MNCs to build stronger linkages between their international operations. Many MNCs have strengthened the inter-unit linkages by developing new structures for their global activities. In particular, many have moved away from country-based structures towards organising themselves around global decisions or regional blocks, so that comparable operations are linked together. For instance, IBM's operations are not structured along the lines of the various countries in which the firm operates, such as IBM China or IBM Canada; rather they are organised into global divisions, such as software and services, and regional blocks, such as Europe, the Middle East, Africa, and North America.

This integration can take two forms, each of which has important implications for IR. International integration can take place through segmentation of operations across countries, with those in one country providing components or services to those in another. For example, firms which have segmented the production or service provision process are the airlines which also use basis in Asia, commonly India, to carry-out routine IT services such as data entry and processing. In this case, the various units across the world are performing quite distinct functions, leading to variations in the type of IR practices that the firm deploys.

International integration can also take place through standardisation operations, with the units in different countries carrying out very similar activity. Examples of this are the automotive and electronic manufacturers which have developed increasingly standardised products and manufacturing techniques. Given the nature of the operations in different countries have important similarities, there is considerable scope for such firms to transfer practices across borders.

Nationality of Ownership of the Subsidiary: As reported by P.J. Dowling and D.E. Welch[2], a number of studies have revealed that US firms tend to exercise greater centralised control over IR than do British or other European firms. US firms tend to place greater emphasis on formal management controls and a close reporting system (particularly within the area of financial control) to ensure that planning targets are met. Hamil found that the US owned subsidiaries were much more centralised in IR decision making than the British owned one. Hamill attributed this difference in management procedures to the more integrated nature of US firms, the greater divergence between British and the US industrial relations systems than between British and other European systems and the more ethnocentric managerial style of US firms.

International HRM Approach: The four IHRM approaches namely ethnocentric, geocentric, polycentric, and regiocentric approaches, have an influence on industrial relations. In the ethnocentric approach, key positions in domestic and foreign operations are held by headquarter personnel. Subsidiaries are managed by staff from the home country (PCNs) and it is presumed that there are not enough qualified host country nationals (HCNs). A parent company wants to have the reins in its hands so that proper coordination and communication can exist and easily translate the parent company's vision and policy into reality without too many hurdles. Because of this approach the local talent is not developed.

When it comes to a comparison of the compensation package of expatriates with that of HCNs, there will be a perceptible gap due to the fact that the expatriates are compensated for their being away from their home. This can create dissatisfaction among the locals and resulting in poor performance. The expatriates may not be sensitive to the needs and expectations of their host country subordinates. Thus, there is the possibility of escalated IR problems demanding parity with expatriates and fair treatment according to the local culture and expectations.

In the polycentric approach of staffing, the multinational company treats each subsidiary as a distinct national entity with some decision making autonomy. Local nationals normally manage the subordinates and they are seldom promoted to positions at headquarters and PCNs are rarely transferred to foreign subsidiary operations. Employing HCNs eliminates language barriers. Bridging the gap between HCN subsidiary managers and PCN managers at the corporate headquarters can become difficult due to language barriers, conflicting national loyalties, and a range of cultural differences. Though IR problems in this approach may be less than in the ethnocentric approach, the career path of HCNs is the bone of contention and conflict.

Geocentricism is a balanced approach in which the MNC takes a global approach to its operation, recognising that each part, whether it is a subsidiary or headquarter, makes a unique contribution with its unique competence. It is accompanied by a worldwide integrated business and nationality is ignored in favour of ability. Here, IR problems will be minimal. But only local governments may act as impediments to corporate policies because the governments may impose certain constraints on immigration policies.

Like the geocentric approach, the regiocentric approach utilises a wider pool of managers but in a limited way. Staff may move outside their countries but only within the particular geographic region. Since local subsidiaries are staffed almost totally by HCNs, this approach reflects some sensitivity to local conditions. While this approach does improve career prospects at national level, it only moves the barrier to the regional level. Staff may advance to regional headquarters but rarely to positions at the parent headquarters. Like in the polycentric approach, here too a career path is in a limited manner, giving rise to conflicts and IR problems.

Subsidiary Characteristics: There are four types of subsidiary characteristics that are relevant to centralisation of employee relations. *First,* when a firm acquires a well-established subsidiary, more autonomy is given to it in its functioning, including in IR. *Second,* if the subsidiary is of key strategic importance to the parent company and it is young, it will expect greater intervention from the parent company in IR. *Third,* where the subsidiary is more dependent on headquarters for resources – financial or operational – there will be an increased tendency of corporate involvement in IR and HRM. *Finally,* where poor performance of the subsidiary is due to IR problems, multinationals tend to introduce parent country HR practices aimed at alleviating industrial unrest or for increasing productivity.

Management Attitude towards Unions: Management attitude or ideology towards unions may provide a complete explanation of multinational IR behaviour. Hence, along with market forces and strategic choices, the management attitude should also have a bearing on the managerial behaviour. If unions are considered by the management as an anathema, there will not be any mutual trust and everything will be looked at suspiciously. This itself will lead to industrial unrest.

Grievance Redressal: The common issues that give rise to formal grievances include terms and conditions of employment, health and safety, work relations, bullying and harassment, new working practices, working environment, organisational change, and discrimination. To some extent, handling of grievances and disciplinary issues varies from one organisation to the other at different levels. In some organisations, disciplinary actions are mostly constructive and rehabilitative, and in some others they are punitive, and a mixture of both. Disciplinary procedures normally provide for fairness in dealing with employees who violate the rules or fail to meet legitimate performance standards.

Legal Context of HRM: In addition to the increasing diversity of the workforce, the problem of managing human resources is also complicated by the emerging body of statutes with respect to the ways in which employers may or may not deal with employees. When managing in foreign countries, managers may come across with quite different local laws. Hence, it is important for all international managers to understand the basic labour laws of that country.

Legal Framework: In every industrialised country, legislation has been passed to perform such functions as fixing minimum wages or maximum hours, or providing health and safety requirements, or requiring payroll deductions for social security and other welfare programmes. In general, industrial relations statutes in most of the countries affirm the right of employees to form unions of their own choosing and to engage in collective action for the purpose of reaching an enforceable written agreement with the management, covering the terms and conditions of employment, and settlement of disputes between the conflicting parties. The statutes also provide legal protection to the employees and their unions, define the boundaries of the negotiation process, and declare certain behaviour and activities of both parties to be unfair labour practices. In addition to statutes, there are administrative and judicial interpretations of these laws that govern the labour-management relations.

TRADE UNIONS AND APPROACHES OF MNCs

The role of labour unions varies from country-to-country, often because of local traditions in management-labour relations. The variations include the extent of union power in negotiations and the activities of unions in general. In Europe, especially in the Northern European countries, collective bargaining takes place between an employer's association and an umbrella organisation of unions, on either a national or a regional basis, establishing the conditions for an entire industry. On the other end of the spectrum, negotiations in Japan are on the company level, and the role of larger-scale unions is usually consultative. Another striking difference emerges in terms of the objectives of unions and the means by which they attempt to attain them. In UK, for example, union activity tends to be politically motivated and identified with political ideology. In the US, the emphasis has always been on improving workers' overall quality of life.

Internationalisation of business has created a number of challenges for labour unions. The main concerns that have been voiced are: (a) the power of the firm to move production from one country to another if attractive terms are not reached in a particular market; (b) the lack of sufficient information, especially financial information, to support the unions' bargaining positions; (c) insufficient attention to local issues and problems while focusing on global optimisation; and (d) difficulty in being heard by those who eventually make the decisions.

COUNTRY-SPECIFIC LABOUR RELATIONS PRACTICES

The country specific differences in laws, customs, values, and norms regarding labour-management relations cannot be ignored by companies when operating overseas. Labour relations practices in six different countries were compared and contrasted.

Great Britain

In Great Britain, union membership is widespread especially among government employees. Strikes by British unions are more common as compared to the United States. This has been accounted for by some with the observation that the public believes that business has a social obligation to attend to the interests of workers, together with the facts that often grievance procedures are not formally structured, and that mediation is voluntary. Disputes can be difficult to successfully resolve, and both parties may resort to confrontation in their frustration (Douglas and Douglas, 1989, Rothwell, 1991).

A number of explanations have been put forward to explain the decline in union membership. Williams and Adams Smith (2005) summarise them as follows:

- the decline of male manual jobs in the manufacturing industries where unions were traditionally well organised
- a weakening of the 'collective identity' among workers which underpins union solidarity
- the growth in unemployment during the 1980s which led to an initial significant decline in union membership
- greater employer hostility towards trade unions
- relatedly, the political climate created by conservative governments which allowed managers to bypass unions to exclude them from the workplace
- the apparent unwillingness of unions to be more proactive in seeking to recruit new members.

A far more significant trend has been the decline in the coverage of collective bargaining in the UK, both in terms of its incidents and the number of employees covered by collective agreements on pay and other terms and conditions of employment.

Australia

In Australia, Workplace Regulations and Other Legislation Amendment Act, 1996 provides freedom of association, voluntary membership, and clauses against discrimination based on membership or non-membership, facilitating the formation of new trade union for increased competition. There is a limited right to strike or lockout during union negotiations and strike pay is prohibited.

The Australian Chamber of Commerce and Industry (ACCI) is one of the councils of the Australian Business Association. The Australian Council of Trade Unions (ACTU) is the national council which represents the Australian workforce.

Industrial Relations Legislation (1987-1998) led to the decentralisation of negotiations. About half of the wage negotiations occur at the state/territory level and half at the federal level. Conciliation and arbitration were compulsory in Australia until 1988. There is no statutory minimum wage, but a multitude of minimum wages for different crafts and occupations have been laid down.

USA

The Industrial Revolution had a powerful effect on both society and labour relations in the US The rise of Marxist philosophy, which pits workers against the capitalist system, was probably the most important reaction to the social upheaval in the US, and found fertile ground among workers during the Great Depression of the 1930s. Most American unions had their beginnings then, being formed under the tremendous pressure of violent confrontations with management. During World War II, confrontational labour relations cooled as they were superseded by a wave of patriotism, and as labour and management met the demands of enhanced industrial production.

With the improved standard of living that most Americans enjoyed after the war, unions seemed less and less necessary. In the late fifties, the image of unions was further tarnished when it was revealed that some large unions were involved with organised crime. More recently, organised labour in the United States has been shaken, as firms threaten to move operations to other countries where labour costs are lower. Although the number of workers represented by unions is considerably lower in the US than in other developed countries, the legitimate representation of workers by unions is supported by federal laws that mandate recognition of unions as legal representatives of workers. There are many reasons which led to the decline in union membership over a period of years.

State laws govern the workers in a firm and they must join the union once a union is certified. In states with right-to-work laws, workers are not required to join the certified union, and thus union solidarity can be eroded to the point that organising unions and sustaining them in those states can be very difficult. In the United States, most unions are organised on the industry level, though many workers are not represented by unions. Unions that are organised on the national level can influence industry-wide wage levels and can wield considerable political power. Collective bargaining talks are held on a company-wide basis with them, often putting local management at a disadvantage. However, much of the responsibility for the day-to-day business of overseeing that the company lives up to their labour contract is left to union locals, which are simply local divisions of the national unions.

Collective bargaining in the United States usually means negotiations between management and trade union locals, but in Germany or Sweden, for instance, the term refers to negotiations between trade unions at the industry level and employer's associations. Although the objectives of the negotiations in the US are primarily financial, they are often viewed in terms of a class struggle by Europeans. The role of government or religious organisations in collective bargaining is minimal and relatively constant in the US, though in most other countries of the world, labour negotiations are seen as having significant social implications which require greater legal or religious restrictions.

American industrial relations have been described as adversarial, as a relationship of confrontation leaving hardly any place for workers' participation, or union activities in the firm, other than the grievance procedure. Non-union firms are still preferred by most managers. There is collective bargaining on wage issues and union recognition has been accepted by both parties.

Germany

The Constitution of Germany guarantees the right to free collective bargaining as well as freedom of association. The Workplace Labour Relations Act regulates the composition and function of the works councils. Works councils can be established in companies with at least five permanent workers who have the right to vote. The participatory rights include the right to be informed, to make suggestions, to be heard and to be consulted. The workers' associations are organised around specific industries regardless of the nature of work. Collective bargaining can take place only between trade unions and individual employers or employers' associations. There is no statutory minimum wage, but collectively agreed wages laid down minimum standards for the establishments.

Italy

The Italian system of collective bargaining is relatively complex. Not only has it undergone substantial structural changes over the past 35 years, but the collective bargaining system is not formally divided into three typical levels, the company level, the industrial level, and the economy-wide level. Instead, significant bargaining is carried out on all levels, because the tasks and issues for each level are unclear. In addition, over time one level may become predominant, indicating the degree of centralisation or decentralisation of the bargaining process.

In 1979, when many industry-wide contracts were expiring, the government intervened on the economy-wide level in an attempt to control high inflation by indexing wages. This had reverberating effects on industrial relations throughout the decade. Strike activity increased, and with a third party involved in the bargaining process, organised labour and management began talking separately with the government, often coming to agreement on issues without corresponding agreements between unions and employers. As labour relations became more politicised, company-level bargaining, which had been consistently wide-ranging, became less autonomous and narrower in scope.

The 1986-87 round of negotiations reflected changes by both unions and management in the traditional view of collective bargaining as being confrontational. Instead, the two groups began to adapt to the changing systems and meet the overall needs of the entire economy by finding many possibilities for cooperation and trade-ups. Greater autonomy returned to company-level bargaining, but it remains restrictive in scope by "functional coordination" clauses which prohibit the renegotiation of issues at a lower level that had been agreed at a higher level.

Because the government took on a larger industrial relations role and changed the old bipolar dynamics, both unions and employers are more willing to assess and modify their demands, despite their ideological differences. Strikes in the private sector have subsided. Innovations in production and economic performance now influence industrial relations more than politics and organisational strength. At the forefront of these positive changes have been the cooperative relations at the company level, and the way in which agreements on that level have complemented industry-wide and economy-wide accords. However, the 1990s are bringing a significant challenge as workers demand higher wages from booming corporate profits against Italian industry's insistence that it must maintain its international competitiveness through wage control.

Japan

The Japanese HR/IR practices may broadly be characterised as follows:

(a) *Lifetime employment*: This means remaining on the payroll but not necessarily remaining in the same job or same plant for the duration of one's working life. As such, it is a guiding principle but not a guarantee, applying only to large industrial organisations.

(b) *Seniority-based pay and promotion*: Regular pay increases and career advancement are provided on the basis of age and length of service in the company. This encourages employees to remain with the organisation and to derive the benefit. However, there is gradual erosion of this system with ability and performance being used as additional criteria for increases in pay and promotion, for example Nissan, Fujitsu, and Honda.

(c) *In-house trade unions*: Unions based on the enterprises and comprising all employees in the company regardless of job or occupation have been the dominant form of trade union; reflecting the principles of loyalty, corporate family, and obedience. They are involved in wage bargaining and resolving workplace problems, but are generally not confrontational (Gill, Wong, 1998).

The Japanese Constitution guarantees certain fundamental rights, namely the freedom of association, the freedom of collective bargaining, and freedom to act collectively. The statutory measures prohibit employers from unfair labour practices, including the refusal to bargain collectively and prejudicial treatment of union members.

The Japanese Trade Union Confederation (RENGO), the main national organisation of trade unions, represents around 60 per cent of total trade union membership. The trade unions offer a proposal and negotiate for wage increases as "pattern setters". The resulting wage increase affects wage negotiations in other enterprises belonging to the same industry and various other sectors. The Labour Relations Adjustment Law provides for a system of addressing disputes between labour and management including conciliation, mediation, and arbitration with a strong emphasis on the voluntary settlement of industrial dispute.

Ishida (1986) concluded that Japanese managers abroad regard the following as the main features of Japanese human resource management:

- Community orientation
- Seniority-based promotion and salary system
- Class egalitarianism and groupism
- Information sharing and employee participation
- Employment security
- Flexible job behaviour.

Industrial Relations Across Europe

European countries feature a variety of industrial relations practices. Some countries have adopted statutory regulations and some others mixture of legal and voluntary elements. Collective bargaining plays a vital role in the EU member states. Works councils and trade unions constitute the two main forms of workplace representation. The coverage of collective bargaining, i.e., the proportion of employees who have their salary and working conditions set by collective agreements varies greatly. The proportion is lowest in the Czech Republic about 25 per cent, whereas it amounts to almost 100 per cent in Sweden. There are substantial differences in union density, ranging from about 15 per cent in Poland to 80 per cent in Sweden and Finland. Codetermination ranges from extensive employee participation such as the legal requirement of including a labour director on the management board of German firms in the coal, iron and steel industry, to no representation at all on the supervisory boards of private companies, for example in Poland. In Finland and Sweden, collective bargaining concerning issues such as wages and working conditions mainly takes place above company level, i.e., at the national or sectoral level, whereas most of the bargaining processes occur at company level in countries such as Poland.

LABOUR RELATIONS PRACTICES OF MNCs

Because there are profound differences in how labour and management perceive each other, a multinational corporation must deal with each group of workers according to the social, political, and religious environment of the country in which it is operating. More often than not, the labour relations strategy used in one country is of limited value in another. In some countries, labour relations are seen in the larger context of a social class struggle, which can often lead to intense labour strike; where this is the case, a firm may have a difficult time gaining cooperation in reaching its goals. In other countries conformity is now the rule, although strike activity was high just prior to World War II.

To understand labour relations in the international context, it is also important to understand MNCs' various orientations toward organised labour. Because labour relations across national boundaries are so diverse, MNCs generally decentralise their labour relations. They sometimes assign the task to their foreign subsidiary, but since labour negotiation in one country can set international precedence, headquarters usually maintain some degree of supervision.

MNCs must plan their labour relations carefully, particularly for their foreign subsidiaries. These subsidiaries are vulnerable to strikes, since halting production in a subsidiary could stop operations worldwide. Union influence thus not only delays the rationalisation and integration of MNCs manufacturing networks and increases the cost of such adjustments, but also, at least in such industries as automobiles, permanently reduces the efficiency of the integrated MNC network. Now the question arises as to what degree the MNCs delegate to their subsidiaries the authority to handle labour relations. On one hand, if they try to centralise the control of labour relations at corporate headquarters, they may fail to understand cultural subsidiaries and run the risk of aggravating a dispute. On the other hand, turning labour relations over to the subsidiary can prevent optimising operations.

In addition to sourcing issues when setting policy on central supervision of subsidiary labour relations, MNCs must consider environmental and safety questions, public image, and ethical practices. The problem for MNCs is that the public holds them to international standards, standards often higher than those of the country in which they are operating. A poignant example of this is the horrible Union Carbide accident in Bhopal, India, in which thousands of people were severely injured or killed by leaking methyl cyanide gas. Few remember, or even care, about the defence offered by the Union Carbide management who claimed, just after the accident, that their work and safety standards were higher than those of other local industries. One thing is absolutely clear that transnational firms must set high standards in their work operations and must consider labour relations central to their strategic plan.

As MNCs grow in size and number, labour unions feel increasingly threatened. Labour unions have responded to the MNC challenge on the international level by forming International Trade Secretariats (ITS) and working through international organisations. Coupled with the resistance from the firms, ITS faces the same hurdles as the MNCs themselves, which are operating in various countries with differing labour laws and customs; and for that reason ITS does not often get support from local unions.

In 1919, the International Labour Organisation (ILO) was formed to set minimum standards for humane labour conditions, including minimum wage standards, child labour practices, and legal restrictions on collective bargaining. Since then, a number of other associations of unions representing workers from specific industry have formed to address those same issues. These include the World Federation of Labour (WFL), the World Federation of Trade Unions (WFTU); the International Confederation of Free Trade Unions (ICFTU); and the Organisation for Economic Cooperation and Development (OECD). The OECD has issued voluntary guidelines regulating multinational behaviour of corporations, within the framework of the law, regulations, and prevailing labour relations and employment practices, in each of the countries in which they operate.

EMPLOYEES' PARTICIPATION IN MANAGEMENT

Over the years, many changes have occurred in the traditional labour management relationships as a result of dramatic changes in the economic environment and the actions of both the firm and labour forces. The role of the worker is changing both at the level of the job performed and in terms of participation in the decision making process. To enhance workers' role in decision making, various techniques like self-management, codetermination, minority board members, and works councils have emerged. In striving for improvements in the quality of work life, programmes that have been initiated include flexitime, quality circles, and work flow reorganisation. Furthermore, the employee ownership has moved into the mainstream in some countries.

Participation in Decision Making: The degree to which workers around the world can participate in corporate decision making varies considerably. Rights of information, consultation and core determination can be developed on three levels:

1. The shop-floor level, which consists of direct involvement, for example, the right to be consulted in advance concerning transfers.

2. The management level, that is, through representative bodies, for example, the participation of works councils in setting up new policies or changing existing ones.
3. The board level, for example, representation of workers on the board of directors.

Yugoslavia, before its breakup, had the highest amount of worker participation in any country; self-management was initiated through workers' councils which decided all major issues including the choice of managing director and supervisory board.

In some countries, employees are represented on the supervisory boards to facilitate communication between management and labour by giving labour a clear picture of the financial limits of management and by providing management with a new awareness of labour's point of view. The process is called *co-determination*. In Germany, companies have a two-tiered management system with a supervisory board and the management board which actually runs the firm. At least one member must be a white-collar employee and one a managerial employee. The supervisory board is legally responsible to the management board. In some countries labour has minority participation. In the Netherlands, for example, works councils can nominate (not appoint) board members and can veto the appointment of new members appointed by others. In other countries, such as the United States, co-determination has been opposed by unions as an undesirable means of cooperation, especially when management-labour relations are confrontational.

In addition to labour groups and media, investors and shareholders too are scrutinising multinationals' track records on labour practices. As a result, a company investing in foreign countries should conform to the international standards of safety and health, not simply the local standards. This can be achieved, for example, through the use of modern equipment and training. Local labour too should be paid adequately. This increases the price of labour, yet ensures the best available talent and helps avoid charges of exploitation. Companies subcontracting work to local or joint-venture factories need to evaluate IR throughout the system not only to avoid lost production due to disruptions such as strikes, but to ensure that no exploitation takes place at its facilities. Several large firms are required to sign agreements forcing them to abide by minimum wage standards.

Participation in Improvement of Quality of Work Life: The term quality of work life has come to encompass various efforts in the areas of personal and professional development. Its two clear objectives are to increase productivity and to increase the satisfaction of employees. Of course, programmes leading to increased participation in corporate decision making are part of the programmes; however, concentration is on individual job-related programmes like work redesign, team-building, and work scheduling.

By adding both horizontal and vertical dimensions to the work, work redesign programmes attack undesirable features of jobs. Closely related to work redesign are efforts aimed at team-building. The team-building effort includes job rotation to enable workers understand all facets of their jobs. Another approach to team-building makes use of quality circles, in which groups of workers regularly meet to discuss issues relating to their productivity.

Flexibility in work scheduling has led to changes in when and how long workers are at the workplace. Flexitime allows workers to determine the starting and ending hours in a given workday. The idea spread from Germany to the European Union and to other countries such as Switzerland, Japan, New Zealand, and the United States. Some 40 per cent of the Dutch working population holds flexi or part-time positions. Despite its advantages in reducing absenteeism, flexitime is not applicable to industries using assembly lines. Firms around the world also have other programmes for personal and professional development, such as career counselling and health counselling. All of them are dependent on various factors, external and internal, to the firm. Of the external factors, the most important are the overall characteristics of the economy and the labour force. Internally, either the programmes must fit into existing organisational structures or management must be inclined towards change. In many cases, labour unions have been one of the major resisting forces. Their view is that firms are trying to prevent workers from organising by allowing them to participate in decision making and management.

EMPLOYEE PARTICIPATION ACROSS COUNTRIES

The practices followed in some countries with respect to employee participation are as follows:

United Kingdom

The idea of the workers' participation in the United Kingdom (UK) began with industrialisation itself and was the result of partly of the compulsion of socialistic thought and partly due to the humanitarian attitude of some of the employers during the eighteenth century who realised the difficulties of the workers and tried to help them by holding informal discussions with representatives of workers. Joint consultation and collective bargaining go together in the industrial relations system in the UK. Joint consultation in the form of joint councils emerged in the British industries with the recommendations of the Whitley Committee which was appointed by the government. As the term indicates, it is consultative and the areas of discussions were confined mostly to health, welfare and safety of the employees. Both the parties lost interest as the councils had no administrative powers. In the UK, both joint consultation and collective bargaining are not very successful.

Germany

'Mitbestimmung' that is, codetermination practices in Germany together make the best experience of participative management. This was introduced by the Codetermination Act of 1976. Presently, the Works Constitution Act of 1972 regulates the practice of codetermination. For almost four decades now, Germany provides the best example of successful implementation of workers' participation in the form of codetermination. It operated as an integral part of the national labour relations system in West Germany. Now it still operates successfully in the unified Germany.

Historically, Germany has been the forerunner in employee participation. The free trade union had demanded codetermination in its tenth Congress way back in 1919. The Works Council Law was consequently passed in 1920. The law for the nomination of Works Council members into the Supervisory Board was also passed in 1922. Both the laws existed in practice until Hitler banned all trade union organisations in 1933. Later, once the Second World War was over, the government realised the need for the close cooperation of workers for the reconstruction of the war-torn economy. A new law was passed in 1946 and, according to it, a parity representation on the Supervisory Board was provided and a Labour Director was nominated in the steel industry.

The Works Council which is a body of workers, plays a very dominant role in the co-determination process, in which trade unions which are exclusively organisations of workers without any nexus with political parties have a notable part. Codetermination is employed in three stages: (a) Works Council, (b) Workers' Representatives on the Supervisory Boards of Companies, and (c) Labour Directors on the Management Boards.

Works Council: It is an important body of workers' representatives elected by the entire workforce in every establishment with five or more employees. Hence, the size of the Works Council depends on the number of workers in the respective establishment.

Supervisory Board: It is a statutory body in companies under the Company Law, and its position is between shareholders' assembly and the management board. The supervisory board appoints members of the management board, oversees its activities and approves decisions of major importance. Normally, the supervisory board meets four times a year. Parity of representation of workers and shareholders is maintained. Shareholders' representatives are elected by the general assembly of shareholders' and workers' representatives. The parity representation of employees and shareholders in the supervisory boards of twelve or sixteen or twenty members works effectively. The Act also lays down that among the workers' representatives, one who is elected by the employees and who represents them, should hold managerial positions. When there is a tie in the voting of a supervisory board, the chairman has two votes in order to break the deadlock.

The supervisory board is another level of workers' involvement in German organisations. This is not a management board, though it appoints members of the management board. It also supervises the activities of the management board on behalf of the shareholders and employees. The Supervisory Board gives its decisions on important matters of policy, such as closure of plant, opening of new plants, major changes of product and, large investment. Its discussions are not made public, but it seems from the information available that, in most cases, decisions are unanimous and voting is avoided at the level of the supervisory board.

Both works councils and supervisory boards work simultaneously and closely cooperate with each other within the company. Close and regular contact between workers' representatives and the supervisory board and those on works councils is the standing practice in most enterprises. The worker-members normally include the company's chairman and vice-chairman.

Labour Director: The labour director is a full-fledged member of the management board, that is, the body responsible for the day-to-day running of the enterprise. The Codetermination Act of 1951 introduced the concept of the labour director, who would be nominated by the workers', and he could be appointed or dismissed only with the consent of the majority of the worker-members on the supervisory board.

The Works Constitution Act stresses that the works councils and the management shall work together in a spirit of mutual trust, and shall discuss matters at issue with an earnest desire to reach agreement and make suggestions for settling their differences. No one is allowed to coerce the other. Workers cooperate with the organisation extremely well, which helps the success of the system. Trade unions cannot shirk their responsibility towards their economic and social developments.

The functions of the works councils are conspicuous over the areas like operation of the enterprise, conduct of employees, hours of work, leave arrangements, prevention of accidents, welfare services, and so on. The council has a considerable amount of codetermination rights in respect of social and staff questions as well as organisation of jobs. At the same time, on financial and economic matters, their rights are limited to information and consultation. The ultimate objective of works councils is to closely cooperate with the management. In almost all the cases of decisions affecting the interest of employees directly or indirectly, the works council is consulted.

The works council members study the situation in the enterprise and are deeply involved in the progress of the enterprise. This is, perhaps, the most important aspect of the success of the codetermination machinery in Germany. Workers are fully involved in their work and workplace. Trade unions are more involved in constructive roles like increasing productivity, maintaining industrial peace, and so on. Strikes and lockouts are, therefore, not common.

Japan

The Japanese system, as combined 'spring offensives' that articulate radical demands with enterprise unions, is almost exclusively devoted to productivity growth. Spring offensives have not been active since 1970. Since then, the enterprise unions have played a dominant role in national industrial relations, shifting the focus of the union from wages to lifetime welfare provisions.

The union role in larger companies has become integrative and cooperative, following the example of the union at Toyota. However, a number of Japanese companies have instituted joint consultation systems with the union or elected worker representatives. Joint consultation decisions need not be limited to social and personnel issues, but may also cover economic questions such as major investments.

Yugoslavia

Workers self-management was the hallmark of erstwhile Yugoslavia. Descending from the dictatorial state ownership of industrial activities, President Tito introduced workers' self-management in 1949 which is the origin of workers' participation in Yugoslavia. Rigid central planning gave way to market forces and workers' self-management with the passing of the Self-Management Law in 1950. Important institutions which functioned under the scheme of workers' participation in Yugoslavia were Workers' Council, Management Board, Director, Local People's Committee, and Trade Unions. The workers themselves constituted the management.

Workers' Council: At the enterprise level, this was the highest body which consists of 15 to 120 members (depending on the size of the enterprise) elected by the workers and the staff for a term of three years. The main functions of the council included: (a) decisions on the basic issues of operational policies; (b) adoption of statutes and other general acts and development plans and programmes; (c) adoption and approval of financial statements of the enterprise; (d) supervision of the work of the management board; and (e) decisions concerning the merger of an enterprise with other enterprises; and (f) any other decision concerning the structure and status of the enterprise.

Trade unions did not have a direct role in the management of the undertaking. But they had the right to present the lists of candidates for election to the workers' council and their approval of the council's decisions relating to wages and distribution of the surplus is necessary. At a higher level, the trade unions are consulted in framing legislation in the field of labour.

Management Board: It was the executive organ of the workers' council, which consisted of a minimum of five members elected from among the members of the workers' council. The director would be an ex-officio member of the management board, three-fourths of whose members were elected from production workers who continue in their normal jobs during the period of their tenure as members of the board. The board managed the affairs according to the council's policy, and held responsible for the efficient running of the enterprise.

Director: He was responsible for carrying out the decisions of the council and the board, as well as the day-to-day functional operations. He used to be selected for a term of four years by the council and the committee of the local people through open competition on the basis of advertisements. He could also be reappointed. He was the person who had to ensure the profitable management of the enterprise. As the council had the powers to remove an inefficient director, he also kept the council informed on all important matters.

People's Committee: The committee of the local people had a voice in the appointment of the director. The committee had the powers to interfere with the management, and to dissolve the workers' management.

Self-management in Yugoslavia has become a story of the past since the country itself disintegrated.

EMERGING TRENDS

The industrial relations practices have its historic origin in different countries and also differ considerably. It is an expression of a society in which it operates and of the power relationships between different interest groups. For example, union structures differ even in Western countries across boundaries, that is, some have industrial unions, others craft unions, and still others have general and conglomerate unions (members of more than one industry). These differences in the union structures have considerable influence on collective bargaining.

The trends in international division of labour are as under:

(a) Countries which do not have supply of cheap labour will concentrate on the production of more specialised products such as in Japan, Germany, USA, and so on. This will result in an increasing demand for highly educated, skilled and creative people.

(b) Those which have cheaper skilled talent available will attract specialised factories, such as IT-enabled services in Bangalore, and the automobile manufacturing units all over India.

(c) Countries which have nothing to offer, naturally, have to face obvious oblivion in the fierce competition that exists.

No multinational corporation can afford to ignore the influence of local culture on industrial relations. The subsidiary's character therefore adds colour to the MNC's role in industrial relations. The MNCs should take note of the following emerging trends:[2]

1. Participation or involvement is one important trend. Participative arrangements differ from country-to-country depending upon its social, economic and political conditions prevailing in that country.
2. Internationally accepted labour practices of the country in which the MNC is operating are expected to be complied with. The conventions lay standards which are in the domain of: freedom of association and the right to organise; collective bargaining; abolition of forced labour; discrimination in employment and occupation; equal remuneration for men and woman in employment; and employment of child labour.

3. MNCs must be aware of and alert to political, legal, socio-cultural, economic and technological aspects and unexpected conditions or significant events in such countries. Ethical norms also influence, for example, corporate social responsibility in land acquisition, bribery, and so on.
4. The use of mediation or arbitration by an impartial party to bring opposing parties together is gaining ground.
5. The growing scarcity of skilled labour and their increased individual bargaining power as well as the increasing mobility and prosperity of skilled labour are the reasons for the decline in the power of trade unions. Other reasons for decline of trade unionism are:
    - Increase in white-collar workers as percentage of total workforce
    - Increase in service sector in relation to manufacturing
    - Rising proportion of women in the workforce
    - Increase in the engagement of temporary employees
    - Trend towards smaller plant size
    - Decline in collectivism among younger knowledge workers
    - Increased mobility of labour
    - Scarcity of skilled labour.
6. Closing of undertakings and retrenching of employees without prior notification has been legalised in some countries.
7. One of the features of international business negotiations is the involvement of the host country's government. So, congruence at various levels and adjusting their styles accordingly are the order of the day for MNCs. They have to sensitise themselves to the difficulties that diversified workforce face in organisations.
8. The soft side of HRM such as motivation, empowerment, involvement, leadership, ethics and the hard side of HRM like performance-related pay, TQM, cost minimisation, and flexibility have led to adoption of company-specific employee-management strategies in most part of the world.
9. With the disintegration of USSR and Yugoslavia and their conversion into capitalist countries, they have integrated on all fronts – economic, social, and political fronts. Further, they are influenced by Japanese concepts like flexibility, employee consultation, and so on. The earlier approach of the welfare state of socialist pattern is getting extinct and IR structures are being characterised by diversity.
10. The state action in IR is generally of three kinds in the European union and in other countries:

(a) *Liberal pluralism:* It upholds the principle of non-intervention. Under this, state regulation of IR is confined to creating a simple legal framework within which individuals and business organisation can conclude agreements, for example, Great Britain.

(b) *The corporatism:* This involves active state interference, but only for the purpose of consultations. For example, in Germany where issues are left for regulation through collective bargaining.

(c) *Statism:* This involves active and direct state interference in the terms of employment and working conditions. For example, in France, wages, work week, period of holidays, social security, and child and family allowances are provided in the law.

The following are the main tactics or strategies adopted by trade unions:

- Information exchanges among unions of different countries which held them refute company claims as well as to cite precedents from other countries during bargaining. The labour unions have formed the International Trade Secretariat which provides worldwide links of national unions in a particular trade or industry. It mainly facilitates the exchange of information.
- The most common union tactic is strike for temporary suspension of functions so as to exert pressure. Though it is a powerful weapon in the hands of unions, the bargaining power of a union may be weakened by MNCs adopting some practices such as sourcing its products or components from different countries, or threatening to move production facilities to other locations. Hence, a union should be cautious in using this weapon.
- The next tactic sought by labour unions is lobbying for restrictive countrywide legislation for overall welfare of labour.
- Finally, labour unions seek intervention from the International Labour Organisation (ILO), the European Union (EU), and the Organisation for Economic Cooperation and Development (OECD), in matters affecting their functioning. For example, in 1997, the ILO adopted a code of conduct for MNCs. The voluntary guidelines cover disclosure of information, competition, taxation, employment, financial and industrial relations, and science and technology.

SUMMARY

- *International industrial relations* addresses significant issues, concerning MNCs and trade unions.
- Industrial relations in each nation are embedded in societal rules, norms, and values and no MNC can afford to ignore the influence of local culture on industrial relations.

- Trends in the context of industrial relations in the multinational show: (a) increased participation in decision making, and (b) participation in work improvement of the quality of work life.
- Regional associations like the European Union (EU) and North America Free Trade Agreement (NAFTA) has brought significant implications on IR.
- The NAFTA has stimulated cross-border collaboration among individual labour unions and their allies.
- The four IHRM approaches, namely, ethnocentric, geocentric, polycentric, and regiocentric approaches, have considerable influence on industrial relations practices.
- The role of labour unions varies from country-to-country because of local variations in labour management practices.
- Industrial relations practices and participative arrangements differ from country-to-country.

REVIEW QUESTIONS

1. What are the factors that influence industrial relations in a multinational organisation?
2. What are the strategies of multinationals that give labour unions cause for concern?
3. What is the impact of European Union and NAFTA on IR? Explain.
4. Discuss the employee relations practices in UK and USA.
5. Critically examine the employee participation practices in some countries with which you are familiar.
6. Discuss the recent developments in international IR in terms of union's and management's approach.

REFERENCES

1. J. Hamil (1984), *Labour Relations Decision Making within Multinational Corporations,* Industrial Relations Journal, Vol. 10, No. 2, p. 34.
2. P.J. Dowling and D.E. Welch (2005), *International Human Resource Management: Managing People in a Multinational Context,* 4th Edition, Thomas Learning.

10

International Mergers and Acquisitions HR Perspective

Objectives

- To explain the role of HR in mergers and acquisitions.
- To appreciate the people part of acquisitions and mergers.
- To anticipate the problems of the employees before and after acquisition.

INTRODUCTION

Mergers and acquisitions are a tremendously important phenomenon in business both because of their prevalence and because of the value involved. While they are important in the global economy, these deals can make or break the firms that take recourse to them. Most research on these shows that a majority of deals fail to create value for firm owners. They are complex transactions that involve teams of lawyers, bankers, consultants, boards, accountants, internal personnel, stockholders, creditors, customers, regulatory authorities and numerous others. Each party plays a role in the process, irrespective of whether it is a complex or simple one. A merger or acquisition is a delicate issue for any organisation. When two distinct corporate entities are fused into one another, rapid change is inevitably sparked off. Consequently, every stage of the ensuing transition has to be mapped and managed; every loose end has to be tied up. There must be a definitive vision for the future not merely economically or commercially, but from a human resources standpoint as well

During mergers and acquisitions, the impact of wide ranging changes is stronger and more visible, among the employees of the organisation more than any other.

PRINCIPLES OF ACQUISITION

Regardless of the size of the company that is acquired, it is possible to state a few more or less uniform principles. Although these principles are not new, they are in the long run, the most important.

Know the People. This cannot be done by long-distance telephone calls. Go out and visit the new people; get to know them and to understand their problems. In trying to evaluate attitudes of newly acquired employees, some companies have used an informal employee survey. Many others feel that direct contact is much more helpful.

Do Not Rush. This is more difficult. In spite of the pressures that tend to force uniformity at an early stage, a persuasive argument can be made for a gradual transition. The people who are new to the company will soon learn those personnel policies which are more liberal than that of the acquired company; let them develop an appetite for them. Then, when the total personnel programmes are integrated, it will be much easier for employees to accept the less desirable part of the change.

Train and Sell. Best results appear to be obtained when the personnel staff and others from the acquired company are thoroughly trained and indoctrinated in the total personnel programme of the acquiring company. Also, best results are obtained when the personnel staff and others from the acquired company then go out and sell and explain these programmes to their own people. The importance of informative group meetings which make use of visual aids cannot be overemphasised.

The technical and financial considerations should not overshadow the "human element" of the acquisition. People are the muscle of any company. Just like the body of a trained athlete, they have a natural rhythm which can be severely injured by improper handling. There is usually only one chance in any one situation to pursue people problems properly. If the approach is considerate and well planned in advance, the handling of these problems can result in growth and profit. Bad handling at the start may lead to countless problems which may last for months or for years – or perhaps forever. Studies show that unresolved human capital issues are often the cause of post-merger diminishing of shareholder value. For that reason, it makes sense to address workforce needs at the earliest during mergers and acquisitions.

Undoubtedly, employees are a key stakeholder group that is often affected in any merger or acquisition. Employees, unless they are stakeholders, have little ability to affect the decisions that are critical to the success of the deal, especially in the post-merger phases. One of the most common reasons for the failure of mergers and acquisitions is the departure of employees, and the inability to integrate employees sufficiently to get them work together.

Of the most common justification for doing mergers and acquisitions, "synergies" often involve cutting personnel. The legal rights of employees differ as per location. Where trade unions exist, they must typically be considered and involved in the whole process. Unions, as supporters of their members, are not likely to support plans that would result in personnel reductions. Depending on the country, the legal rights of unions also differ. For example, in certain countries unions are given the right to be involved at the negotiating table and must, by law, be informed of different ongoing deliberations.

COMMUNICATION FRAMEWORK

The communication framework can well be the single most important factor for smooth integration in an acquisition. With effective communications, the acquiring firm can develop a climate of confidence and, hopefully, eliminate much of the friction which frequently occurs. The acquiring company in the pre-acquisition phase should obtain samples of internal reporting systems and evaluate them carefully. Usually, the acquiring company will want such systems to parallel its own. During the period immediately following the acquisition, however, the amount of such reporting may vary, depending on the differences between the two companies.

Good communication is an essential part of good human relations. The timing and setting of communication is very important in a process of merger and acquisition. The best time to start the communication programme is before the acquisition talks begin. The effect and meaning of what is said to be employees are of prime importance. The need is to start the process as soon as the idea of an acquisition is first mentioned. Remember, rumours and half-truths travel faster than the facts. One company handled the rumour problem by saying: "Let us know the rumour, and we will put out the facts". To combat rumours of the sale of the company, they announced that their management had some discussion with another about merging, but they had been terminated. This direct and frank approach greatly increased the respect of the employees for their top management. It is necessary, of course, that information be screened to ensure that it is factual and that the distribution is effective. Premature leaks on acquisitions can lose the battle before it begins. The basic objective is to inform employees about an acquisition as quickly as possible. Top management to an extent communicates through formal channels, but it does not by any means control all the means of communication. We must realistically accept that employees talk to each other, to their union leaders, to the press, television, and radio. If we do not make an accurate statement at the right time, facts are replaced by rumour and speculation. We also have to be ready to try and answer the employee's questions.

Acquisitions and mergers are a fact of corporate life. Since there are sound reasons for acquisitions, they will probably continue at a rapid rate, and employee communications aspects in future mergers, as in previous ones, will present many and varying challenges.

RESPONSIBILITIES OF HR

HR has always been an important participant in the process of mergers and acquisitions, aiding both growth and economies of scale through knowledge management, assessment of employee needs and seamless integration of people and procedures. But perhaps its most important function is to help employees come to terms with all the changes around them and help them adjust into a new and unfamiliar working routine, and under a new set of rules. This is done by ostensibly demonstrating an understanding of the target company's culture, identifying employees for their worth, and deciding how they can be made to fit into the new scheme of things in the quickest possible time. HR should in fact, make its presence felt from the deal or due diligence stage onwards, by understanding how interaction with a new set of people, cultures and systems will mould the future for both companies – the acquired, and the acquirer. One of HR's biggest responsibilities after taking over the reins of the target organisation would be gauging the effectiveness of its existing HR function and weighing it against that of the acquiring organisation. This helps in preparing the ground for an integration programme. The most important thing is to decide whether to build an integration team, assimilate new cultures, or to have clear-cut job descriptions for employees.

Once the integration programme has been launched, the human resource function can be summed up in one word: communication. HR should do everything it can, to facilitate two-way communication between the target and the parent company, thus paving the way for the formulation of a comprehensive staffing programme that takes into account the present crop of talent, newly-created and redundant positions, and benefits and compensation strategies. Communication is the key, and more so with the employees who are going to stay on. In the absence of proper communication, rumours and gossip become the prevailing truth.

Organisations also need to pay special attention to retaining highly skilled or experienced workers. Mergers and acquisitions are seen by head-hunters and competitors as a good time to lure away employees who might be anxious or insecure about their future. It is always a small set of managers that contributes to most of the effectiveness of a company. This group has a reputation from across the levels and departments, and often have a good market-value. This means, in the state of uncertainty and confusion, the company may lose its best managers. HR must also guard against flagging morale and motivation levels of the employees concerned, and consequent low productivity.

When it comes to formation of the integration team too, management should ensure that the team in charge of the merger has members who have the necessary skill and experience. Decisiveness, balance and discretion in evaluation, sensitivity to employee attitudes, familiarity with the nuances of integration projects, and being able to bring out the best in other people by employing the right means at the right time, are other qualities that a specialist team need to possess.

PERSONNEL CONSIDERATIONS

A common representation made during negotiations for the acquisition of a company is, "there will be no changes in your policies and programmes. You will continue to operate exactly as you did before. The only difference is that we, rather than others, will own the stock of your enterprise."[1]

In considering the people part of acquisitions and mergers, one should answer the following questions:

- Just how much weight do personnel factors carry in an acquisition?
- Why is there a continuing and increasing concern about personnel considerations when one company acquires another?
- How many acquisitions have failed, and how many of these failures are due to the improper handling of the human element?
- Finally, just how often has this human element been the difference between the success and failure of an acquisition?

For the purpose of discussion one should accept the premise that to buy a business is to buy people. Assuming this, how does this blending and complementing of the human element before, during, and after the acquisition result in the difference between profit and loss, success and failure, and growth and stagnation. No matter how one initially faces the situation, there is always a change when one organisation is acquired by another. Circumstances will indeed be different after the acquisition. The acquired unit must tune into the parent company and live according to its rules. Moreover, there is the need for realistic evaluation of the human factors long before making decision to acquire. The real goal here seems to be: (a) obtaining the facts, (b) recognising these facts for they really are, and (c) evaluating such facts in a meaningful manner.

There are also many important considerations in the compensation area: What is the acquired company's compensation philosophy and policy? Are employees at various levels receiving high, low, or middle-of-the-road pay? What is the method of compensation? Does the company grant a higher level of non-cash compensation and lower level cash compensation than the acquiring company? What are the costs of other benefits, such as company cars, expense accounts, and club memberships? How does the acquired company approach control of wages and salaries? How are wages and salaries administered? Are the controls and administrative systems of the two organisations compatible? Will changes be necessary? If so, how much, how many, and when should they be made?

Many questions are to be answered and many points to be resolved in dealing with employee compensation and benefit plans when two companies merge or when one company is acquired by another. Many possible answers can be given to these questions. But just as no two mergers are exactly alike, neither are there any standard answers to the treatment of benefit plans that can be stereotyped and followed time-after-time in each merger situation. The compensation and benefit problems arising out of any merger must be considered unique, and specific solutions to the problems should be tailored separately for each situation.

The multitude of labour relations considerations must be given an early and thorough evaluation and analysis. What is the union relations history? What unions represent the employees? How many strikes? What is the grievance and arbitration caseload? Is the company a pattern setter or follower in contract negotiations?

ANTICIPATION OF EMPLOYEE PROBLEMS

The problems of the employees that may arise as a result of mergers and acquisitions may be considered under the following two areas:

Before the Acquisition: It is practically impossible to anticipate all the problems of the employees which might occur as the result of an acquisition. Likewise, it is almost impossible to compile an all-inclusive check list of actions to be covered for solution of these problems. However, to try and minimise these potential problems, an organised research of the subject is possible. To aid the acquiring company in considering the human problems before taking on the responsibility for the people involved, a checklist, in the form of a series of questions, will be helpful in identifying the problems.

Answers to the following questions are necessary in order to make a meaningful evaluation:

- What are the specifics as to employees, numbers, jobs they hold, sex, age, and service?
- What is the turnover in the workforce? High or low, why?
- What are the principal sources from which the company obtains its employee?
- What is the labour relations history?
- What are the principal unions involved?
- What is the thrust of the union-management relationship?
- Is there a heavy grievance case load? If so, why?
- What is the basis on which new labour contracts are generally determined? Industry pattern, area pattern, or any other?
- Is the company a pattern setter or pattern follower in contract negotiations?
- If it is non-union, why?
- If it is non-union, what unions appear to be most likely to be candidates for organisational entries?
- What is the industrial relations climate in the area of the company's locations?

- Is there an incentive plan? Who are covered? What does it cost? How does it work?
- How is the personnel function organised as to: (a) organisational structure, (b) salary administration, (c) employment procedures, (d) compensation and benefit plans, (e) training and development, (f) labour relations, and (g) community relations?
- What are the major strengths of the human resource department?
- What are its major weaknesses?
- How does it compare with the HR functions in the acquiring company as to status in the organisation and level of contribution?
- What is the anticipated structure of the new organisation? Which positions will be upgraded? Which ones downgraded? Which ones eliminated?
- What is the policy (or what will be the policy) on termination and voluntary retirement?
- What is the best way to go about a careful personal explanation to each employee who will be affected one way or the other, as a result of the acquisition?
- What should be done to change the personnel policies in the acquired company to fit those of the acquiring company, or *vice versa?*

After the Acquisition: As most problems concerning people arise after the acquisition, a thorough examination of the post-merger difficulties concerning management and employees must be done. Many corporate procedures and check lists for acquisitions tend to overemphasise the money aspects of the matter and forget the people factor. Most top managers know the importance of the people side of the business – but, at the same time many acquiring companies completely ignore it.

People are the catalyst in the acquisition process. Apart from the profit and loss statement and the balance sheet, the human element is to be considered with utmost importance. The people consideration route in an acquisition should be fair and objective. It also needs lot of patience that induces confidence and respect, and permits the needed time and consideration for the integration of the people problems involved. A major staff responsibility for implementing people considerations in the acquisition in a timely manner rests with the chief personnel executive of the acquiring company. Before there is an analysis of the acquired company, it is essential that the personnel executive of the parent company establish good relationships with all the officers, including his own counterpart, of the newly acquired company (division). Without first establishing such good relationships, it will be difficult, if not impossible, to identify the real problem areas.

Of even greater concern to the management group of the acquired company is the uncertainty of their own future. After good working relationships have been established analysis of policies and programmes can proceed under favourable circumstances

Recommendations and actions growing out of such a study will, of course, be guided by many different factors in each organisation.

Although the corporate personnel are concerned with all aspects of the newly acquired unit's personnel operation, efforts must be concentrated in those areas in which the problems are most acute. In addition to analysis of the new unit, the corporate personnel staff can encourage exchange of experiences of the personnel organisations in the various divisions, especially that of the new unit, with one another, through group meetings. Such meetings are of immeasurable help in promoting understanding. The success or failure of any acquisition depends to a great extent on the degree of harmony and relationships developed between the acquiring and acquired company. Those engaged in the personnel function – whether called human relations, employee relations, industrial relations, or personnel – can make a major contribution to the success of acquisition.

PRE-MERGER CONSIDERATIONS

For the post-merger treatment of employee benefit plans, it is important that prior to the merger the acquiring corporation review the employee benefits programme of the corporation to be acquired for a number of reasons. It should be determined in advance whether any benefits problems exist which might present impediments to the merger.

Special attention should be given to the pension programme (including the plan or plans for union employees). Eligibility for participation, vesting conditions, and the amounts of benefits provided should be compared to those of other companies in the same industry and/or geographic areas, and this comparison should extend to comparable elements in the acquiring company/s pension plan (or plans). What is desirable is to issue a sufficiently informative statement to employees, satisfactory to both companies that will counter any feelings of apprehension employees may have.

Most mergers and acquisitions are driven by apparent cost-cutting synergies and stock prices. In most cases, the merger partners do not look closely enough at the 'people component – strategic variables at the very heart of the deal. Infact, strategic vision needs involvement of HR professionals from the beginning to assess the people implications that do not feature in balance sheets or income statements. HR specialists are left with the difficult role of developing communication strategies; aligning payroll, benefits and compensation systems; and unifying different and possibly incompatible processes and cultures. Clemente and Greenspan (1999, p. 1) point out that there are literally hundreds of reasons why mergers and acquisitions failure rate is so high. But many can be traced to the exclusion of human resource professionals in the pre-deal planning phase and the function's last-minute inclusion after the transaction has closed.

CASE 1

Acquisition by Asian Paints

In the case of Asian Paints, with 51 per cent acquisition of Singapore company Berger International in 2002, Vice-chairman and MD Dani says he was clear that his company will be choosy in its operations and not necessarily operate all the ten subsidiaries of Berger. In the four years since the acquisition, Asian Paints has sold three subsidiaries in Malta, Philippines and Myanmar. Dani's motive is clear: to be present only in emerging markets and in markets that generate cash flows. "Surely, cultural issues play an important role in an acquisition. To handle this carefully, we spent time with the employees and worked as a team to thrash out the synergies such that the acquisition generates value", says Dani.

Critical size helps you to spread your fixed costs. At the same time, one must always be prepared for making course corrections on the way. We exited out of our ventures in Mauritius and Malta because after operating for a while, we found out that the growth of the paint market as well as the economy was stagnating. So, we took out call and I feel companies should always be prepared to make such decisions but what counts in today's age is the speed of integration, opines Dani.

One of the most essential learning from the acquisitions was realising the importance of local knowledge. When the companies went abroad, they realised that it was a whole new ball game; the market dynamics were altogether different. They have to align their products and customer offerings to cater to each individual market. Along with local understanding, comes the core issue of localisation of talent and the need to develop a strong local cadre. A local workforce brings with it a better understanding of the market, operating environment, and consumer preferences. The greatest challenge for Indian MNCs lies in the area of attracting and acquiring local talent for their overseas ventures. As Indian companies globalise, they have to acquire size and market share to stay afloat.

The process of integration follows an acquisition, but what counts in today's age is the speed of integration and how fast you are able to share organisational best practices within different units. Along with technology and intellectual integration, emotional integration is also critical, because in the end one needs to realise that while there are brands, there are also customers and there are employees.

For its international operations, Asian Paints accomplished the process of clearing apprehensions about acquisitions through its various connect initiatives, where communication played a key role, followed by effective action. It is now implementing systems and processes to make them as efficient as any world-class entity. Asian Paints has implemented ERP across its units to make the transaction process more robust. It has flown in people on special assignments, wherever any unit had any concern area, be it pertaining to supply chain, marketing or any other function. It has recently rolled out a mega operational efficiency initiative which focuses on issues like productivity, safety, environment, reducing factory level losses, planning and control systems, thus adding value to its acquired operations. (*Source: Business Today*, December 3, 2006.)

Discussion Questions

1. How did Asian Paints handle cultural issues in the acquired companies? What are its essential learnings from the acquisitions?
2. What steps did Asian Paints take in the process of integration following the acquisitions?
3. How did Asian Paints accomplish the process of clearing apprehensions about its acquisitions?

CASE 2

Tata Acquires Corus Group

It is not often that a company is able to buy another that is four times as large, but the largest ever overseas acquisition by an Indian company seems all set to succeed with the board of the Anglo-Dutch company, Corus Group, responding positively to Tata Steel's 4.3 billion pounds takeover offer. Tata Steel has a capacity to make 5 million tonnes of steel a year and Corus about 19 million tonnes; together they will become the world's fifth largest steel maker that will be a welcome development for the global steel industry, which remains fragmented despite the Arcelor Mittal merger earlier this year. Like Mittal, Tata Steel is attempting to buy a quintessentially European institution with its shareholders spread across the European Union.

Like Arcelor, Corus was the outcome of a merger between companies that were already well known in their respective countries. Tata Steel's bid has not evoked any such protests. As in Mittal's deal with Arcelor, significant synergies may spring forth from Tata Steel's merger with Corus. Tata Steel will get a foothold in the European markets, where Corus has a strong presence in the value-added products such as steel used in automobiles and aircraft. For Corus, the attractions are the large reserves of ore that Tata Steel commands, more important, the access to the managerial and technical resources of India's most widely admired business group.

The Tata Group's outward looking focus is in ample evidence once again. It comes in a year when Indian companies are emerging as significant players in cross-border acquisitions. In the first nine months, they have invested $ 7.5 billion to acquire some 115 companies abroad against the $ 8.3 billion foreign companies have brought in to fund their acquisitions in India. The bid for Corus is a telling demonstration of India's competitiveness in the manufacturing arena. Indian manufacturers are scaling up to the level of world leaders on the back of strong engineering and managerial skills.

Ratan Tata, Chairman of Tata Sons, said "Corus and Tata Steel are companies with long, proud histories. We have compatible cultures of commitment to stakeholders and complementary strengths in technology, efficiency, product mix and geographical spread. Together we will be even better equipped to remain at the leading edge of the fast changing steel industry. The managing director of Tata Steel sought to allay fears of job losses at Corus as a result of the takeover and planned cost-cutting. He said the threat to jobs would have been greater had the deal not taken place. The deals make it more competitive and that means more job security, though he didn't rule out redundancies in future." Jim Leng, Chairman of Corus, said "This creates a well-balanced company, strategically well-placed to compete in an increasingly competitive global environment. The deal was prompted by his company's decision to seek access to low-cost production and high-growth markets.

The President of Confederation of Indian industry said "The Tata Steel-Corus is a sign of a confident India Inc. being recognised as a significant global economic player. The internationalisation of the Indian corporate sector has reached a new high with this landmark deal." (***Source:*** The Hindu, October 21, 2006.)

Discussion Questions

1. Why there was no protest from European countries for Tata's acquisition of Corus Group, a European institution, whereas there was vehement opposition when another European company Arcelor was taken over by Mittal Steel?
2. What are the significant synergies that will accrue to Tatas by the acquisition of Corus Group?
3. "The internationalisation of the Indian Corporate Sector has reached a new high with Corus Group landmark deal" – Comment.

SUMMARY

- *International mergers and acquisitions* portray various human resource issues and considerations that weigh in any such activity.
- No two mergers or acquisitions are exactly alike.
- There must be a definite plan and vision for the future, not merely from economic or commercial point of view, but from a human resource standpoint.
- HR is an important participant in the merger and acquisition process, right from the beginning to the end.
- Communication framework is the single most important factor for smooth integration in a merger and acquisition.

- The questions usually asked by employees during mergers and acqusitions are: (a) reasons for the merger; (b) facts about the company with which his organisational plans to merge; (c) general changes that might result from the merger; (d) changes likely in terms of specific job and income; and (e) changes in terms of future responsibilities and compensation.
- It is to be recognised that people are often the only variable between the success and failure of a merger and acquisition.

REVIEW QUESTIONS

1. What is the role of HR in mergers and acquisitions?
2. What are the HR considerations which weigh in any merger and acquisition process?
3. What are the issues to be considered before and after acquisition and mergers?

REFERENCE

1. Myles L., Mace, and George G.M., *Management Problems of Corporate Acquisitions,* Division of Research, Harvard Business School, Boston, 1962, pp. 258-259.

11

Cultural Dimensions of IHRM

Objectives

- To explain cultural differences and similarities in a global perspective.
- To discuss the Hofstede's framework of cultural differences.
- To identify different strategies for managing diversity.

INTRODUCTION

Many think that the way we dress or behave with others is culture. To some it means refined behaviour or sophistication in living, yet others think it is the way we speak. If we are involved in international businesses, it is essential to have a clear understanding of culture and cultures of different countries. The management is required to cope with problems of alien cultures, unfamiliar laws, languages, attitudes, practices, competitors, managerial styles, work ethics, and so on. Human resource function such as hiring, maintaining and remunerating must acquire global perspective to face this challenge. The management must be flexible and proactive, and execute the company's strategy on a global scale, so that it can become a source of competitive advantage for the company. By helping the best qualified people execute the company's strategy on a global scale, the management can become a source of competitive advantage for the company.

CONCEPT OF CULTURE

'Culture', in simple words, means the way of life of a group of people. It is shared by all or almost all members of the social group. It applies to most of the people most of the time, never to all the people all the time. We think of people belonging to another culture if their way of behaviour is significantly different. Anthropologists describe culture as a whole that includes beliefs, morals, customs, knowledge, law, art, and habits, acquired by a person as a member of society. It includes behaviour which may be considered as right or wrong, admirable or absurd, by people from a different culture. This is because behaviour is driven by beliefs and different people hold different beliefs about what is right or wrong.

Social and cultural factors in various countries of the globe affect the international human resource management. These factors include attitude of the people to work, attitude to wealth, family, marriage, religion, education, ethics, human relations, and social responsibility. Culture is socially shared, learned, subjective, cumulative and dynamic.

In terms of organisational culture there would appear to be three levels at which it is used:

1. *Perceived culture*: What is usually observed and experienced by those working within it.
2. *Common values*: The beliefs and values that underpin and determine the perceived culture.
3. *Underlying assumptions*: Behind the common values are the underlying assumptions about the world and how it functions.

STRATEGIC AND CULTURAL VALUES

As the company grows and becomes successful, it usually develops a culture that distinguishes it from other companies and that is one of the reasons for its success. The process of creating an organisational culture is really a process of linking its strategic values with its cultural values. Strategic values are the basic beliefs about an organisation's environment that shape its strategy. Strategic analysis evaluates economic, demographic, public policy, technological, and social trends to identify needs in the marketplace that the organisation can meet. Cultural values are the values employees need in an organisation to carry-out its strategic values. Organisations that attempt to develop cultural values that are not linked to strategic values may end up with an empty set of values that have little relationship to its business.

After developing its strategic and cultural values, the organisation must establish a vision of the organisation's direction. This "vision" is a picture of what the organisation will be like at some point in the future. It portrays how the strategic and cultural values will combine to create the future. For example, an insurance company might establish a vision of "protecting the lifestyles" of two million families by the year 2015. In effect, it synthesises both the strategic and cultural values as it communicates a performance target to employees. Operationally, development of culture would involve developing a strong corporate identity, development of important values, building healthy traditions, and developing consistent management practices.

What is considered good in one culture may not be considered so by people in other cultures. When people go abroad and find people behaving in different ways, they are perplexed. They may not even understand why people in other countries are not behaving like themselves. They may find such behaviour 'strange', and even wrong.

Values are general beliefs about what is right and wrong and determine general preferences. They drive, often unconsciously, our thinking and action. Managerial values influence all managerial activities such as communication, superior/subordinate relationship, selection and reward systems, leadership, and so on. To cite an illustration of value system, Latin American managers feel they should recruit members of their family wherever possible. Americans depend totally on track record and qualification. Indians believe that happiness of one's entire family, including the extended family, should be of utmost importance to all. But Americans believe that individuals should achieve more and more success and accumulate more and more material things like money, houses and cars for themselves, even if it leaves little time for the family.

Exhibit 11.1

The Hewlett-Packard Way

Enduring Values through Changing Times

Based on the belief that people are committed to doing their jobs well and are capable of making sound decisions, Hewlett-Packard practices a highly innovative style of management known simply as the HP Way.

The HP Way engenders a very open and informal corporate culture. Consistent with this, the company has developed a matrix style of organisation rather than the more formal pyramid management structure popular among many companies.

It has been the policy of the company not to have a tight military-type organisation, but rather to have overall objectives which are clearly stated and agreed upon, and to give people the freedom to work towards these goals in ways they determine best for their own areas of responsibility.

The Hewlett-Packard work environment fosters individual dignity, pride in accomplishment and the motivation to produce quality work. In return, the company ensures that employees share in the success which their efforts make possible.

Organisational values

- Trust and respect for individuals.
- A high level of achievement and contribution.
- Conducting business with uncompromising integrity.

→

- Achieving common objectives through teamwork.
- Encouraging flexibility and innovation.

Corporate objectives

- Profit.
- Customer respect and loyalty.
- Participating in relevant fields of interest.
- Growth.
- Helping people in sharing company success.
- Fostering initiative and creativity.
- Corporate citizenship and responsibility.

Strategies and practices

- Management by wandering around.
- Management by objectives.
- Open-door policy.
- Total quality control.

Culture is mostly determined by the economic level and conditions and climate of a region or a country. Since economic level and conditions and climate differ from region-to-region and country-to-country, culture also differs from region-to-region and country-to-country. However, certain needs of the people like physiological and sociological, *viz.*, food, water, clothing, housing and security are common irrespective of the region or country. Therefore, economic and social behaviour of people across the world have some common features though the presentation of the general behaviour may vary.

CULTURAL SENSITIVITY AND CULTURAL SHOCK

Cultural sensitivity is to have the empathy to accept cultural differences without allowing one's own values to surface in unproductive or confrontational ways.[1] Therefore, individuals have to understand cultural differences and follow them rather than be openly judgemental of the culture of the land.

According to Hall[2], cultures also vary based on the manner of information processing. Cultures which handle information in a direct, linear fashion are called, "*monochromic*". Americans are more monochromic. The other type of culture is "polychromic". In this culture people work on several forms simultaneously instead of pursuing a single task. Japanese and Indians belong to polychromic culture.

A study on Japanese managers working in Germany reveals that the Japanese viewed their counterparts as abusive, argumentative, blunt and uncooperative; while German managers viewed Japanese managers as arrogant, reclusive and indecisive. Both the groups tried to understand other group negatively, due to lack of cultural sensitivity. This attitude caused strained relationships.

Cross-cultural communication process and negotiations are important in understanding cross-cultural sensitivity. In some countries like the USA, Canada, Germany and Switzerland, the messages that the people convey are explicit and clear. They use the actual words to convey the information. These cultures are called 'low-context cultures'.

In countries like India, Japan, Saudi Arabia, and other Middle East Arab countries, communication is mostly indirect and the expressive manner in which the message is delivered becomes critical. Much of the information is transmitted through non-verbal communication. These messages can be understood only with the reference to the context. Such cultures are referred to as, 'high-context cultures'.

People have more or less the same needs irrespective of the religion, race, region, and caste. These common needs are referred to as 'cultural universals'. Murdock has identified cultural universals like athletic, sports, bodily adornment, cooking, dancing, singing, education, joking, kin groups, status differentiation and dream interpretation. The cultural universals enable the businessmen to market the products in many foreign countries with modifications, e.g., TVs, cars, and videogames.

International human resource managers have to take care to avoid misunderstandings by understanding cultural differences as one has to be sensitive to the culture of the host country. Infact, all cultures are good as they are evolved over a period of time based on the then local conditions. However, culture can be changed when such conditions tend to change or disappear.

To become more sensitive to a new culture, (a) watch body language. Body language provides different signals in a foreign country; (b) learn some of the key words of the country, which will also provide tips on how people communicate in their country; (c) learn certain customs of new country; and (d) learn how to communicate for getting a job done in a foreign country.

According to anthropologists, cultural shock involves anxiety and doubt caused by an overload of unfamiliar expectations and social clues. Because of differences in cultures, an employee posted outside his or her home country will experience confusion, alienation, disorientation, and emotional upheaval. This is known as culture shock. An executive transferred from India to Korea, for example, would experience anxiety because of alien culture, foreign language, unaccustomed climate, and unfamiliar food habits. But the anxiety is less when he or she is posted to Singapore where one comes across large number of Indians and hotels run by Indians.

Many employees of multinational corporations do not know how to deal with a cultural adjustment process. This experience can be painful and devastating. At its extreme, it can prevent growth and self-actualisation. When an individual's psychological security is threatened, the consequences may not be healthy for him, his family, or the organisation he represents.

Increasing numbers of multinational organisations, inter-company interactions among them, and cultural adjustment problems, are a compelling reason for cross-cultural training. The importance of cross-cultural sensitivity, empathy, and ability to communicate with people from different cultures are of great concern worldwide.

Exhibit 11.2

Cultural Sensitivity

Example 1

An Indian businessman on his first trip to Japan negotiated a very large deal with a Japanese company. On his return to India, he sent an e-mail to the Japanese party expecting to receive a reply by the next day. When he did not receive any reply he thought that the deal was off. He panicked and diverted his team to a different project. But he received an encouraging reply after a week. The problem was lack of knowledge of a different culture. Indians expect a quick reply to their e-mails. The Japanese check all aspects from all concerned people before replying.

Example 2

Mohan joined a firm in Japan as a senior manager. On the day of joining, he was asked if he would like to pick up the appointment letter and other related forms. Mohan thought it was a suggestion and said he would pick it up later. By saying this he lost the goodwill of his employers without even realising it. The Japanese communicate indirectly. What they actually meant was that Mohan should pick them up the same day. But Mohan failed to understand it because different cultures communicate in different ways. In addition, the Japanese expect people to respond quickly. By saying that he would pick them up later, he created a negative impression.

Example 3

Shalini's husband had been relocated to China as procurement manager by his company. She was told by one of her Indian friends that personal relations are very important for doing business in China. She called one of the biggest and most important suppliers of her husband for dinner. In her desire to please this important person, she decorated her house with Chinese lanterns. The guest looked upset. He stiffly bowed and walked out. She did not know that Chinese use different lanterns for different occasions and she had decorated her home with funeral lanterns.

It is apparent from the above examples that knowledge of different cultures is essential for operating successfully in a globalised world.

CULTURAL DIFFERENCES AND SIMILARITIES

Cultural factors influence human behaviour. Human behaviour that affects business includes: employee behaviour, consumer behaviour, and behaviour of other stakeholders. People with different cultural backgrounds behave differently even at the workplace.

Cultures sometimes clash due to different behavioural expectations. For example, problems in Japan and India are normally resolved behind closed doors. But in most of the Western cultures, including that of the USA, the conflicts are to be brought out in the open and discussed face-to-face in public. For understanding cultural issues in organisational setting against international perspective, it is essential to understand employee behaviour. Four basic conclusions can be drawn about cross-cultural impact on employee behaviour:

First, individual behaviour in organisational setting varies across cultures. Thus, employees based in India, Japan, US and Germany are likely to have different attitudes and patterns of behaviour. The behaviour patterns are likely to be widespread and pervasive within an organisation.

Second, culture itself is an important variable for this variation. There are also other factors like differing standards of living and varied geographical conditions which cause variations in behaviour. However, culture is a significant factor.

Third, although behaviour within organisational setting remains quite diverse across cultures, organisations themselves appear to be increasingly similar. Hence, managerial practices at a general level may be alike, but the people who work within organisations differ markedly.

Fourth, the same manager behaves differently in different cultural settings. A manager may adopt one set of behaviours when working in one culture, but may change those behaviours when moved into a different culture. Businesses should identify the cultural variations in foreign countries and evaluate their influence on human resource management, marketing, and stakeholder relations.

Making adjustments wherever necessary: Business firms after evaluating the influence of cultural variations on business practices and processes should decide the nature and degree of adjustments necessary. Host country's culture, in certain areas, does not expect foreigners to adjust to them. However, human resource practices need to be adjusted based on the host country culture.

Communication: Communication plays a vital role while doing business in various foreign countries. Businesses should be cautious in spoken and written language, translation, and the silent language; otherwise they face serious problems in various transactions. Poor translations may also result in tragic consequences. The collision between aircraft from Air Kazakhstan and Saudi Air in New Delhi was due to inaccurate translations. Therefore, appropriate technical words should be chosen in advertisements, reports, agreements, and in all other business transactions.

Competitive advantage: Culture of a country determines cost of doing business, productivity, entrepreneurship and innovation. Japan's culture emphasises on teamwork, loyalty, honesty, and reciprocal obligations. These factors ultimately improve competitive advantage of the business.

Culture and business ethics: Though the basic ethical principles are more or less the same throughout the world, specific issues are closely related to the culture of a country. Thomas Donaldson suggests that international business firms should be guided by the following ethical principles:

- Respect for core human values and human rights.
- Respect for local traditions.
- Taking the situational factors into consideration while deciding what is ethical and what is unethical.[3]

HOFSTEDE'S FRAMEWORK

There are many models that seek to explain cultural differences between people. An important study of cultural differences was made by Geert Hofstede of the Netherlands. He found in his study that all people were mentally programmed at three levels.

Universal Level: Almost all people in the world are mentally programmed to a considerable extent in the same way. They are stimulated by hunger, thirst, anger, pain and pleasure, affection for children and attraction towards the opposite sex in almost the same way.

Collective Level: This kind of mental programming is shared with some, but not with all people. It is common to people belonging to a certain group or category. The best way to recognise this commonality is to find how it is different from people belonging to other groups or categories. It can be seen in the language in which people express themselves, the degree of respect they show to elders, the physical distance they maintain from other people in order to feel comfortable, the way they carry-out basic human activities like eating, marrying, and the ceremonials surrounding them, and so on.

Individual Level: As we all know, not even identical twins raised together are programmed exactly alike. Due to this there exists a wide range of alternative behaviour patterns within the same collective culture.

Hofstede studied 1,60,000 employees of IBM subsidiaries in 60 countries. He discovered that national cultures have a profound effect on work-related values and attitudes. He saw highly significant differences in behaviour and attitudes of managers from different countries, even though they worked in the same multinational company. He also discovered that these differences did not change over time and that they were more due to national differences than due to age, gender or position.

Cultures vary on following dimensions, although subcultures and individuals variations exist. He found that cultures basically differ from each other in following dimensions:

- Individualism vs. Collectivism
- Power Distance (high power distance vs. low power distance)
- Uncertainty Avoidance
- Career Success vs. Quality of Life (also called masculine vs. feminine)
- Confucian Dynamism

These dimensions are used as a tool to compare cultures. Each of the above dimensions are explained below:

Individualism vs. Collectivism: Individualism pertains to societies in which the ties between individuals are loose. Collectivism as its opposite pertains to societies in which people from birth onwards are integrated into strong, cohesive in-groups. People characterised by individualism culture, tend to put their careers before their organisations and usually assess how situations will affect them personally. People in a culture dominated by collectivism tend to place organisational needs before their own needs. Canada, New Zealand, Netherlands, UK, USA are some of the countries characterised by individualism. Collectivism is said to dominate in India, Japan, Germany, Peru, Columbia, Greece, Mexico, Pakistan, and Singapore. India and Japan are characterised by a high level of collectivism.

Japan has a collective culture and they strongly feel that the behaviour, and even the beliefs, of members of any group should be determined by the will of that group. North Americans, on the other hand, are individualists and believe that every individual can behave in the way he chooses to, subject only to the laws of the land. Individualism is measured by the degree to which individuals in society prefer to act as individuals rather than as a group. Every emphasis is on the individual who is personally accountable for his/her actions. Self-respect in individualistic societies is based on the achievements of the individual who is expected to provide only for and be concerned with the interest of himself and his immediate family. All his commitments are primarily to himself.

Collective societies, on the other hand, believe that group is more important than individual. In a collective culture, social networks are very strong. People clearly distinguish between their own groups and others. Groups have common goals and objectives, not individual goals. Groups are expected to look after their members and also protect them when they are in trouble. In exchange, they owe absolute loyalty to the group. People prefer to work within a group rather than individually. The individual draws his self-respect from the success of the group.

Power Distance: Power distance is defined as "the extent to which the less powerful members of institutions and organisations within a country expect and accept that power is distributed inequally" (Hofstede, 1991). It refers to the acceptance of the idea by employees that in an organisation people will have different levels of power. In a high-distance culture boss is supreme and he or she alone can make decisions. Others cannot question but simply follow orders and instructions. In a low-power distance culture, employees accept the boss as long as he or she is right.

Norway, Germany, Ireland, Denmark, New Zealand, Austria, and USA represent cultures with low-power distance. Brazil, Mexico, Indonesia, Spain, France, Japan, India, and Singapore are examples of societies with a high power distance. Japan and India are known for their high level of power distance. In India, power distance is operated not through the managerial hierarchy but also through the social system of segmentation and stratification. Power distance explains why there is a great interest in the study of leadership in India and Japan.

Here is an interesting story of culture and cultural differences. A high powered Chinese delegation had gone to Canada to negotiate a financial deal with a leading bank. The bank management was anxious to please the delegates and organise a reception in their honour and gave the responsibility to host them to one of their bright young managers. This person took the help of another young manager to make sure that nothing went wrong. They hired a very expensive place, carefully chose the menu, and made the best possible arrangements. After the Chinese arrived, the managers were shocked to see that they were not pleased or comfortable. As soon as the meal was over, instead of staying back they rose and left. The hosts just could not understand what had gone wrong. The difference in power distance in their respective cultures was the culprit. The Chinese have great regard for age and all their senior positions are filled by older people. When they found that their hosts were much younger than them they assumed that they were not managers of an equally high rank and felt insulted. Also, the Chinese are formal and start all such receptions by drinking toasts to each other's health. The young Canadians, on the other hand, did not go through this social ritual. Further, the Chinese failed to understand clearly who is in authority because they saw there were two hosts that clearly confused them.

Uncertainty Avoidance: Uncertainty avoidance is defined as "the extent to which the members of a culture feel threatened by uncertain or unknown situations" (Hofstede, 1991). Extreme uncertainty creates high anxiety. Uncertainty is alleviated by technology, law, religion, and by written and unwritten codes of behaviour.

People in uncertainty avoidance societies believe that the future is uncertain anyway. They are comfortable with uncertainty and handle it with ease and without getting too disturbed. They are more comfortable with taking risks. But uncertainty and lack of clarity can cause a high degree of stress, nervousness, and aggression in people in these societies. Hofstede describes these societies as high in uncertainty avoidance. Some consequences in management is that people in these societies look for lifetime employment and have low job mobility. Canada, US, Australia, Denmark, Norway, Singapore, and Hong Kong belong to the first category, whereas France, Belgium, Peru, Argentina, Italy, Austria, Japan, and Israel are said to possess people who are motivated to avoid uncertainty in their worklines.

Career Success (Masculine) vs. Quality of Life (Feminine): Masculinity pertains to societies in which social gender roles are clearly distinct; femininity pertains to societies in which social gender roles overlap. Some societies rigidly define men's and women's roles. Their social roles are clearly different from each other. Men are expected to be assertive, tough and focused on the acquisition of money and material things. Women are expected to be modest, tender, and concerned with the quality of life. Hofstede calls them masculine societies.

In some other societies, the quality of life is much more important. They are also called feminine cultures. The sexual roles in these societies are not clearly differentiated. Both men and women are supposed to be modest, tender, and concerned with the quality of life. In this context, femininity refers to the relationship among people, concern for others, and interest in quality of life. Such a society emphasises the well-being of its members, quality of relationships, and standard of living.

The degree of masculinity or femininity is seen as the extent to which cultures value qualities like assertiveness and materialism on the one hand, and people and quality of life on the other. Masculine societies are characterised by extensive divisions of social roles by sex and the divisions are narrow in feminine societies. Japan, US, Austria, India, Germany, and Israel are masculine, whereas Finland, Denmark, Sweden and Norway are feminine societies. The cultural value of masculinity/femininity has an impact on the study of employee well-being and related issues.

Employees expect the organisation to have a high level of concern for their employees and their families and nurture them. One example is to give paid paternal leave to male employees to look after their children. These are diffused societies. Also, managers are expected to show interest in employees' personal lives.

Confucian Dynamism: Hofstede, and Bond at a later period, conducted a survey of Chinese managers and employees and identified a fifth dimension which they called Confucian dynamism. They found that these societies have strong work ethics and commitment to traditional Confucian values. Many attribute the extraordinary success of China to Confucian dynamism.

KLUCKHOHN-STRODTBECK FRAMEWORK

Hofstede's work is magnificent and monumental and of immense help to global managers. In addition, there are other important ways in which cultures differ, according to the framework of Kluckhohn and Strodtbeck. They found that cultures differ across the following six dimensions:

Relationship with the environment: Societies differ significantly in their approach to nature and external environment. For example, North Americans feel that people can, and should, modify nature to enhance their own well-being. They see nature and the external environment almost as a challenge and spend enormous amounts of money and effort to control nature and feel very frustrated when they have to succumb to the forces of nature.

In domination societies, goal achievement is important because the general belief is that people can and should make a difference. Penalties for failure, therefore, can be severe. In harmony societies, people try to do their best but the belief is that ultimately everything depends on 'god's will'. Hence, slippages from targets and deviations are expected. Penalties for failure are minimal. In subjugation societies, since everything is in the hands of gods or forces of nature, failure to achieve goals by people is tolerated.

Time-oriented: Time orientation refers to past, present, and future. Past oriented societies believe that plans should be evaluated in terms of their fitness with the customs, traditions and the wisdom of society. They feel that preserving history and past traditions is important and changes should fit with past experience. Future-oriented people justify innovation and change to meet a changing and dynamic world and in terms of future benefits. They have less regard for past customs and traditions. Past, present, and future-oriented people can be found in all societies. In certain societies such as in the US, time is considered as fleeting and scarce. According to them, time is money. In others, time is considered as a 'river' available in large measures. Cultural differences, therefore, explain the relative importance of deadlines, definition of being late, length of assignments, and so on.

An example illustrates the impact of cultural difference. An American company had been given a contract to set up a turnkey project in Bahrain. Due to certain reasons, the project could not be completed within the deadline. The American manager became very nervous. He went to the Bahrainian, profusely apologised and said that the project may not be completed for another six months. An American company in this situation would have sued the contractor for damages worth millions of dollars. The Bahrainian, however, was not at all disturbed. He told the distrust American, 'it is okay. We have lived without this facility for the last five thousand years. Surely, we can live without it for another six months.'

Nature of people: Some societies view people as basically being honest and trustworthy and may prefer a participative style of management. In such societies participative style is possible. There is the well known story of the American who had gone to Cairo on business. He met with an Arab businessman. They liked each other, became good friends, and struck a handsome deal. The American was very happy. He immediately called his lawyer, drew a contract and sent it over to the Arab for signing. He waited and waited but the contract was never signed. The problem was that Arabs expect that friends should trust each other. The immediate response of the American sending a contract full of penalty clauses and provisions for arbitration, offended him. On the other hand, certain other societies view people with suspicion and distrust. In such societies where people do not trust each other, obviously, a participative style is not possible. They will prefer an autocratic style.

Activity orientation: An American company operating in a remote Mexican town increased the wages of workers to motivate them to work even harder. The effect was the opposite showing high rate of absenteeism. The reason was that societies like Mexico want to experience life and fulfil their desires. They want to work only as much as needed to enable them to earn just enough to live. Malaysians are also more interested in spending their extra hours with family and friends than in earning more money by working overtime. Decision making in such societies is likely to be emotional. Americans believe in working hard and being rewarded for it. Decision-making in such societies is usually rational and pragmatic.

Focus of responsibility: Some societies believe that responsibility lies with the individuals – be it for performance, for success or for failure. In certain other societies, responsibility lies with the group. Here loyalty, harmony and unity are very important because in their absence the group will not be effective. These societal attitudes also affect management. In societies where responsibility lies with the individual, hiring is based on educational, professional and personal qualities. In group-oriented societies, qualities like compatibility, trustworthiness, and the ability to work with others are equally important. Group decisions, for instance in Japan, take longer because concurrence of members must be taken prior to taking a decision, but here implementation is much faster.

Concept of space: Some cultures conduct business in public view. In Japan, managers and staff work in the same room. The executives may hold meetings in moderate sized offices or in open areas, with many interruptions from visitors and employees. In the US privacy and offices reflect status. Executives hold important meetings behind closed doors with a secretary screening interruptions. In some cultures, there is a blend of the two. In the Middle East, many persons can be present during a meeting.

WORKFORCE DIVERSITY

Globalisation provided an opportunity to business firms to expand geographically by entering into new markets. This opportunity converted domestic companies into multinational companies and MNCs into transnational companies. Consequently, a new competitive environment has been created. This competitive environment forces the MNCs to compete with domestic companies in the host country, compete with other MNCs in the same country, in addition to competing with home country MNCs at home as well as in foreign markets. For example, Coca-Cola competes with Pepsi-Cola in the USA, in India and other countries, in addition to competing with domestic companies of India. Workplaces in MNCs today are highly diversified with the employees of different countries, different age groups, religions, races, ethnic groups, colour and gender. People from various countries and societies bring varied cultures to the workplace in addition to the best talent.

In recent years, diversity in organisations has been an exciting, stimulating, frustrating, and intriguing topic. Some organisations continue to struggle for diversity, whereas others have a fully integrated diverse workforce. The challenge to increase and manage diversity continues to be critical to organisational goals, particularly as more organisations, large and small transact business internationally. Some organisations work to appreciate diversity and value differences, whereas others continue to discount differences and diversity. Learning to manage and ultimately appreciate differences requires learning, emotional growth, and stretching the boundaries of all participants. Although differences can be challenging, they also lead to very important benefits to individuals, groups, and organisations.

A more diverse workforce will increase organisational effectiveness. It will lift morale and enhance productivity. Today, many organisations conduct diversity audits for various reasons such as determining the effectiveness of diversity recruiting and retention efforts, measuring the value of diversity training, and surveying workers about the success of diversity initiatives. These audits reveal whether a gap exists between what is being done and what the organisation should do in terms of diversity and are used as a basis for action planning.

The following are the strengths of diversified workforce:

1. Employees with diversified background bring diversified skills, knowledge, and culture in addition to talent needed by the job. In addition, employees with diversified backgrounds can bring original ideas and approaches to the workplace that help a company target products and services to a marketplace that itself is becoming more and more diverse.
2. Diversified workforce brings varied knowledge about the availability of resources in terms of quality, price, and delivery from different countries.
3. Diverse workforce with varied economic backgrounds understands the tastes and preferences of customers of all income brackets.
4. Workforce diversity allows the organisation to be more flexible and adaptable and response to the environmental demand aptly.
5. Diversified workforce mostly avoids conflicts and disputes at workplace and strives for harmony and congenial relations.
6. Diversity in workforce contributes to the increase in productivity and helps cost-minimisation in all spheres.

The following are the weaknesses of diversified workforce:

1. Cultural diversity when poorly managed can lead to a host of problems such as higher turnover and inter-group conflicts.
2. Diversity in workforce mostly results in misunderstanding caused by perceptual differences.
3. Cultural difference cause the employees to take more time to understand the view points of others causing considerable delay in decision making.
4. Workforce diversity results in communication distortions in terms of language, and psychological and semantic barriers.

In spite of various weaknesses, workforce diversity provides relatively more concrete strengths to an organisation as compared to its weaknesses.

STRATEGIES FOR MANAGING DIVERSITY

Workforce diversity or cultural diversity can be an important source of energy in enhancing organisational effectiveness. More and more organisations are realising the virtues of such diversity, but surprisingly, little do they know how to manage it.

The following are the five-fold strategies for managing workforce diversity or cultural diversity.

Individual Strategies

Individuals with broad minded approach can formulate strategies based on the situations, ego-state, and cultural background of other persons at the workplace in order to manage the diversified cultural situations. The individual strategies include:

- *Understanding the cultural background of others*: Individual employees before transacting the business should understand the cultural background of his/her colleagues and/or others. This would enable them to understand their behavioural patterns.
- *Belief that all cultures are good*: Cultures are evolved over a period mostly based on the climatic and economic conditions of a region or a country. Cultures in different parts of the world are formed in response to the environmental factors that existed in the region concerned. Therefore, all cultures are basically appropriate and good.
- *Perceive from others' perspective*: Perceiving a situation/transaction from the perspective of the other person and act accordingly would invariably result in harmony as the transaction ultimately takes place by convincing other person or being convinced by the other person to the situation.
- *Approach of not-winning over others' culture*: Individual employees should not adopt the strategy of winning over the other's cultural issues or values. At the same time, one should not try to convince others over their cultures or 'trade-off over the cultural issues'. Rather, one should adjust himself/herself according to others culture, unless the organisational policies/rules/customs are otherwise.
- *Clear communication*: Communication is a prime factor in cultural diversity. Therefore, individual strategies should concentrate on the language and using appropriate words while communicating under the situations of cultural diversity.

Group Strategies

Group of employees belonging to the same culture can understand the cultures of other groups and cultural differences between the two groups. They can also formulate appropriate strategies for managing cultural diversity. The group strategies include:

- *Knowledge sharing*: Expatriates from the same nationality meet, discuss and share the information and knowledge with regard to the culture of the host country and from other nationalities. They also share their experiences of cultural conflicts as well as cultural harmony.
- *Advising and cautioning*: Expatriates of a particular nationality living in a foreign country for a quite long time acquire cultural values and cultural practices of the host country. These experienced expatriates impress upon the new immigrants from their home country about the cultural expectations in the host country. In addition, they also caution the new immigrants about the possible cultural conflict areas and appropriate strategies that can be adopted to prevent as well as to solve them.
- *Cultural exchange through socialisation programmes*: Expatriate groups of various nationals as well as host country nationals organise formal and informal socialisation programmes. These programmes encourage the participants to speak about their cultures and listen to the others' cultural practices with an open mind.

Organisational Strategies

Organisations can formulate effective strategies to manage cultural diversity at the workplace, in addition to the strategies adopted by individuals and groups. Organisational strategies include:

- *Recruitment and selection strategies*: MNCs follow different approaches in recruiting and selecting the prospective employees, *viz.*, ethnocentric, polycentric, regionocentric and geocentric. These approaches have their own advantages and disadvantages.
- *Organisational policies and practices*: The cultural policies of an organisation normally include matters relating to recruitment/selection from different cultures, payment of salary and benefits, work distribution, training and development, and employee relations. Policy implementation should be equal and fair rather than favouring certain cultures and disfavouring others.
- *Cultural training*: MNCs, in addition to job training, should also arrange for cultural training. The purpose of the cultural training basically is to manage the cultural diversity in order to maximise its advantages.
- *Formal socialisation programmes*: MNCs organise socialisation programmes in the form of outings, company annual days, and special celebration, wherein cultural

events and programmes of cultural understanding and exchange are widely organised.

- *Structuring work teams*: MNCs structure the work teams by drawing the employees across the functional departments in order to take-up and complete a project or a specific task. MNCs should include employees across the cultures within each functional area in the project teams.
- *Communication teams*: Information sharing, consultation, negotiations, bargaining, networking, and working together need effective communication. Communication and consultation across cultural groups helps different groups and individuals to adapt themselves to organisational culture.
- *Special benefits to women and old people*: Women, old people, and physically disadvantaged people though they broadly belong to the same cultural group, they bring slightly different cultural values and norms in many respects. Therefore, MNCs are expected to provide special benefits and concessions to them.

National Strategies

National strategies towards management of cultural diversity include:

- *Legislative approach towards equal employment opportunities*: Various governments enacted laws forcing the companies to employ minority and disadvantaged communities.
- *Efforts of the cultural associations/societies*: Various cultural associations and societies like Indo-American Cultural Society and Indo-German Cultural Society spread the cultures of their countries in all those countries they operate. Efforts of these societies enable the people in various countries to understand the cultures of their respective countries.
- *Efforts of the diplomatic missions*: Diplomatic missions like embassies and high commissions of various countries established in foreign countries initiate special efforts to spread the culture of their respective countries in addition to carrying out the cultural values of the foreign countries to their home countries.

International Strategies

International strategies include:

- *Economic unions and regional integrations*: Growth of economic unions like European Union and regional integrations like North American Free Trade Agreement and Asia-Specific Economic Cooperation formulate policies for free flow of human resources among the member countries. This, in turn, results in spread of cultures of member countries within the region.

- *Efforts of international trade organisations and financial institutions*: International trade organisations and financial institutions like World Trade Organisation, International Monetary Fund and World Bank aim at the growth of the world economies through a number of efforts including free movement of human resources across the countries. In addition, these institutions conduct training programmes in technical skills and cultural aspects, thus contributing to easing the management of cultural diversity.

Exhibit 11.3

Hewlett-Packard's Diversity Management Programme

Hewlett-Packard conducted an employee attitude survey and found that its minority employees were particularly dissatisfied with the company's style of management, its pay and benefits programmes, the work environment and the firm's promotional opportunities. The following steps were taken by the company to resolve these problems:

1. It conducted diversity training sessions for all its managers.
2. It informed its managers that they would be held accountable for achieving the firm's diversity objectives, which include new hiring policies, new approaches to employee development, and efforts to remove artificial barriers to success.
3. It established employee development and mentoring programmes to help a broader range of employees move-up in the organisation.
4. It formed employee support groups, such as the Black Managers' Group to address the needs of specific groups of employees.

Source: Caudron S., *Training Can Damage Diversity Efforts,* Personnel Journal, April 1993, pp. 50-62.

BEHAVIOUR VARIATIONS ACROSS CULTURES

In a global village, human resource management and organisational behaviour are expected to play a crucial role in the process of internationalisation of business. Globalisation has its impact on people management. The management is required to cope with problems of alien cultures, unfamiliar laws, languages, attitudes, practices, competitors, managerial styles, work ethics, and so on. Human resource function such as hiring, maintaining and remunerating must acquire global perspective. To face this challenge, the management must be flexible and proactive. There are cross-cultural and cross-national differences in individual behaviour, managerial attitudes, values and beliefs. Behaviour variation can be studied in terms of individual differences, managerial responses, motivation, rewards, leadership, power conflict, communication, and environment and technology across cultures.

Managerial response: Just like individual responses, managerial responses also vary across cultures. Specific behaviours depend upon attitudes managers hold about employees. Managerial responses are shaped by the cultures of the land. Managers in Japan, for instance, strongly believe that a manager should be able to answer any question he or she is asked. On the other hand, Swedish managers have the least concern for knowing all the answers. In France, the manager's role is thought to be that of an expert, whereas in the US the manager is viewed as a problem-solver.

Managerial behaviour is rapidly changing, particularly among European managers. In general, these managers are becoming better educated, career-oriented, more willing to work co-operatively with labour, more willing to delegate, and more cosmopolitan. Even if people were to follow the same basic steps when making decisions, there exists a widespread difference in the way people from various cultures may go about doing so.

There exist cultural differences with respect to who is expected to make decisions. In Sweden, for example, it is traditional for employees at all levels to be involved in the decisions affecting them. However, in Pakistan, where autocratic decision making is expected, it would be considered a sign of weakness for a manager to consult his subordinate about a decision. Another cultural difference in decision making has to do with the amount of time taken to make a decision. For example, in the US one mark of a good decision maker is that he or she is "decisive", and make it without delay. On the other hand, in some other cultures time urgency is downplayed. In Egypt, for example, the more important the matter, the more time the decision maker is expected to take in reaching a decision.

Motivation: Motivation theories and approaches are mainly developed in America. Nevertheless, some of the theories and techniques do apply to other societies as well.

Rewards: Employees' expectations from their jobs depend on respective cultures. Naturally, rewards also vary across cultures. For example, job security is more valued in some cultures than in others. In certain societies like the US for example, individual rewards like recognition, promotion and merit pay increase are more valued. On the other hand, in Japan, employees place a higher value on group rewards and recognition. It is essential that a manager must understand the varying expectations and rewards of employees and try to provide them accordingly.

Leadership: Cultural factors influence the effectiveness of specific leadership actions, and determine varying leadership styles in different countries. In a society with a high-power-distance, employees routinely expect the leader to make decisions, solve problems, and assign tasks. In such a culture, any effort by the leader to promote participative style of management will be opposed. On the other hand, under conditions of low-power-distance any directive behaviour by the leader will not be tolerated, as employees expect empowerment from the leader.

Power and conflict: Power and conflict are a part of organisational life in certain countries. For instance, in the United States power and conflict are accepted and attempts are even made in organisations to create and sustain moderate level of conflict. Such a level of conflict is perceived to be beneficial for organisational effectiveness. In Japan, attempts to increase one's power are frowned upon, and instigating or promoting conflict is considered unseemly. Instead, the focus is on conformity, group harmony, and the like.

Communication: Different words may mean different things to different people. In addition to different vocabularies, cross-cultural communication is made difficult by the fact that in different languages even the same word can mean different things. For instance, General Motors produced a car called the Nova, which did not sell well in Italy where "no va" means "does not go". In China, Coca-Cola means "bite the head of a dead tadpole".

Even non-verbal communication varies across cultures. Colours and body language, for example, can convey quite a different message in one culture than in another. Thus, managers should be forewarned that they cannot take everything for granted while dealing with people from another culture. They must acquire familiarity with verbal and non-verbal languages of that culture.

Communication across countries has another dimension namely, the need for coordination. For example, when an Indian executive talks to his or her counterpart in Germany, he must not only contend with differences in language, but also with a time difference of several hours. Studies suggest that even when both persons in an international transaction know each other's language, communication may still suffer. In addition to the most basic verbal communication skills, non-verbal communication may create serious misunderstandings. Even though we share many values, beliefs and attitudes, we misinterpret and misunderstand each other. This is so even when we are dealing with our own people. The problem simply becomes accentuated when we deal with persons of foreign origin.

Environment: Environment in certain countries is stable and predictable, whereas in other societies it is dynamic and turbulent. The economies of Japan, Sweden and the US, for example, are fairly stable. Although competitive forces within them vary, they generally remain strong free-market economies. Environment also varies in terms of its complexity. The Japanese environment, though stable, is highly complex. India has a complex environment reflecting unity in diversity.

Technology: More and more companies are becoming international and to cope with the demands of varying cultures, these firms adopt different organisational structures, and technology. International conglomerates have international headquarters that coordinate the activities of businesses scattered across the globe. There are two aspects of technology which have their impact on organisational effectiveness. One is variations in available technology, and the other variations in attitudes towards technology. With regard to availability of technology, there are wide variations across cultures. Some countries are highly backward and unable to absorb imported technology. Attitudes towards technology also vary across cultures. Western countries generally have a positive attitude towards technology, but most Asian countries tend to view it with suspicion.

CASE

Cross-cultural Managerial Differences

Setex Inc. is a Japanese American joint venture that manufactures car sheets in South Western Ohio. The company gets high marks from its blue-collar workers for the way they are treated. The factory is immaculate, well lit, ergonomically designed, and air-conditioned. Every worker (or 'associate') is part of a team and team-members build camaraderie and avoid boredom by rotating jobs every two hours, moving through all eighteen assembly jobs in a few days.

Setex's American managers, however, are not as positive when they talk about their Japanese bosses and use of Japanese work practices. The American managers particularly complain about Setex's decision processes, the lack of feedback from their Japanese superiors, cross-cultural communication barriers, and the long hours the Japanese executives expect their American managers to put in.

The US managers say they are not allowed to make decisions or fully use their talents. The Japanese approach to decision making – shared consensus building – frustrates American managers who are used to individual responsibility and recognition. Aggressive, ambitious Americans often feel out of place.

American managers complain about lack of feedback from their Japanese bosses. Even when their work is outstanding, some managers contend they are not promoted simply because they are not Japanese.

Communication presents another problem. Language differences, for example, hinder mutual understanding. The English spoken by the Japanese is sometimes difficult for the Americans to understand. And Japanese terminology often confuses Americans. For instance, one American manager asked, "What difference it makes whether you call a worker hourly or an associate?" But to the Japanese it matters! Add to the fact that the Japanese bosses often talk among themselves in Japanese and fax messages back and forth to Japan in their native language. As a result, non-Japanese-speaking Americans begin to feel left out of the loop.

The Japanese managers come from a culture that stresses company teamwork, harmony, and consensus. They see the workplace as an extended family. As such, they expect the American managers to place the company ahead of their personal lives. While Americans typically look forward to time-off with their families, the Japanese spend long hours after work socialising together and piling up years of unused vacation time. Setex's managers find it hard to adjust to jobs that seem to consume their entire lives.

Discussion Questions

1. Why are American managers feeling aggrieved particularly when American workers appear to be quite happy? Do you agree with their reasons?
2. Does it really matter if the workers are called hourly workers or 'associates'? Why are the Japanese insisting on it?
3. What should the Japanese do to improve the situation?
4. What should the Americans do to improve the situation?

SUMMARY

- *Cultural dimensions of IHRM* deals with the cultural differences and similarities in a global environment.
- Culture is learnt from the environment and interaction at workplace and social spheres.
- Culture is made up of assumptions, values, beliefs and attitudes set by the society based on the changing environment.
- Hofstede found in his study that all people were mentally programmed at three levels: universal level, collective level, and individual level.
- Cultural insensitivity can result in missed opportunities, loss of business, bad relations, and ruffled feelings on both sides.
- A thorough cultural orientation for expatriates and their families is a good investment in their future success and also worthwhile in terms of public relations and goodwill for the company.
- Cultural diversity has certain strengths and weaknesses. More and more organisations, however, are realising the virtues of cultural diversity.
- Strategies for managing cultural diversity include individual strategies, group strategies, organisational strategies, national strategies, and international strategies.

REVIEW QUESTIONS

1. What is culture? What are the various factors that contribute to the formation of culture?
2. "All societies are mentally programmed at three levels." Discuss.
3. What are the strengths and weaknesses of workforce diversity?

4. What are the individual, organisational, national and international strategies for managing workforce diversity?

REFERENCES

1. Richard Mead, (1994), *International Management: Cross-cultural Dimensions,* Back Well Publishers, Cambridge, pp. 390-93.
2. Edward T. Hall, (1976). *Beyond Culture,* Anchor Press, Garden City, New York.
3. Donaldson, (2003). *Values in Tension: Ethics Away from Home,* Quoted in Charles W.L. Hills, International Business, Tata McGraw-Hill, New Delhi, p. 118.

12

Cross-cultural Communication and Negotiation

Objectives

- To understand five dimensions of human communication in any cultural context.
- To identify different barriers to cross-cultural communication.
- To explain the concept of cross-cultural negotiation and various stages of the negotiating process.

INTRODUCTION

Communication is the flow of material, information, perception and understanding between various parts and members of an organisation. The process by which verbal and non-verbal language is shared in communication. There are five fundamental dimensions of human communication described in this chapter. There are difficulties of communicating across cultures because of various barriers to effective cross-cultural communication. There are three broad categories of communication barriers, namely, (a) physical, (b) psychological, and (c) semantics. Negotiations are a major aspect of international management and are fundamentally influenced by communication as well. There are many models that seek to explain cultural differences between people. Hofstede (1980) concluded that there were four main factors, namely, individualism, power distance, uncertainty avoidance, and masculinity that explained the differences found in national culture.

VERBAL AND NON-VERBAL MESSAGES

Verbal: Learning a foreign language improperly, even if just a few words are involved, can create immediate difficulties. For example, a Japanese businessman who was transferred to the United States explained his frustration in trying to find affordable housing; he kept asking about renting a "mansion", the word he had been taught instead of "apartment". Language differences can go much deeper than simple translation ambiguities. Even when we can manage to translate from one language to another with literal accuracy; the failure to understand idioms or slang creates many misunderstandings. Similarly, the deeper meanings of individual words – with their web of rich associations – are often lost because they are rooted in the culture of the language. Also, literal translations from one language to another can also create misunderstandings because they do not account for culture-based linguistic styles.

Non-verbal: Non-verbal communication systems vary from culture-to-culture just as verbal systems do, but often we overlook the symbolic nature of non-verbal communication. Many American travellers abroad have been embarrassed when they discovered that the two-fingered gesture they used to mean "give me two" is assigned a different, obscene meaning in many countries. They have also been mistaken when they assumed that a nod always means "yes". In some countries, a nod means "no". Confusion in non-verbal indicators may be much more complex.

DIMENSIONS OF HUMAN COMMUNICATION

There are five dimensions of human communication:

1. To assume that our communication relationships with the same people will always remain the same, misunderstandings are bound to happen because people change, the circumstances around the relationship change, and topics of communication change.
2. Communication involves purposive and expressive messages. When people communicate they exchange verbal and non-verbal messages with each other. One kind of message is a purposive message, that is, a message that communicates the direct intention of the sender of the message. In contrast, expressive messages are those unintentionally sent along with a spoken message.
3. Communication is made up of multiunit signals. Human communication travels through a variety of signals, not just words. Kinesic, proxemic, olfactory, and other signals picked up by the five senses are methods or "units" of human communication. These do not occur one at a time in human communication, but simultaneously. If the combined package of the units is comfortable, understandable, and known to the receiver, clear communication takes place.

However, if the units present confusing stimuli to the receiver, misunderstanding will occur.

4. Communication depends on the context for its meaning. "Context" means the degree to which the communicator and the listener share a common background of knowledge and experience. This occurs when both individuals have a common history or, at least a shared understanding, of each others' lives, intentions, and experiences. When a context is understood to a great degree between two communicators, much can be said even though little is actually spoken; they can "read between the lines" of each other's statements. In high context cultures, their members share many cultural norms, and do not really need to talk that much to communicate.

   High and low-context cultures have several important differences. Members of high-context cultures are more skilled in reading non-verbal behaviour, and they assume that other people will also be able to do so. Thus, they speak less than members of low-context cultures and they listen more; in general, their communication tends to be indirect and less explicit. Members of low-context cultures, on the other hand, stress direct and explicit communication. They emphasise verbal messages and the shared information they encode.

   In high-context cultures, because everyone understands the nature of and requirements for communication, a simple nod, grunt, sigh, or wave of the hand may communicate a lot of information. Japan is an example of high-context culture. Canada and the US are considered to be low-context cultures, because there are many subcultures in these countries; and people do not widely share exactly the same norms regarding communication. Many researchers link high-context communication style with collectivist cultures and low-context communication style with individualist cultures.

5. Communication is dependent on the competence of the communicators. If a person is able to send and express messages clearly and receive and interpret messages correctly, communication is enhanced. The degree to which a message is poorly expressed and incorrectly interpreted is the degree to which misunderstandings occur. These can happen at different levels of communication. For example, if an expatriate cannot speak the local language very well, misunderstanding may occur due to the expatriate's inability to express clearly basic sentences. If the expatriate is fluent in the language, misunderstandings may still occur because the host nationals may interpret the purposive message correctly but also pick-up an unintended expressive message negative in nature. The two examples cited earlier involve instances where both parties lacked the competence necessary to communicate cross-culturally.

Each of these five dimensions of human communication apply to any culture. However, how each dimension is manifest and carried out in each culture is unique to each culture. That is why living and working with people with diverse cultures can be both irritating and interesting. To communicate with someone from a different culture, one must first learn not only the language, but also the rules as to how the language is used in different contexts and situations.

BARRIERS TO CROSS-CULTURAL COMMUNICATION

Cross-cultural communication and negotiation are of particular importance in international HRM as they are significant areas of organisational functioning and are particularly susceptible to cultural influence and hence, misunderstanding among the employees in the organisation.

To communicate effectively with someone from a different culture, there are certain barriers that must be understood and surmounted. These are ignorance of cultural rules of communication, perpetual biases, faulty attributions, and stereotypes:

Ignorance of cultural rules of communication: It has been estimated that approximately 65 per cent of our communication is non-verbal in nature. Each culture has different rules regarding non-verbal communication. There are five types of non-verbal communication: kinesics, proxemics, fixed features of space, semi-fixed features of space, and personal space.

Kinesics: Kinesics refers to gestures, facial expressions, body positions, body movements, and their relation to communication. It is common in Indonesia to converse with someone, while in their home, by sitting on the floor and talking. As one sits down on the floor, great care must be taken not to point the soles of one's shoes or feet toward the host. Doing this is a great offence, as the gesture indicates that the person is seen as being inferior (Dodd, 1977).

Without knowledge of basic kinesics for the culture in which one is operating, misunderstandings and bad feelings can be caused rather easily. Edward T. Hall, a noted anthropologist believes that by holding that kinesics is one of the most basic of all modes of communication and is only partially readable across cultural boundaries. The only way this barrier can be overcome is to study the kinesics of the culture in which one will be living and to memorise the behavioural patterns.

Proxemics: Proxemics is the study of the spatial relationships in human communication. The field includes the study of fixed features of space (such as architecture and buildings) and how they influence human relationships; semi-fixed features of space (such as, seating arrangements, office layouts) and how they influence communication; and human use of personal space when communicating (Dodd, 1977, p. 55).

Fixed features of space: One example of a fixed feature of space that influences organisational behaviour is room size. Different cultures design offices and workroom layouts differently to reflect cultural preferences. For instance, "a large office in the United

States communicates status and perhaps power. The smaller the office, lesser the status appears to be connected with the occupant of the office. In contrast, in India, high government officials may share a room with six other lesser employees in a room, perhaps "15 feet by 20 feet" (Dodd, 1977).

Semi-fixed features of space: How companies layout office furniture and work space directly influences how people communicate with each other. High-context cultures tend to have more open and less private work spaces. Japanese norms reinforce working groups and being part of a group. There are no partitions separating desks, so everyone can overhear what everyone else is saying on the telephone or in work-related conversations. Compare this with the strong perceived need for privacy in North American companies. Large work spaces are partitioned and subdivided with movable "walls" in such a way that cubicles are formed. In each cubicle a person has his/her own desk, often surrounded with personal items marking that territory as the worker's private working space. North American cultural values of independence, individualism, and privacy dictate to a large degree how work space is arranged, and the resulting structures reinforce the norms associated with those values.

Personal space: Researchers have found that human beings unconsciously structure and measure the space around their bodies. The normal conversational distance between strangers illustrates the importance of dynamics of space interaction. Different cultures have different measurements of personal space. For North Americans, there is a radius of 18 inches around them that they view as "intimate space". People who are physically allowed to enter that space are people whom the North American knows and trusts and is comfortable with. Conversely, Latin Americans and people from the cultures of the Middle East have relatively small intimate space. In some of these countries, "being close enough to breathe on another person during a conversation is deemed appropriate. Infact, the breath is like one's spirit and life itself, so sharing your breath in close conversation is like sharing your spirit" (Dodd, 1977, p. 58).

Perceptual biases: Researchers studying cognition have found that in order to store information, make sense out of what we perceive in the world around us, and simplify the world around us. There are four important reasons why humans have developed this capacity for information categorisation:

1. To reduce the complexity of the environment. There is no way humans could remember 7,500,000 different words for different colours – we would undergo information overload.
2. To identify objects and behaviours in the environment. English speakers have chosen over time to rely on the primary colours or variants of them (for example, "light" and "dark" green) to identify the colour of objects.
3. To reduce the necessity of constant learning and reclassifying. Simplifying colours to the primary colours and their general variants enables English speakers to

classify the colour of something quickly without having to undergo long mental-processing episodes.

4. To construct a ready knowledge of appropriate and inappropriate action to take in any situations. For example, a yellow light on a traffic signal means "slow down to stop"; the driver doesn't have to think about the shade of the colour before taking the appropriate action.

The mental categories by which a person sorts out and responds to the world reflect the culture into which that individual was born (Bruner, 1957). Thus, people from different cultures attach meaning and expect certain responses in various situations according to learned experience and socialisation. In other words, our categories are to a large degree taught to us by others (parents, teachers, peers). The research seems clear that people from different cultures process and categorise information differently.

Triandis (1964) notes that as we utilise the categories in our minds to make sense out of the world around us, we have positive and negative experiences associated with those categories. For example, even if an Indonesian knew that Westerners might not be expected to know that they should not show the soles of their feet to him, if the Westerner did do so, he would still feel revulsion, shame, or other negative emotions associated with his/her mental category of appropriate non-verbal behaviours.

Faulty attributions: When we judge the motives behind why people do what they do, we attribute reasons to their behaviour. For example, if while you are driving down the freeway, a car races up to you from behind, passes you, and then continues to weave in and out of traffic while exceeding the speed limit, you may attribute the driving behaviour of that person to a number of reasons: the driver has no regard for the rights of others, is drunk, is late for an important appointment, or has a sick wife in the backseat and is speeding to the hospital. The possible attributions you could make are numerous.

The following are the steps involved in attributions:

Perception: The first step in attributing motive or reason behind a behaviour is to observe that behaviour.

Category retrieval: Once behaviour is observed, in milliseconds our brain goes through a kind of "library index card" retrieval until it finds the category in our mind that makes sense out of the behaviour we observe.

Estimation of motives: Once evaluations about, and emotions toward, the observed behaviour have been triggered, the next phase is to estimate why that behaviour occurred. Human beings seem to have a strong need to understand why things happen. Evaluations and emotions kindled will likely influence the correctness of the attribution. Researchers have found that human beings make two general kinds of attributions about behaviours they observe: internal and external. Internal attributions are made when the behaviour is viewed as being caused by the other individual's internal characteristics, personality, or psyche.

External attributions are made when the behaviour is viewed as being caused by external factors or conditions that impinge on the other individual.

Behavioural response: Based upon the attribution made, the observer selects a behavioural response. Based upon one's personality traits, one chooses a response. If that response is inappropriate in a cross-cultural business setting, such as during a negotiation, devastating results can occur.

Final analysis: Once attributions have been made, that information is fed back to the category, and the category is updated. If the category is fed with faulty information, the category will not be accurate. Then, when a similar incident occurs, the category will cause inaccurate evaluations and trigger inappropriate emotions in the individual. Conversely, the more accurate the information fed back into the category, the more effectively the individual will be able to deal with his/her environment. To make correct attributions cross-culturally, it is important to put one's attributions on hold and not automatically assume that one's evaluation of the situation has been correct. Research shows that successful expatriates compare their evaluations with host nationals to make sure they are accurate before they permanently store them in their memory categories: that is, they consult an expert on the culture.

Stereotypes: Another barrier to cross-cultural communication is stereotyping – categorising a group of people based upon some feature they hold in common, such as nationality, race, or religion. Studies show that once the categorisation takes place, an individual tends to favour his/her own group in nearly every respect and disfavours the other group attributing more positive attributes to one's own group and more negative ones to the other. Furthermore, such research has firmly established that the favouring of one's group can be attributed to the existence of a perceived out-group, regardless of any actual differences among people that would merit division (Oddou and Menden Hall, 1984).

Once one feels part of an in-group, individuals not part of that group are categorised on a variety of issues (intelligence, industriousness, education, and accent) and are seen as similar to one another. Stereotyping is a powerful barrier to cross-cultural communication because interactions with people from out-groups are processed through the categories that make up the stereotype. If a group is classified as being dishonest, for example, whenever one interacts with a member of that group, it will be difficult for the holder of the stereotype to trust anything the outsider does or says. Prejudice and racism are difficult to eradicate because the categories that make up discrimination interpret the world in such a way that the categories are reinforced, even if reality is different.

CROSS-CULTURAL NEGOTIATION

Negotiation is the process of bargaining with one or more parties to arrive at a solution that is acceptable to all. Business negotiations often involve one party attempting to influence another to make a particular decision or sign a contract. A negotiation becomes cross-cultural when the parties involved belong to different cultures and, therefore, do not share the same ways of thinking, feeling, and behaving. Negotiating cross-culturally is one of the single most important global business skills. Global negotiations contain all of the complexity of domestic negotiations, with the added dimension of cultural diversity.

Negotiation is not always the best approach to doing business. Many times such strategies as 'take-it-or-leave-it' or bargaining become more effective. Negotiating, compared to bargaining or the take-it-or-leave-it approach, is time-consuming and patience-testing. As a rule, managers should negotiate when any one of the following conditions exists.

- Their power position is low relative to their counterpart.
- The trust level is high.
- Sufficient time is available to explore each party's multiple needs, resources, and options.
- Commitment, not mere compliance, is important to ensure that all parties carry-out the agreement.

One of the most important arenas of cross-cultural communication for international business people is negotiation. People from different cultures use different negotiating styles and approaches. They have different communication styles, different strategies for persuasion and a different set of protocols. Differences occur in the way a conflict is viewed, managed and resolved.

Negotiating is all about attitude. There are two basic approaches to how a final outcome is viewed. Some cultures view the negotiating process as a 'win-win' situation – a process through which both sides gain. Other cultures adopt a zero sum mentality where someone's gain must always equal someone's loss. Yet, if both parties come to the negotiating table without having done some serious thinking about the barriers to and complexities of cross-cultural communication, there is a low probability that the negotiations will be successful.

One important finding about cross-cultural negotiation is that within any culture, people go through four stages in the negotiation process. These stages are relationship building, exchanging task-related information, persuasion, and making concessions and agreements. However, cultures differ in the degree to which value is placed on each stage of the negotiation relationship.

Relationship building: The first stage of negotiations involves building interpersonal relationships between the negotiating parties. For Japanese this is a very important part of the negotiation process, and they spend considerable time in building relationships with the other party. Conversely, Americans rate building relationships as less important and spend much less time on this phase than do the Japanese. For the Japanese, it is important to spend a lot of time in the town after the official meetings, in eating and drinking with the members of the other party. In this way, formal barriers are broken down between the parties, and a sense of trust slowly develops. During the first meetings when Americans may want to get down to business, the Japanese will likely talk in generalities, for in their minds the preliminary sessions are simply to assist in building relationships.

Exchanging task-related information: The second phase of cross-cultural negotiations involves information exchange and understanding each other's situation and needs. It is difficult enough to understand other party's situation, interests, and needs in a negotiation situation in one's own culture. As is well known, people from differing cultures commonly view problems, reality, and business operations in different ways. It takes a sustained, sincere effort both to clearly articulate one's own situation and to understand that of the other party in a cross-cultural negotiation.

Persuasion: Persuasion involves influencing the other party to adopt one's view point, position, or beliefs. For example, Americans quickly persuade the other party to agree with their offer bid, contract, and so forth. Americans view this phase as the most important part of the negotiation process and spend quite a bit of time in the use of persuasive tactics. The Japanese also rate this phase as important and spend a fair amount of time on it as well. However, for the Japanese, persuasion should only take place after mutual trust has been established; for Americans, persuasion can take place quickly with appeals to logic and rationality overriding the need for warm interpersonal relationships.

Concession and agreement: The Japanese value this phase less than Americans do, though they spend about the same amount of time in this phase as Americans. Adler (1991) notes that, "Americans negotiate sequentially; they discuss and attempt to agree on one issue at a time. Throughout the bargaining process, Americans make many small concessions, which they expect their opponents to reciprocate; then they finalise the list of concessions into an overall agreement." The Japanese, on the other hand, do not tend to spend a lot of time and energy on making small concessions that reciprocate their opponent's concessions. Instead, they like to view the process holistically, trying to understand each side's views and needs, build trust, and then make concessions, if any, at the end as a form of wrapping up the negotiations. Collectivist cultures tend to avoid open conflict while individualist cultures meet confrontation head-on, often believing that confrontation is the quickest route to problem-solving. In cross-cultural negotiations, conflict may be evident even before the two parties sit down to talk.

When locked in negotiations, it is important to take into consideration the differences in the decision making process between cultures. In some cultures where power is decentralised (United States, Australia), decisions can be made quickly, and often by a single individual. However, in cultures with collectivist values (Japan, China), decisions are made by consensus and can take longer. However, implementation of decisions is quicker in collectivist cultures as opposed to individualistic cultures that often demand the right to question the decision handed down.

SUMMARY

- *Cross-cultural communication and negotiation* throws light on five dimensions of human communication and negotiating cross-culturally.
- Cross-cultural communication is the communication between people not only based on different national cultures but also on the basis of race, religion, educational and economic backgrounds.
- Three stages of communication are perception, interpretation, and evaluation of events. Various factors that influence cross-cultural communication are roles and status, decision making style, symbols, chromatics, and proxemics.
- Various methods for effective cross-cultural communication are: (a) communication through multiple channels; (b) paraphrasing to ensure correct understanding of meanings; and (c) double checking to verify that the receiver has understood correctly.
- Different stages in the negotiation process are: (a) relationship building, (b) exchanging task-related information, (c) persuasion, and (d) making concessions and agreements.
- Different barriers to cross-cultural communication are: (a) ignorance; (b) biases; (c) faulty attributions; and (d) stereotypes.
- Negotiating across cultures is the single most business skill.
- Successful international negotiation requires effective cross-cultural communication.

REVIEW QUESTIONS

1. What is cross-cultural communication? Why is competence in this area essential for success in global business?
2. What are the major problems in cross-cultural communication? Explain.
3. What is perception? Why does misperception occur so often in cross-cultural communication?
4. Identify specific non-verbal aspects that are important in communicating? Discuss how these non-verbal activities influence communication effectiveness.

13

Global Occupational Health

Objectives

- To identify the key occupational health issues faced by different countries.
- To highlight the basic principles of occupational health.
- To trace the history of occupational health over the years including the contribution made by different international organisations.

INTRODUCTION

Occupational health is a multi-dimensional field encompassing social science, economics, law, employment studies, and issues common to every family. The health and safety of people at work is a critical concern for all societies and all countries. The field of occupational health touches on fundamental aspects of working life and has become a centre of social and political issues in countries with progressive policies and a tradition of social responsibility. These countries have developed systems of occupational health protection, social insurance, and medical services that reduce the burden on the worker and the loss to the economy. However, these systems are not perfect, and they are often under scrutiny. Developing countries often lack these systems or have them only in rudimentary forms. Occupational injuries and illness can become a significant drag on the economy, as it reduces productivity, increases the burden of disability and illness on people, and causes financial insecurity.

HISTORY OF OCCUPATIONAL HEALTH

Occupational health developed in parallel with technology and industrial activities. In the early days of industrialisation, the poor social conditions of workers living in urban industrial areas were inhuman and miserable. Inside the factories and mines of the 19th century, the workers were exposed to the hazards of occupational disease and injury, and the adverse effects of excessively long hours of work. Little attention was paid to safety devices and the workers training to handle new machinery. Toxic hazards increased due to prolonged exposures to a wide range of new elements which were introduced without considering their possible effect on workers. Moreover, in the 19th century, manufacturers generally believed that it was economically viable to keep their new machines running continuously with cheap labour.

In the middle of the 19th century, the above conditions created concern among enlightened industrialists and physicians. Occupational health conditions were first documented in Italy by Bernardino Ramazzini (1633-1714), then in England by Percival Pott (1713-1788) and Charles Turner Thackrah (1795-1833), and spread gradually to the whole industrialised world. With this, a proper study of the health of the worker can be said to have taken place. Subsequently, there grew up the practice of industrial medicine dealing in the earlier years largely with treatment of injury and sickness, but tending gradually to become more interested in preventive work. Now, managements and workers find industrial medicine as essentially preventive in character rather than curative. Prevention is now the key note, especially in more hazardous industries.

The second wave of occupational health interest started between the 19th and 20th centuries, approximately 100 years ago. Scientists and medical practitioners investigated singular causal factors and their relationships with single disease outcomes. Prevention and control became an important priority, particularly in the leading industrialised countries, where occupational safety and health legislation and legislation for workers' compensation for occupational injuries and diseases were passed. These activities stimulated specific preventive practices. This second wave lasted approximately 70 to 80 years. During this period, the most important focus in the work environment included machine safety, prevention of injuries from falling and slipping, and prevention of explosions of pressure vessels and boilers. Since World War II, occupational or industrial hygiene as a technical field has developed to measure and access hazardous factors at work.

The third wave of occupational health started in the 1980s when Scandinavian scientists first considered the psychological and psychosocial aspects of work. Occupational stress, psychological hazards, workload psycho-sociology at individual and group levels, and work organisation became subjects of active discussion and targets for research and preventive control actions. These studies paralleled work in occupational psychology on issues of job satisfaction and work motivation. This research led to the improvement of the overall quality of work life and to help promotion, work ability, and the well-being of working people. All three waves of occupational health history have been responsive to the needs of work life in its various developmental stages.

The health problems arising from industrial progress in developing countries today are, in many aspects, similar to those during industrialisation in the 19th century; these countries also have to face major threats from each endemic disease and generalised poverty. During the 20th century, the trade unions in many countries began to exert influence on occupational health by pressing for improvements in legislation and for the extension of employee compensation laws to cover occupational injuries and diseases.

In 1973, WHO listed three major tasks in occupational health: (a) identify and control known or suspected work factors that contribute to ill health, (b) educate management and workers to fulfil their responsibilities towards health and safety, and (c) promote health programmes not primarily concerned with work-related injuries and diseases.

CONCEPT AND OBJECTIVES

Occupational health includes studies on all factors relating to work, working methods, conditions of work, and the working environment. It implies not only health protection but also health promotion which includes everything that can promote the health and working capacity of the worker.

Occupational health approach covers: (a) the protection and promotion of health, work ability, and well-being of workers; (b) continuous improvement and development of safe and healthy work environment; and (c) psychological, psychosocial, and organisational aspects of work, and the adoption of work and management cultures conducive to health and well-being.

International organisations such as the World Health Organisation (WHO), and the International Labour Organisation (ILO) have given much attention to health and safety of employees, as evidenced by the WHO Global Strategy on Occupational Health for All that was adopted by the 49th World Health Assembly (1996), and by the ILO Convention No. 161 on Occupational Health Services (1985). The European Union includes occupational health as a part of its employment and social policy programmes. Although much effort has been made toward the worldwide implementation of those authoritative policies, much remains to be done in the sphere of occupational health for all.

According to the joint ILO/WHO Committee on Occupational Health, "Occupational health should aim at the promotion and maintenance of the highest degree of physical, mental, and social well-being of workers in all occupations". Occupational health covers a wide field and calls for specialised knowledge from many disciplines like medicine, engineering, chemistry, toxicology, psychology, physiology, and statistics.

In 1988, the WHO Expert Committee on Health Promotion in the Work Setting (thereafter called the WHO Expert Committee) declared that "the work environment constitutes an important part of man's total environment, so health is to a large extent affected by work conditions..... Work is a powerful force in shaping a person's sense of identity. It can lend vitality to existence, and establishes the cyclical patterns of day, week, month and year." It referred to the positive influence of work on health, which is included with the concept of health promotion. WHO repeatedly emphasised that occupational health programmes should not be limited to the prevention and control of work-related hazards, but should deal with the full relationship between work and health and include general health promotion.

Thus, health promotion is not confined to disease and injury prevention. It is a strategy to improve the ability of workers to live their lives and to function in their family and community roles. The key insight of health promotion in the context of occupational health is to perceive the workplace as a community.

Exhibit 13.1

Key Objectives of ILO Convention No. 161 and Recommendation No. 171

1. Principles of national policies concerning occupational health services.
2. Functions of occupational health services:
   - (a) Surveillance of the working environment
   - (b) Surveillance of workers health
   - (c) Information, education, and training advice to workers and employers
   - (d) First-aid treatment and health programmes
   - (e) Other functions including analysing surveillance results, reporting on occupational health service activities, and participating in research and with other services in environmental protection activities.
3. Organisation of occupational health services.
4. Operational conditions of occupational health services including provisions for composition of competent occupational health service teams, protection of confidential health information, and professional independence of occupational health service personnel.

Exhibit 13.2 The 10 Objectives of the WHO Global Strategy on Occupational Health for All
1. Strengthening international and national policies for health at work and developing the necessary policy tools.
2. Developing health and environment.
3. Developing healthy work practices and promotion of health at work.
4. Strengthening occupational health services.
5. Establishing support services for occupational health.
6. Developing occupational health standards based on scientific risk assessment.
7. Developing human resources for occupational health.
8. Establishing registration and data systems, developing information services for experts, effectively transmitting data, and raising public awareness through public information.
9. Strengthening research.
10. Developing collaborations between occupational health and other activities and services.

PRINCIPLES

Five basic principles have been identified as the basis for successful occupational health systems in a WHO/EURO survey of legislation in European countries concerning occupational health services (Rantanen, 1990). The five principles are as follows:

1. *Protection and prevention*: This principle is the core of occupational health activities and includes the following:
   - identification of hazardous exposures and factors causing overload or other adverse work conditions;
   - assessment of the distribution and levels of exposures, identification of exposed groups or individuals, and sources of hazards;
   - assessment of risks to health and safety from exposures or adverse conditions; and
   - initiating, instituting, and advising on needs and means for preventive and control actions aimed at protecting workers health and safety.
2. *Adaptation*: Not all workers have equal work ability, health status, or competence. In this context, the ageing workers, adolescents and young workers, pregnant women, handicapped workers, migrant workers, and workers with chronic diseases may need adaptation of work, working methods, or work environment.
3. *Promotion and development*: Optimally organised work can have a positive effect on workers' health and work ability — it can develop physical, mental, and

professional capacities, and can contribute to the development of safe working practices and healthy lifestyles.

4. *Cure and rehabilitation*: Work-related diseases, accidents, status of physical and mental overload, and acute and chronic illnesses do occur among a substantial proportion of the workforce.
5. *Primary health care*: In some countries primary care or general practitioner-level health care is a part of occupational health services wherein workers have access mainly to primary health care.

One important principle of occupational health is equity. Equity as a concept is closely related to ethics and justice. Equity in work life enables employees of all backgrounds to obtain employment, to develop their skills at work, and fulfil their roles in society. Determining and safeguarding ethical principles and professional independence are key issues in ensuring the sustainable future, and credibility and trust for occupational health professionals. The Code of Ethics of the International Commission on Occupational Health (1992) provides authoritative guidance for occupational health professionals.

ISSUES

Occupational health issues are deeply embedded in society and have a profound but largely unacknowledged effect on economic development. Some of these issues include:

- the health risks that workers pay to earn a living
- the consequences to their families when workers become ill or injured
- the social contract between workers and employers and the responsibility to keep the workplace safe
- the financial loss to workers and their families from a prolonged illness or disabling injury
- the cost of providing medical and rehabilitation care to injured workers
- the hidden cost to the health-care system of illnesses
- the cost of providing benefits and wage replacement to workers who are injured
- the loss of productivity that results from avoidable injuries and illnesses
- the development of new technology, the cost of production, and return on investment
- the statutory compliance by way of employee's compensation or rather insurance plans
- management and of minimisation of the risk of disasters.

The various questions that can be raised in this context are:

- How to create a safe working environment?
- How to protect the health of workers and their families?
- How to prevent disability due to occupational disorders?
- How to ensure intervention of the society in all matters relating to occupational health services?
- How to make occupational health services a shared responsibility of the public and private sector organisations and government?

SYSTEMS

The minimum structure for a national system in occupational health can be drawn from international conventions, national regulations, and international and national guidelines provided by international organisations and national bodies and authorities. Some countries have much more than this, but all should have at least a minimum structure.

The following are the minimum requirements for a national system of occupational health:

1. Legislation should set forth the basic requirements, responsibilities, and rights of authorities, employers, and workers in occupational health services.
2. Competent authorities should be appointed for enforcement of legislation; who are to be assisted and advised by a national occupational health committee appointed on a tripartite basis by the government. In most countries, the authority consists of the Ministry of Labour or the Ministry of Health.
3. A national policy programme should organise services, develop contents, provide human resources, and plan for the development of occupational health services.
4. Infrastructures for providing services at the workplace level should utilise several options such as in-plant services, group services, private health centres, hospital-based occupational health services, or services provided by the primary health-care units and social security institutions.
5. Human resources personnel should have proper competence in qualitative and quantitative aspects of the management of human resources. This includes training as to how to deal with issues of compensation, insurance, accommodation, employment security, rehabilitation, and retraining.
6. Specialised support and advisory services are needed to provide guidance and assistance to the "frontline occupational health service".
7. Occupational health, as a specialised activity, primarily requires competence in occupational medicine, occupational hygiene, and occupational psychology.

Several countries have set-up separate institutes for training occupational safety and health personnel.

8. Employers, workers, and their organisations should be involved to ensure the successful implementation of occupational health and safety at the workplace.

Occupational health practice rests on scientific knowledge, which comes largely from research. Without research, occupational health would remain backward, inefficient, inflexible, and unable to adapt to new technologies or challenges. Hence, the focus of research should be on several scientific disciplines in natural sciences, basic medical sciences, physiology, behavioural sciences, and technology.

SERVICES

Occupational health activities vary from country to country due to differences in legislation, national tradition, and medical practices. It is supported by a worldwide network of practitioners, public and private facilities, and institutions and organisations that are guided by laws, government agencies, and professional standards of practice. The infrastructure for occupational health protection, management of occupational injuries and illnesses, and compensation and public policy is called occupational health services.

The principles of occupational health services were laid down in the ILO's Occupational Health Services Recommendation 1959 (No. 112), with the following aims:

- Protecting the workers against any health hazards which may arise out of their work or the conditions in which it is carried on.
- Contributing towards the workers' physical and mental adjustment, in particular by the adaptation of the work to the workers and their assignment to jobs for which they are suited.
- Contributing to the establishment and maintenance of the highest possible degree of physical and mental well-being of the workers.

According to international guidelines, including ILO Convention 161 and national legislation, all people who take part in the workforce shall have access to occupational health services. That should be provided either at the workplace or in a nearby facility, and should carry out a minimum set of service activities. The precise content of services may vary according to national law and practice and local conditions and needs, but a certain minimum should be found everywhere. Each worker should be provided with such services.

Occupational health services are a special, separate set of health services for workers and workplaces to prevent and control health and safety hazards at work and to promote good practice and guidance in the field of occupational health. Occupational health services should cover all workers in all workplaces, in all sectors of the economy, including industry, private and public services, agriculture, self-employment and informal work, and also work done in all environments – for e.g., on land, at sea, in the air, underground, and even underwater.

Occupational health services shall be provided by competent and accredited personnel including occupational health physicians, occupational health nurses, occupational hygienists, occupational psychologists, physiotherapists, ergonomics experts, and others as defined by the national laws and regulations. Occupational health services personnel should have a certified competence in the tasks for which they are responsible.

In most countries, occupational health services apply the principle of participation – the workers and employers have a right to participate in the decisions on how the occupational health services are organised and provided. According to the ILO Convention 161, the employer is responsible for financing and regularising free occupational health services for his or her employees.

Since health is now viewed as an integral part of socio-economic development, "an acceptable level of health for all", as laid down by WHO, cannot be achieved by the health sector alone. It requires an inter-sectoral approach, i.e., the coordinated efforts of the health sector and relevant activities of other social and economic development sector.

MEASURES TO IMPROVE

A healthy and productive workforce is the key factor behind the social and economic development of any country. Originally, occupational health programmes were designed during the advent of industrialisation to prevent and treat acute and chronic illnesses and injuries among working population. Gradually, as public health programmes were developed, occupational health adopted a more specific role in the prevention and control of occupationally determined outcome. Overtime, occupational health shifted its emphasis to the overall health and well-being of the working population. Today, occupational health services in their most advanced forms are comprehensive, covering the control of hazardous factors in the work environment, promotion of work ability, and promotion of workers general health and healthy lifestyles.

Developing countries struggling to improve their standard of living should avoid the enormous loss of work ability of the workers by supporting and sustaining occupational health services. Industrialised countries face growing problems due to the shortage of young workers and the ageing of the working population. To ensure the availability of a sufficient workforce, unnecessary losses of work ability need to be eliminated. As adverse working conditions and occupational health and safety hazards are in principle preventable, the strategies for preventing such hazards and risks starting with high-risk occupations and the most adverse conditions will have an equalising impact on all occupations. Many differences in health outcomes are related to social and economic factors and are thus manageable with the help of social policies. This is particularly true within the areas of occupational injuries and diseases.

Legislation is also used in many countries to improve occupational health at the national level. Legislation on workers protection lays down minimum standards of health and safety at work and is usually enforced by the factory inspection service. At the national level, occupational health and safety is currently implemented in many countries in three main ways: (a) legislation in establishing statutory minimum standards of health and safety at work, (b) occupational health services at places of employment or other workplaces, and (c) research and field surveys as well as education and training by national or regional occupational health institutes.

ROLE OF INTERNATIONAL ORGANISATIONS

The major international organisations in the field of occupational health are part of the United Nations system or have a close working relationship to UN agencies. In addition, there are occupational health associations or societies in almost every country, usually representing certain professions and sometimes specific to certain industries.

World Health Organisation (WHO)

WHO has a long tradition in occupational health dating back to the design of its constitution in 1948. The famous *Alma Ata Declaration* (1978) called for the provision of health services in places where people work and live. The Health for All by the year 2000 strategy included concrete objectives for occupational health. In 1996, the 49th World Health Assembly adopted the Global Strategy on Occupational Health for All which contains comprehensive and ambitious objectives for occupational health that are currently implemented in all WHO regions.

International Labour Organisation (ILO)

ILO has worked on occupational health issues for over 80 years. One of the first health-related conventions of the ILO was Convention No. 13 in 1921 on the prohibition of white lead paint that was found to be toxic to both workers and children. In 1985, the International Labour Conference adopted Convention No. 161 and Recommendation No. 171 on occupational health services. The current Safe Work Programme consists of occupational health elements, including the Global Programme for Elimination of Silicosis.

International Commission on Occupational Health (ICOH)

ICOH is a professional association of occupational health experts whose mission is to advance research, training, and information on occupational health. The ICOH has about 35 scientific committees active in various fields of occupational health research. The most important ICOH document is the 1993 International Code of Ethics for Occupational Health Professionals. The Code defines the basic ethical principles for occupational health practice, obligations of health professionals, and professional independence of occupational health experts. The Code stipulates 26 different duties and obligations for occupational health professionals, and guides them in various practical activities as per the ICOH's ethical principles.

Other important professional organisations relating to occupational health are the International Occupational Hygiene Association (IOHA), the International Ergonomics Association (IEA), and the International Social Security Association (ISSA).

FUTURE CHALLENGES

The global need for occupational health will exist as long as human resources are regarded as the most important asset in an organisation. In the changing world of work, the field of occupational health and its expertise must continuously develop to meet new challenges and opportunities in modern work life.

Change in the practice of occupational health is inevitable because there have been and will continue to be massive changes where occupational health services are provided – in the workplace, in large enterprises, and in public and private sector organisations.

Outsourcing has stimulated the growth of contract services. Now, even routine services are provided under contract. Individuals and groups of occupational health professionals, usually at a senior level, have always worked as consultants and under contract to organisations to do certain jobs. Occupational health professionals often have many clients but can give only a small amount of time and attention to each. Obviously, organisations like this arrangement because they do not have to pay the salary and benefits for a full-time employee, and they can discharge him/her easily whenever the job is finished or if they do not like the result.

A key characteristic in the global economy is flexibility. Flexibility is required to satisfy market needs and to survive in more competitive environments. This requirement will only increase as the human capital is the most flexible production factor, even in modern work life.

On health care services new structures need to be developed, and the infrastructure at the national level needs to be rationalised in every country. Promotion of occupational health among large and medium-sized companies is needed in all countries. Scattered agricultural workers, self-employed workers, micro-enterprises, and small enterprises need to be covered by some sort of public occupational health services system.

In future, the occupational health professionals will confront new problems and different approaches in health and safety arising out of new technologies, new work organisations, or new work practices. Further, this will require new skills in collaboration, communication, business management, and problem solving on the part of occupational health practitioners. Teamwork, new job demands for innovations, and continuous learning at work, are the other requirements for the success of occupational health professionals.

Occupational health professionals cannot cover the wide range of issues now emerging without help from other disciplines. Hence, a multidisciplinary and multiprofessional approach might include specialists in toxicology, occupational hygiene, safety, psychology, ergonomics, medicine, and other fields. Also, this approach in future will include not only prevention, control, and curative treatment but also health promotion and eradication of poverty.

Research in occupational health will be as important as it has ever been. Various new technologies, working methods, and work organisations are introduced in the workplace without prior testing. Sometimes, these innovations work well and succeed, and sometimes they are a failure. Therefore, research in this field has to cover many more complex multidimensional issues and problems than before.

Occupational health services will have to follow a multidisciplinary approach in the future, as occupational health problems will have a much wider scope than in the past. Continuous change calls for continuous professional development. Professionals who are active in this field need to update their knowledge and skills to keep pace with rapid changes in work life.

Occupational health professionals must take a more comprehensive approach in order to predict future changes and challenges and to be able to operate in expanded international environments. Occupational health is an information-rich activity. Occupational health professionals can make effective use of information and communication technologies in occupational health practice. Moreover, they have to: (a) maintain and expand their competence and skills, (b) adopt a multidisciplinary work culture, and (c) safeguard ethical principles and professional independence.

Ethics is a crucial issue for occupational health, as it is for business and for the society. Maintaining and promoting ethical conduct in the rapidly changing world of work is an important challenge to all occupational health professionals.

SUMMARY

- *Global occupational health* lays stress on different principles and issues on occupational health services and systems.
- Occupational health is a multidimensional field touching upon fundamental aspects of working life.

- Many countries have developed occupational health systems covering occupational health protection, social insurance, and medical services.
- Occupational health programmes were developed globally during the advent of industrialisation to prevent and treat acute and chronic illnesses.
- Today, the occupational health services cover hazardous factors in the work environment, and promotion of healthy lifestyles.
- The five basic principles in occupational health activities are: (a) protection and prevention, (b) adaptation, (c) promotion and development, (d) cure and rehabilitation, and (e) primary health care.
- Occupational health is supported by a worldwide network of practitioners and institutions.
- Occupational health systems and practices were developed in parallel with technology, industrialisation, and in response to the challenging health and safety issues of workers in various developmental stages.
- It is, however, very challenging to provide occupational health services in a dynamic environment.
- The key insight of health promotion in the context of occupational health is to perceive the workplace as a community, a social environment in which people produce goods and services.
- A properly designed workplace will achieve the benefits of: (a) greater efficiency, (b) more productivity, (c) lower acute injuries, (d) less fatigue among workers, (e) higher quality of products or levels of service, and (f) more satisfied workers.
- The major international organisations in the field of occupational health are: (a) World Health Organisation (WHO), (b) International Labour Organisation (ILO), and (c) International Commission on Occupational Health (ICOH).

REVIEW QUESTIONS

1. What are the main issues in occupational health?
2. Bring out the various principles of occupational health.
3. Trace the growth of occupational health systems with specific reference to the contributions made by global organisations.

14

Global Ethical Environment

Objectives

- To understand the role of ethical issues in international business.
- To explain the ethical philosophy that impinges on management practices.
- To discuss the nature of unethical activities in international human resource management.

INTRODUCTION

International business ethics are as old as international business itself. Every executive, regardless of where it sits, has at some point faced a decision that challenges their ethical standards. Anyone who has done much travelling around the world knows that countries differ in their approach to punishing certain kinds of behaviours. Many countries have laws "on the books" regarding the criminal nature of certain behaviours, yet the daily practice is to disregard the law. When an expatriate enters a new country and begins doing business there, he/she may be confronted with business practices that are not just different, but unethical from his/her perspective. The expatriate might also act in a manner that is deemed illegal locally, though considered legal at home. In order to be effective, multinational organisations need to adapt to specific ethical requirements of different societies. In this regard, HR has an important role to play in incorporating ethical behaviour among the employees and in building, maintaining, and developing a corporate identity of its own.

ETHICAL DECISIONS

Virtually, all societies have developed rules and regulations about how business should be transacted and how business organisations should be managed. In other words, based on experience and the philosophical and/or religious values of a society, rules of acceptable and non-acceptable behaviours evolve and are encoded into society. Such an evolved business ethics is based on basic beliefs about human beings, their proper relationships, and the value of human life. Business ethics can be defined as "the moral principles and standards that guide behaviour in the world of business". (Ferrell and Fraedrich, 1991).

Managerial decisions are woven through with ethical issues. Brady (1990) lists several reasons why managers, both international and domestic, should be concerned with ethics. In this context, the following four points are listed by him.

1. Managerial decisions affect people's lives and well-being. Brady notes that in each case a poor or unwise decision on the part of the manager can adversely affect the lives of many people. Often the answers to such questions are not clear, yet they always involve issues of what is right or wrong, and what should be good or bad for employees.
2. Managers must distribute organisational resources fairly. This managerial responsibility is clearly influenced by ethical concerns. Brady notes that "such decisions are ethical because of the need to be fair, and fairness is a strong component of the daily managerial routine. But this is not as simple as it sounds. A fair distribution is not always an equal one… where special ethical needs exist, there may be ethical justification for skewing an otherwise equal distribution in favour of those needs."
3. Managers create rules and policies. Managers create, implement, and enforce rules and policies in companies – as one of their major roles. Brady notes that "the relationship of a manager to the rules is not merely mechanical. If it were, there would be no discretionary power, and there would be less reason for supposing the situation to be ethical. Most managers do have discretion to waive rules or to change them, or at least decide in any particular case whether a rule applies. Therefore, we hold managers responsible for the proper development and application of organisational rules."
4. Managerial decision making tests one's personal values. Managers sometimes are faced with decisions that test their own personal values; that is, the decision that seems best for the organisation or the situation conflicts with their own sense of right and wrong. Brady further notes that "it is in the managerial arena that

organisational dominance over personal judgement may be most intense". This incongruence between the organisational values, situational needs, and personal values can be especially marked in cross-cultural situations, when managers and employees have differing value systems. Thus, the issue of business ethics permeates organisational life – especially the organisational life of the manager.

International standards of ethics should address six major issues: economic relations, political relations, customer relations, organisational relations, technology transfer, and employee relations.

INTERNATIONAL BUSINESS ETHICS

To explore the issues associated with international business ethics, it is helpful to distinguish between three concepts: individual relativism, cultural relativism, and universalism.

Individual relativism: The idea of individual relativism, in its extreme position, is that there is no absolute principle of right and wrong, good or bad, in any social situation. What is right and what is wrong should be left to the individual or individuals involved in the situation at hand. A pure individual relativist might claim that practices which are universally banned by most societies are neither right nor wrong – they simply depend on the beliefs of each individual and each individual alone.

Cultural relativism: According to Norman Bowie (1990), cultural relativism is, "the doctrine that what is right or wrong, good or bad, depends on one's culture". Societies, through experience have developed rules that benefit most of the people, most of the time. And because each society has faced different situations over time, each society has evolved different rules to create order, justice, predictability, and to ensure their smooth functioning. Thus, applied to business, cultural relativism holds that business people operating in foreign countries should follow the practices in that country; that is, "when in Rome, do as the Romans do". One should respect the values and standards of other cultures and conform to them when on their soil.

Universalism: Universalism holds that there are universal and objective ethical rules. The assumptions within universalism are that there are core universal ethical principles that guide societies' social behaviours and that, often, apparent differences in rules between societies really come from the same core ethical principle.

Those who take the universalist position observe that there is a wide acceptance of many core business principles around the world. For example, take bribery. Michael Bogdan (1979) has shown that bribery is prohibited officially in laws in virtually every nation of the world. Some governments may not enforce those laws as rightly as others – but universalists believe that there is widespread conceptual agreement among all people regarding the ethicality of this.

Another contention of the universalists is that, if the world is to have any hope of enduring social stability, values will have to be negotiated and adopted globally. Thus, for the universalist, international social stability, especially in the business world depends on a universal view as the best approach.

For the ethical relativist, there are no universal or international rights and wrongs; it all depends on a particular culture's values and beliefs. According to them, when in Rome, one should do as the Romans do. While relativism may be appealing to those who fear cultural imperialism, it is a logically and ethically incoherent theory.

Unlike the relativist, the ethical absolutist (or imperialist) believes that when in Rome, one should do what one would do at home, regardless of what the Romans do. This view of ethics gives primacy to one's own cultural values. Opponents of this view argue that ethical absolutists are intolerant individuals who confuse respect for local traditions with ethical relativism. It must be noted that while some behaviours are wrong wherever they are practised (e.g., bribery of government officials), other behaviours may be tolerated in their cultural context (e.g., the practice of routine gift giving between Japanese business people).

In contrast to the ethical relativist, the ethical universalist believes there are fundamental principles of right and wrong, which transcend cultural boundaries, and that multinationals must adhere to these fundamental principles. However, unlike the absolutist the universalist is careful to distinguish between practices that are simply culturally different and those that are morally wrong. The difficulty for managers operating in diverse cultural environments is to identify moral norms, which transcend cultural boundaries, and then, without compromising those norms, recognise and respect diversity where it is morally appropriate to do so. One useful way to determine the ethical dimensions of a proposed project, policy, or behaviour is to consider consequences, as well as rights and justice claims, for all stakeholders.

CORPORATE ETHICS CODE

One of the most interesting initiatives in international business self-regulation is the Caux Roundtable Principles for Business Conduct, developed in 1994 by Japanese, European, and North American business leaders meeting in Caux, Switzerland. This is the first international ethics code for business and aims to set a global benchmark against which individual firms can write their own codes and measure the behaviour of their executives. The Japanese concept of kyosei means living and working together for the common good – enabling cooperation and mutual prosperity to coexist with healthy and fair competition. Human dignity relates to the sacredness or value of each person as an end, not simply as the means to the fulfilment of other's purposes or even majority prescription.

The Basic Elements of a Corporate Ethics Code: The corporate ethics code plays a key role in creating an environment of predictability and consistency for the behaviour of employees and suppliers. Codes also address the relationship between organisational control and an individual's moral judgement. Codes in use by international business organisations typically contain provisions about the following:

- A general statement of the values of the organisation and its guiding principles.
- Definitions of what constitute both ethical and corrupt conduct.
- Competence requirements and professional standards.
- Directives on personal and professional behaviour.
- Affirmations of fairness, equity and equal opportunity.
- Stipulations on gifts and conflicts of interest.
- Restrictions on the use of organisational facilities for private purposes.
- Guidelines on confidentiality, public comment, whistle-blowing and post-separation use of company/organisational information.
- Identification of different stakeholders and other interested parties and their rights.
- Interpreting and implementing the code.
- Mechanism for enforcing the code.

A corporate ethics code needs to be more than the rules of the road; it should include a statement of the company's core values. If the company does not have such a statement, then the first words they put on paper should be the statement of core values. The code should be organised around the core values.

Codes of conduct must provide clear direction about ethical behaviour when the temptation to behave unethically is stronger. The pronouncement in a code of conduct that bribery is unacceptable is useless unless accompanied by guidelines for gift-giving, payments to get goods through customs, and "requests" from intermediaries who are hired to ask for bribes.

Obviously, any person or team charged with writing a corporate ethics code should know the ethically sensitive areas within their operation. But writing a code involves much more than simply putting words on paper. How the code is written and developed is probably just as important as the final product. Code writers must develop a process that ensures as to how the code will guide practice and how it will be used to inject desirable practices.

Industries or individual firms can also develop self-regulatory codes. A corporate code of conduct is a public statement of the firm's values and guiding principles. For example, we are responsible to our employees, the men and women who work with us throughout the world. Everyone must be considered as an individual. We must respect their dignity and recognise their merit. They must have a sense of security in their jobs. Compensation must b fair and adequate, and working conditions clean, orderly, and safe. We must be mindful of ways to help our employees fulfil their family responsibilities. Employees must feel free to make suggestions and complaints. There must be equal opportunity for employment, development and advancement for those qualified. We must provide competent management, and their actions must be just and ethical. We are responsible to the communities in which we will live and work and to the world community as well. We must be good citizens – support good works and charities and bear our fair share of taxes. We must encourage civic improvements and better health and education. We must maintain in good order the property we are privileged to use, protecting the environment and natural resources.

A common difficulty with codes of conduct is their enforcement. The attitudes of senior management play a crucial role in developing, implementing, and sustaining high ethical standards. Expatriates, line managers, and HR professionals may also play a role in institutionalising adherence to ethics codes through a range of HR-related activities, including training and the performance-based reward system.

BRIBERY

Bribery and corruption top the list of the most frequent ethical problems encountered by international managers. Bribery involves the payment of agents to do things that are inconsistent with the purpose of their position or office in order to gain an unfair advantage. Bribery can be distinguished from so-called gifts and "facilitating" or "grease" payments. The latter are payments to motivate agents to complete a task they would routinely do in the normal course of their duties. While most people do openly condone bribery, many argue for a lenient approach based on the view that bribery is necessary to do business. However, it is now generally agreed that bribery undermines public confidence in markets, adds to the cost of products, and may affect the safety and economic well-being of the general public.

Bribery is a practice that can be found in almost all cultures around the world. It is known by different names. In the Middle East, the word used for bribery is *baksheesh,* which is technically defined as the tip given by a boss to his/her subordinate. Its origin may be referred to the money that a new sultan would give to his troops upon acquiring his position.

The Russians call it *na leva,* and the Chinese *hongbao.* It is *kitu kidogo* in Kenya. In most Spanish speaking countries bribery is referred to as *el soborno,* meaning "pay off". In Mexico, bribery is often called *la mordida,* which means "the bite". In Germany, bribery is called *schmiergeld* which means "grease money". In France, bribery is referred to as *pot-de-vin* which means "jug of wine". The Americans sometimes call it grease, the British just call it plain bribery or perhaps more politely "a transaction expense". No matter what you call it, the plague of bribery and corruption perpetuated by the givers and takers in the business world has a much greater impact on the lives of hundreds of millions of people than you would think.

Bribery can take other forms than money. In Mexico, bribery can include lavish entertainment in exclusive restaurants and weekend trips to resorts. In Malaysia, bribery can be conducted by wisely losing games of chance. In Argentina, bribery can take the form of expensive gifts, such as post-impressionistic paintings or jewellery. Whatever form it takes, it can add significantly to the cost of doing business. Many firms have policies regarding "questionable payments" in foreign countries. These provide guidance for managers faced with situations where they are unsure how to respond to a request for payment.

SOCIAL RESPONSIBILITY

There are many definitions of social responsibility, but in general it means that a corporation has responsibilities to society that go beyond the production of goods and services at a profit; they are more than economic institutions and have a responsibility to devote some of their resources to helping solve some of the most pressing social problems.

Many people do not subscribe to this view; nevertheless, significant pressure is put on corporations to consider the social impact of their products, services, and practices. In case of a multinational company, corporate responsibility sometimes becomes a major issue. A striking example of this is Union Carbide. Conforming to local laws is exactly what Union Carbide did when it constructed a plant in Bhopal, India. The Indian government's desire to produce pesticides and fertilisers to increase the agricultural productivity of their country led to Union Carbide's venture in India. This plant brought many jobs to the area, and until the accident, the relationship between the local government and community and Union Carbide was a positive one.

The Bhopal incident was considered a watershed for awakening multinational corporations to the demand for greater accountability outside their home country. This incident is cited as a factor in the development of industry standards and the development and implementation of US environmental legislation and regulations.

The Chernobyl nuclear accident in April 1986 was kept secret by Moscow for almost a month and caused an international furore. It underscored the potential international implications governments face if, they choose to act in an unethical manner. Moscow's initial silence on the affair was an amazingly unethical act despite the tendency of communist governments to control information flow.

There are a number of international agreements and treaties in place which provide guidelines for managing corporate social responsibility across a wide range of problems in the multinational context.

1. *Organisational relations* – including competition, strategic alliances, and local sourcing;
2. *Economic relations* – including financing, taxation, transfer prices, local reinvestment, equity participation, and fiscal policies;
3. *Employee relations* – including compensation, safety, human rights, non-discrimination, collective bargaining, whistle-blowing, training, and sexual harassment;
4. *Customer relations* – including pricing, quality, and advertising;
5. *Industrial relations* – including technology transfer, research and development, infrastructure development, and organisational stability/longevity; and
6. *Political relations* – including legal compliance, bribery, and other corrupt activities, subsidies, tax incentives, environmental protection, and political involvement.

To achieve the goal of corporate social responsibility, HR professionals in multinationals may be required to:

- Minimise the exposure of employees to corrupt practices by assisting in the development, publication, and implementation of appropriate codes of conduct.
- Ensure that the training programme covers areas of ethical concern, such as bribery, human rights, justice, fair play, the common good, in a manner consistent with the multinational's policies and practices.
- Align performance appraisal and compensation systems so that they support the ethical parameters.
- Converse with the required skills to handle problem situations that may arise at the international level.
- Ensure that the employees understand the difference between corrupt bribery payments, gifts, and allowable facilitation payments and they are fully briefed on their responsibilities in this regard.

ETHICAL DILEMMAS OF MNCs

The objective of the MNC is to optimise its operations globally; conversely, the policy of the host country's government is to optimise its operations locally. In essence, the implication of this dilemma is often an MNC cannot simply come into a country, set up a shop, and organise itself to make the company as efficient as possible. Host governments may fear by MNCs inherent economic power. Thus, the host government may try to gain control over MNCs – and make use of MNCs – to meet their own goals, which may include creating a more equitable distribution of wealth or increasing their country's economic self-determination (Garland, Farmer, and Taylor, 1990). Sometimes, to facilitate the latter goal, the host government may require that MNCs hire a high percentage of host country managers to staff the MNC's subsidiary rather than allowing expatriate managers to do so.

The following examples from Garland, Farmer, and Taylor illustrate other issues involving ethical dilemmas.

- If an MNC installs state-of-the-art labour saving technology in a foreign subsidiary, the host government may not be very pleased. If there is a high incidence of unemployment or underemployment in the country, the government may prefer the MNC to use older, more labour-intensive technology to create more jobs for its people. Such provisions may even be part of the agreement in the initial negotiations with the government. Once the MNC decides to use labour-intensive technology, over time, the government may begin to criticise the MNC for not gradually introducing more labour-reducing technology. The MNC may, over time, begin to be accused of not assisting the country in developing its technological base.
- If the MNC repatriates most of its profits, it is accused of depriving the host country of money that was generated within the host country. However, if a decision to reinvest profits in the host country is made, the MNC might be perceived to be adding to its economic control of the local economy or in a sector of the local economy.
- If the MNC pays local wages to its workers, it might be seen as an exploiter of low-cost labour; however, if it pays above average wages to local workers it might be accused of emasculating the competitiveness of local firms and hoarding the brightest talents from the labour pool.
- If the MNC does not promote local managerial talent, it might be seen as being discriminatory. If it does, however, it might be seen as creating a "braindrain", that is, taking out of the country some of the country's brightest people.

Positive relationships, between the MNC and local government, and business and labour leaders, are key to the success of an overseas subsidiary. Usually, MNCs want to keep a low profile overseas. However, the more successful an MNC is in overseas, the less likely it will be able to keep a low profile.

There are no easy solutions to these dilemmas. For example, consider an MNC which decides to pay local workers in excess of the average salary of that company. Such a step may be lauded by the press and other watchdog groups in the home country, yet such a step may lead to other problems.

When the tension between the MNCs' interests and those of the local community become strained and out of balance, it can result in a public relations nightmare, which in turn can influence profits negatively. Garland, Farmer, and Taylor suggest the following four reasons for this tension:

1. Multinationals serve as convenient targets when governments are unable to satisfy the needs and aspirations of their people.
2. The multinational is foreign, and is seen as an alien influence subverting the indigenous culture and acting as a tool of its home state.
3. The multinational is typically private, and is viewed as a rapacious pursuer of its own gain at the expense of the public welfare.
4. The multinational is the most visible symbol of a world order that discriminates against the developed countries and in that sense the legitimacy of the multinational corporation is inherently subject to dispute.

Because of these perceptions, multinationals should pay constant attention to the quality of their relationships with the local communities around the world in which they have set-up operation. They have to maintain good relation with the key players in the community in which they work, such as government officials, union leaders, activist groups, the media, charitable organisations, and religious organisations. The role of "bridge builder" is a significant one in the job description of an expatriate manager.

INTRA-COMPANY ETHICAL ISSUES

Business ethics are based on broad principles of integrity and fairness that tend to focus on shareholder and stakeholder issues such as product quality, customer satisfaction, employee wages and benefits, as well as local community and environmental responsibilities that a company can actually influence.

Business ethics defines how a company integrates its core values – such as honesty, trust, respect and fairness – into its policies, practices, and decision making. Business ethics, of course, also involves a company's compliance with legal standards and adherence to internal rules and regulations.

There are laws in many countries (for example Australia, Canada, and Europe) that equally try to reinforce and ensure fairness in terms of job selection, and promotion in the workplace. Firms based in these countries face issues similar to those faced by US firms. In addition, international firms often face the challenge of complying with two sets of regulations – home and host – which are sometimes incongruent.

Expatriate managers and their families often do not receive adequate cross-cultural training before going abroad. The challenges an overseas assignment brings can cause high levels of stress, which in turn can adversely affect family relationships and consequently the manager's performance at work. All jobs have a stressful component in them, but it is common sense to train someone before he or she undertakes a new task. It would be unwise as well as unethical from a "productivity" standpoint.

Many companies send people to operate in a new business culture, with different business norms and customs, with little or no preparation, and expect them to perform well immediately upon arrival. Without training, it is unethical and irrational to expect high levels of performance. Further, it is unethical to expose employees to the negative emotional and psychological side effects that result from lack of training. It is important to understand that internal company policies can affect people adversely as much as the external environment of the international business world.

GUEST WORKERS AND IMMIGRANTS

Throughout the world, there are many "guest workers" (including migrant workers, immigrants, and illegal aliens) who have left their country of origin to work in a country which offers higher pay and a better standard of living. These guest workers are brought in to work in jobs that the local populace choose not to hold, for example, garbage collection, maid service, repetitive factory work, and manual labour.

Guest workers increasingly make up large portions of the labour force around the world, yet they are almost always denied citizenship in the country in which they work. They can be deported in an economic downturn; their career mobility is often limited; and their quality of life is usually much lower than that of most of the citizens of the country in which they work, even though their contribution is significant to the GNP. Whether they are illegal aliens or legal short-term residents, the life of a foreign guest worker tends to be one of uncertainty, unequal treatment compared to the country's citizens, and poor upward mobility. They hold different religious beliefs, eat different foods, wear different clothes, and hold cultural preferences that differ from the local citizens. These often lead to conflicts between the communities.

The treatment of guest workers is clearly inequitable because they are not considered equal to the citizens of the country. To many people, this treatment is therefore unethical, but at the same time the guest workers themselves choose to work in spite of the treatment Managers in these countries are faced with the issue of whether they should provide work for these guest workers when the differential treatment is seen as unethical.

During the 1950s and 1960s, countries such as France, Germany, Austria, and Italy relied heavily upon guest workers from Algeria and Turkey, who created social problems because they often did not return home. More recently, migrant workers from Eastern Europe are arriving in large numbers in Western Europe, as their own countries underg tumultuous political, economic, and social upheavals.

Some governments are rethinking their policies towards the use of guest worker because of concerns about social issues surrounding their working conditions and abou indigenous unemployment. To stem the tide of migrant workers, political pressure i mounting on the European Union (EU) to adopt a migrant labour policy. Standards c fairness, equality, and human dignity come into play when governments and managers try to wrestle with the guest worker issue. Should guest workers' conditions be judged against the standards and values of their home cultures or the culture in which they are presently living and working? If they contribute to the economy, should they be given the same rights and privileges of the local citizenry who also contribute to the economy? And what about guest workers who are willing to work in very low-paying jobs as compared to citizens who work in high paying jobs? Many governments are wrestling with these issues, all of which are mainly related to the question – what is the right thing to do?

ETHICS PROGRAMME

A code of ethics fulfils many purposes within an organisation. It increases the ethical sensitivity and judgement of employees, strengthens support for individuals' moral courage, and helps to hone an organisation's sense of identity. The following are the six steps for an effective ethics programme:

1. Tailor ethical standards to the company's business needs.
2. Designate high-level managers to oversee compliance.
3. Educate employees in the company's standards and procedures through publications and training.
4. Design a compliance system that includes auditing and monitoring procedures and mechanism that encourages employees to report potential violations.
5. Enforce standards through consistent discipline.
6. Report all violations and take appropriate action to improve the programme.

When business is conducted across nationally and internationally, the operationalisation of an enterprise's ethics programme takes on added layers of complexity. In particular, questions about the existence of universal ethical standards and global values are raised. The question of ethical relativity arises where human rights are habitually violated. It comes up not only in the context of different home and host country employment practices but also in the policies and programmes of multinationals. Consequently, multinationals have to develop codes of ethics and behavioural norms for expatriates, TCN and local HCN staff. Hence, an ethics component should be incorporated in their pre-departure training and orientation programme.

HR has a specific role to play in the formulation, communication, monitoring and enforcement of an enterprise's ethics programme. It is well positioned to make an important contribution for creating, sustaining, and implementing ethical behaviour within a strategic HR paradigm. HR professionals have specialised expertise for integrating ethics into all aspects of organisational life.

While people involved in international business activities face many of the ethical issues as those in domestic business, the issues are made more complex due to the different social, economic, political, cultural, and legal environments in which multinationals operate. Many firms have to place more emphasis on pre-departure training and in-country orientation of expatriates. Such programmes should include an ethics component covering basic ethical standards. If not, difficulties may crop up in implementation of responsibilities of multinationals.

SUMMARY

- *Global ethical environment* covers certain perplexing issues that may arise while doing business internationally and possible efforts one can make to behave ethically.
- Managerial decisions at the domestic and international level are woven with inter-organisational and intra-organisational issues.
- Three concepts, namely, individual relativism, cultural relativism, and universalism are associated with international business ethics.
- Every decision that an international manager takes involves issues of justice, legality, fairness, equity, and human decency.
- Bribery exists, more or less in all countries of the world, as a cross-cultural manipulation of ethical behaviour.
- Ethical tensions are associated with social responsibility issues in MNCs operating overseas.
- Fair management of ethical issues and drafting a suitable ethics programme are the most important aspects of an international manager's job.

REVIEW QUESTIONS

1. Discuss the two main contrasting approaches of ethics presented in this chapter.
2. Explain the ethical concerns of company managers posted in a multinational company.
3. What initiatives do you suggest for criminalising foreign bribery? Justify your answer.

15

Leadership and Motivation in a Global Context

Objectives

- To describe the origin of leadership and motivation.
- To study the cross-cultural issues pertaining to leadership and motivation.
- To understand different leadership styles across a variety of cultures.

INTRODUCTION

Great leaders have existed throughout history and can be found in all cultures. Since World War II, leadership has been a hot topic within the social sciences. Numerous books and articles have been written on the subject. Many social scientific theories of leadership have been constructed, but few studies have been done to test their effectiveness in cross-cultural settings. The "universal theories" of McGregor, Likert, Blake and Mouton, Misumi, and others have not been adequately substantiated by the research literature. After reviewing these theories, Yukl (1989) noted that the empirical research provides only limited support for the universal theories. The Vroom and Yetton model, though promising, deals only with a small part of leadership (decision making), and more research is needed to test each of the model's elements. Despite the lack of testing of Western leadership models, much writing and research has been done on differences of leadership in different cultures.

LEADERSHIP ACROSS CULTURES

Leadership involves influencing individuals both separately and in groups, and to act in a desired manner. In general, executive leadership calls for three skills, namely, technical, human, and conceptual. A multinational leader needs to possess certain unique qualities (apart from those listed in the trait theory) to become successful in global settings. What an international manager needs is emotional intelligence. Emotional intelligence refers to a set of five individual and social competencies, including self-awareness, self-regulation, motivation, empathy, and social skills.

Self-awareness is the ability to recognise and understand one's moods, emotions, and drives, as well as their effects on other people. Leaders with a high level of self-awareness exhibit self-confidence, a realistic self-assessment, and a self-deprecating humour.

Self-regulation is the ability to control or redirect disruptive impulses and moods – the ability to think before doing. Leaders with a high level of self-regulation exhibit trustworthiness, integrity, comfort with ambiguity, and openness to change.

Motivation is reflected in a passion to work for reasons that go beyond money or status. Leaders high on motivation exhibit remarkable organisational commitment, drive to achieve, and optimism (even in the circumstances of failure).

Empathy refers to understanding the emotional make up of other people and skill in treating people according to their emotional reactions. Leaders with a high level of empathy demonstrate an ability to build and retain talent in their organisation, show cross-cultural sensitivity, and become known for offering great service to clients and customers.

Social skill refers to the proficiency in managing relationships and building networks, along with an ability to find common ground and to build rapport. Leaders with a high level of social skill are effective at leading change, show a superior ability to build and lead teams, and become known for their persuasiveness.

UNIVERSALISM IN LEADERSHIP

In international settings, leadership needs to be situational, that is, leadership in multinational companies requires that managers adjust their leadership styles to fit different situations. This adjustment must occur not only in response to traditional contingency factors such as subordinates' characteristics but also in response to the cultural and institutional context of the multinational's country locations.

In recent years, a new issue has cropped up in the literature on leadership. The issue relates to the universalism of leadership. That is, whether or not effective leaders act similarly regardless of their respective cultures. Transformational leadership is projected as an approach which can cut across all cultural barriers and be effective in any organisation anywhere in the world and represents a higher level of leadership. Transformational leaders are visionary agents with a sense of mission who are capable of motivating their followers to accept new goals and new ways of doing things. Specifically, the transformational leader:

- *Articulates a vision:* Presents in vivid and emotional terms an idealised vision of future for the organisation – what it can and should become – and makes this vision clear to followers.
- *Breaks from the status quo:* Has a strong desire to break from tradition and do things differently; is an expert in finding ways to do things differently; and challenges subordinates to find new solutions to old problems.
- *Provides goals and a plan:* Has a vision that is future-oriented, and provides clear steps for followers to transform the company.
- *Gives meaning or a purpose to goals:* Places the goals in emotion-laden stories or a cultural context so that subordinates see the need to follow the leader's ideals and to share a commitment to radical change; helps subordinates envision a future state of a better organisation.
- *Takes risks:* Is willing to take more risks with the organisation than the average leader.
- *Enthusiastic to lead:* Seeks leadership positions and displays strong enthusiasm for the leadership role; acts as a role model.
- *Builds a power base:* Uses personal power based on expertise, respect, and the admiration of followers.
- *Demonstrates high ethical and moral standards:* Behaves consistently and fairly with a known ethical standard.

Contrary to popular belief, transformation leaders are not new to the present century. The German sociologist Max Weber recognised the existence of transformational leadership throughout history. This type of transformational leadership he called 'charisma' and he noted that it had existed in all cultures. According to Weber, Jesus Christ and Muhammad were among the first transformational leaders. Most people also consider Mahatma Gandhi and Martin Luther King as representatives of transformational leadership.

Transformational leaders succeed because subordinates respond to them with high levels of performance, personal devotion, reverence, excitement regarding the leader's ideas, and a willingness to sacrifice for the good of the company. However, true transformational leaders are rare. They seem to arise when an organisation needs a change or faces a crisis.

Does transformational leadership really work equally effectively in all cultures? The answer does not seem to be a definite 'yes'. Leader behaviours need to vary from country-to-country. For example, transformational leaders need to be more directive in less developed countries than in developed ones. Moreover, cultures can create some problems in using universal leadership concepts in countries such as Japan, where the use of contingent reward systems is not as widely used as in the West. These reward systems can also become meaningless in Arab and Turkish cultures where there is a great belief that things will happen 'if God wills' and not because a leader has decided to carry them out. Obviously, though transformational leadership has universal appreciation, it needs to be fine-tuned when applying in any particular country.

CROSS-CULTURAL DIFFERENCES IN LEADERSHIP

While the leadership is exhibited in all societies, cultural norms influence what kinds of leadership behaviours are appropriate in a particular culture. By definition, leaders stand out from their peers, yet they stand out without pushing the constraints of cultural norms too far. If leaders attempt to behave too differently from cultural norms, they will be rejected; however, if they adhere to all cultural norms in letter, they will not be leaders. Leaders must break some norms to be seen as different by their fellow men and women.

While the general observations about leaders hold true across cultures, the manner in which the leaders inspire others to follow their vision, motivate them to work to accomplish the vision, communicate the vision to elicit followers, organise their followers, and reward their followers, differs from culture-to-culture.

LEADERSHIP STYLES

In discussing the differences in leadership across cultures, the research has largely been driven by the economic success (or potential for economic success) of various nations. For example, the leadership styles of Japanese executives are known more than the leadership styles of executives in Bhutan. A few countries namely Japan, the Arab world, and France have been selected as useful contrasts in the way leadership is manifest in different cultures.

Japan: Dorfman and Ronen (1991) observed that influence to achieve high performance levels in Japanese work groups, "flows from the norms themselves, [and] not from an active or hands-on directive leadership style….. Detailed organisational charts and job descriptions are not the norm in Japan, but procedures for formalising the structure of an organisation are ubiquitous in US companies. In Japan, organisations do have rules, but they are not as important as the underlying norms of organisational behaviour in the workplace. Rules are seen as flexible in nature, easily meant to meet different situations, and not ironclad and dangerous if broken."

When an employee in Japan goes to his/her manager and seeks the manager's advice about a personal problem, the manager will take the time to listen, advise, and help the subordinate. Bolon and Crain (1985) found that Japanese managers take more steps when dealing with a problem subordinate, and spend more time in trying to understand the situation compared to American managers.

Though Japanese society is undergoing shifts in its values, business, and economic systems, traditional leadership norms are holding firm. Nakane (1970) summarises the issues of Japanese leadership by stating the following general principles:

1. In comparison to leaders in other societies, Japanese leaders have less authority and control, as they are expected to maintain warm relations with their followers. The followers are allowed to influence the decisions of the leader to a great degree.
2. The loyalty of a subordinate to a superior is a virtue in Japanese ethics. The leaders allow subordinates to show this loyalty. The leader, to a large degree is expected to be dependant on the followers – it is seen as positive if the leader has some weaknesses that the followers can compensate and make up for it.
3. Leaders must keep conflict, contention, anxiety, and tension to a minimum among the workers they lead. An important value in Japanese intra-group relations is conflict avoidance.

The Arab World: Leadership behaviours in Arab societies are closely linked to tribal traditions as well as Western influences. Ali (1990) notes that most Arab organisations, whether public or private, are highly centralised and adopt an authoritarian structure (functional-type), regardless of corporate strategy or technology. Further, he observes that the tribal-kinship influence on managers does not facilitate a willingness to work with groups outside the family, engage in creative problem-solving, seek alliances with outsiders, or break or test established organisational norms. It is not unusual for organisational problems to be solved according to cultural values of the tribal-kinship group.

The legacy of being ruled by the Ottoman and Europeans has left a legacy of administrative orientation towards centralisation, rigid rules, and clear divisions of labour. These systems combined with tribal-kinship values have developed into the leadership style of "sheikocracy". The characteristics of sheikocracy are:

- Hierarchical authority.
- Rules and regulations contingent on the personality and power of individuals who make the rules.
- Subordination of efficiency goals to human relations and personal friendships.
- Indecisiveness in decision making.
- A patriarchal approach to leadership.
- Nepotism at upper levels of organisations.
- Open-door policies.

Western influences in management methods have also influenced Arab managers, but the use of participative and other more democratic approaches to leading workers is difficult because of resistance on the part of political rulers, conservative segments in society, and other managers who are not as Westernised in their approach to management. These influences have produced a "duality" in Arab managers' approaches to leadership.

The effects of the cultural values of personalism and individualism in Arab society create organisations where systems of rules, procedures, regulations, and protocol do not solve problems regularly. In other words, organisational problems are viewed subjectively by managers, and when managers feel they have a solution, they tend to be rigid in their decision making processes.

When control devices such as committees, rules, and handbooks are ignored in Arab organisations, a kind of leadership vacuum exists. Someone or something must enter the vacuum and restore order and guidance. According to Khadra (1990), in the Arab cultural context, seeking out new management ideas, new training programmes, and so on are not thought of to solve organisational stagnation. In Arab cultures, the most important element in filling the vacuum is a person, "a great man", who will make things right. Thus, a great man is expected to emerge and is waited for by all the members of the organisation, and there will be a free disposition to accept him in his role once he emerges.

Khadra emphasises that stability, progress, and growth of the system depend on whether the leader is an ordinary man or a great man. If the leader happens to be an ordinary man, the model of leadership is the "caliphal model"; if the leader happens to be a great man, the model becomes a "prophetic model". The factor that distinguishes the leader who emerges between becoming a great man or an ordinary man is the ability to accomplish a superior feat. In order for the ordinary man to lead the group, he must use coercion and authoritarian measures, as well as ingrate himself, to maintain his status as leader. For the great man, however, a different situation exists. His power and influence depend on showing love, a minimum use of coercion, and submission to his instructions by his followers. Followers feel free to express their opinions and emotions to a great man because such a leader by nature and custom must show his interest and concern in diverse ideas.

France: Leadership in business and government organisations in France is heavily based on belonging to the cadre. Obtaining cadre status is important, for it changes social and legal status relating to pension entitlement, self-perception, and the way others perceive a person.

One attains cadre status in three ways, the most common being to excel in high school and be admitted to one of the *grandes ecoles* – professional schools that admit only the best and the brightest of France's high school graduates. Upon graduation from such a school individuals are automatically positioned for success in a company or in the government (Barsoux and Lawrence, 1991). The second way to obtain cadre status is to get a job after or before graduation from a university other than one of the *grandes ecoles* and wait five to ten years to gain cadre status. Thus, cadre status must be earned "on the job". The third way is to enter a firm without any higher education and, over a period of several years, prove oneself to be outstanding.

This system of producing leaders from the cream of the crop has predictable effects on leadership style. Barsoux and Lawrence(1991) observe that: "French managers see their work as an intellectual challenge, requiring the remorseless application of individual brainpower. They do not share the Anglo-Saxon view of management as an interpersonally demanding exercise, where plans have to be constantly 'sold' upward and downward using personal skills. The bias is for intellect rather than for action."

The design of French organisations reinforces the isolationist, intellectual, and analytical orientation of the cadre. French organisations are highly centralised, have rigid hierarchies, and positions of authority are respected. At the top of the firm in France is the PDG (president-director-general). In US terms, this position is akin to the chairman of the board and the CEO together. The person who occupies this position in a French organisation has complete decision making power and control of the company. Senior executives in France believe they owe their high position to their intelligence and should make all the critical decisions. Because of this rigidity, French managers resist adopting a more flexible organisational system.

French leaders are expected to make decisions based on careful quantitative analysis and prefer to communicate by memo and letter. All of this reinforces norms of formality and authoritarianism. French executives command respect and obedience from their subordinates and in turn give their own superiors the same. Such norms reflect a larger national organisational culture where leaders are expected to display behaviours that relate to intellect, analysis, and independence in thinking.

In 1988, General Electric (GE) got the French medical-equipment maker *Cie Generale de Radiologie.* Because the French company had been struggling, GE attempted to boost the morale of their newly acquired co-workers. The result of this approach was a conflict in leadership styles between the Americans and the French. After takeover the morale was low, the best French managers and engineers left for other firms, and it was difficult to recruit qualified replacements. GE leaders did not communicate their vision, inspire others to work for achieving the vision, and did not organise their French workforce to work effectively because they engaged in leadership behaviours that did not fit with French expectations of organisational leadership.

Leadership Tips: The role of leadership in business is critical. An increased emphasis on global-team-building has created demand for business leadership. So far, companies have failed to develop enough global leaders to meet their needs, resulting in what many call a global business leadership crisis.

A leader is supposed to inspire great performance. There are ten basic leadership behaviours that differentiate between excellent and mediocre business leaders. A successful global leader should:

- Provide clear objectives
- Build teams
- Achieve unit goals
- Enhance individual and team performance
- Make the difficult decisions
- Generate enthusiasm and pride
- Make the team feel important
- Teach and learn from honest mistakes
- Manage creative talent effectively

THEORIES ON MOTIVATION

The purpose of motivation is to create conditions in which people are willing to work with zeal, initiative, interest and enthusiasm with a sense of responsibility so that the goals of an organisation are achieved effectively.

A brief description of some of the important theories on motivation is as follows:

Maslow's Hierarchy of Needs: The famous psychologists Abraham Maslow contributed to the human relations school. Despite the fact that he did not develop a theory of management, his work in psychology was applied by others to the organisational context. Lowest on the hierarchy is the *physiological* – needs that have to do with satisfying hunger, thirst, shelter, and sex. Next on the hierarchy is *safety* – needs that involve ensuring personal safety and income. Following this need is the category of *belongings* needs; these have to do with the needs for social acceptance as shown by rewarding interpersonal relationships. *Esteem* is the next category on the hierarchy, and this involves the desire for prestige, to feel valuable in the eyes of only self and others. Finally, the highest needs of all are those of *self-actualisation*; these needs involve the desire to feel competent, authentic, self-expressive, creative, and unique.

Maslow assumed that an individual will not be concerned with higher needs in the hierarchy until lower needs in the hierarchy are met. Maslow's ideas were applied to organisational setting by variety of academics, writers, and consultants, and the need for self-actualisation was elevated as the ideal state for people to see. Much attention was paid to how organisations could facilitate conditions that allow people to pursue self-actualisation at work. One problem with this theory is that individuals often pursue self-actualisation outside their work. Many people may not want to be self-actualised at work, and programmes that promote such an environment may, therefore fail. Nevertheless, Maslow's model of needs has had a powerful effect on how training programmes and management education programmes are conducted. The content of such programmes often have assumed that if a manager meets workers' needs, they will be motivated.

Maslow's hierarchy was the first motivation model to be tested internationally. Compared to the number of studies that tested Maslow's model in the US and in Canada, the number that tested his model internationally is relatively small. Some studies found that Maslow's hierarchy was the same or very similar across cultures, while other studies found some similarities along with significant differences in needs hierarchies across cultures. While complete support was not found for Maslow's hierarchy, there is clear evidence that the need types in his model manifests itself across cultures. Though Maslow's hierarchy itself may not be universal, the needs within that hierarchy do seem to reflect universal needs. For example, Badawy (1979-80) found that the Arab managers preferred to do business with people whom they knew and trusted. The Saudis were much more concerned about issues in the social needs category and less concerned about self-actualisation needs than the Americans.

Herzberg's Two-Factor Theory: Frederick Herzberg developed a different needs-oriented theory. He believed that when an organisation satisfies a worker's lower-order needs, the worker will reach a "zero-level" of motivation. In other words, if a company pays a fair wage and has a safe workplace and decent interpersonal relationships between supervisors and employees, then the worker will show up to work on time. Doing all that is not enough to motivate the worker. Rather, it is a prerequisite for motivation to occur. Herzberg labelled these lower order needs "hygiene factors". When they are not present, or are inadequate, they create dissatisfaction. When these needs are met, they create "motivational neutrality".

Herzberg believed that higher-order needs must be met for motivation to occur in the workplace. He argued that jobs must allow for a sense of individual achievement, challenge, and recognition for a person to feel motivated at work. He advised companies to take care of the lower-order needs first and then enrich the nature of jobs, so that they will allow workers to meet their higher-order needs.

Herzberg's model has been tested outside the US and support for it cross-culturally is mixed. Though some studies found support for the model, others did not. In general, not enough of studies found that people across cultures view the same kinds of work-related issues as motivators and as hygiene factors. In some cases, people viewed hygiene factors as being highly motivating to them at work. Herzberg's model has not found clear support in North America. However, the theory may be useful as a diagnostic tool for tailoring specific motivation programmes in the workplace.

McClelland's Needs Theory: David McClelland's research findings support the facts that humans tend to have dominant need clusters and that those needs may not exist in any kind of hierarchical ordering. McClelland's work would suggest that individuals acquire dominant need groupings as they grow up, and these are influenced both by nature and nurture. People are not necessarily born with these needs, but can acquire them over time and through experience. The three needs he studied were the need for power, the need for achievement, and the need for affiliation.

People who have a strong need for achievement desire to accomplish challenging tasks, seek success, and always try to excel. They are often entrepreneurs. People who have a high need for affiliation seek to have rewarding interpersonal relationships, develop friendships, and avoid conflict. These individuals often work as "integrators" whose role is to facilitate the work of several departments or work groups. This role requires communication skills and the ability to develop good working relationships with a diverse group of people. Further, people who have a high need for power and desire to be in authority over others influence organisations. Numerous studies have been conducted worldwide to test the general validity of McClelland's work. These studies provide for the cross-cultural general validity of his model and indicate that the need for achievement exists in varying degrees across cultures.

Expectancy Theory: The expectancy theory assumes that individual motivation level is a function of perceived probability that one's work will, in fact, result in the desired performance. Expectancy theory does not try to define specific needs of people; rather, it acknowledges that employees value different kinds of outcomes and that one's organisations understand the expectancy mindset of each employee, the correct outcomes can be held up as goals. The employee must not only desire the outcome, but believe that he/she can do the job and that once the job is accomplished, the outcome will in fact be given to him/her.

Equity Theory: Another model that has received a lot of attention by management researchers is equity theory by J. Stacy Adams. The principle behind it is: "if people perceive their compensation as equal to what others receive for similar contributions, they will believe that their treatment is fair and equitable" (Daft, 1991). Perceived inequity, i.e., dissatisfaction, anger, frustration, and other conditions do not contribute to motivation, but wherever perceived equity exists, people are motivated to work hard. When workers compare themselves to one another, they take into consideration differences in terms of experience, age, education, performance, and a host of other variables. Equity theory holds that employees calculate their level of performance in relationship to their "inputs" (experience, education, effort, ability, potential) against the level of our "outputs" (actual performance, status, pay). Very few studies have been done on expectancy and equity theory internationally, so it is difficult to comment on their cross-cultural general validity. However, the studies that have been done have supported both equity and expectancy theory.

MOTIVATIONAL ISSUES

One of the most difficult tasks for international managers is to motivate and lead people from cultural backgrounds different from their own. Motivation is probably the most researched areas of management. If a manager can grasp what will motivate his/her employees, then that manager will have a more productive workforce. Being able to understand what motivates employees is thus a key diagnostic skill for a manager to possess. The actions a manager takes to motivate his/her subordinates depend on that manager's assumptions about what motivates people. Most of the research undertaken in this area has been carried out in the US, Canada, and Great Britain. The most common approach, historically, to answer the question of what motivates workers has been to focus on satisfaction of needs. One of the earliest researchers that took this approach was Frederick Taylor. He believed that workers were motivated to work by the need for money. His model is based on the idea that people work hard when they are given more money. He held that a company should break work down into its most efficient components to use workers' time on the job more productively. By doing this, profits would increase, and the company would have more money to increase workers' pay, which in turn, would keep them motivated to work hard.

Taylor's ideas seem to work best when the nature of the job is routine and predictable (such as basic assembly-line work), when little judgement is required from managers, and when workers are willing to comply with organisational rules. Motivation is not really that simple. People seem to be motivated by more than just money; and individual differences exist in workers – some may be more interested in receiving more leisure time instead of money, for example.

In reaction to Talyor's ideas, a new approach to worker motivation developed, namely, the human relations school. This assumes that individuals are motivated by more than just money. It is the study and practice of utilising human resources through an understanding of the activities, attitudes, sentiments, and inter-relationships of people at work. Human relations seek to emphasise employee aspects of work rather than technical or economic aspects.

Some scholars have criticised the validity of all research done on motivational issues. They claim that superimposing a model that has inherent Western assumptions about the nature of human needs may not apply to non-Western cultures. For example, a Cambodian manager may understand concepts such as self-actualisation differently from a North American or a European manager.

One problem for researchers is that it is often difficult to translate survey questionnaires so that the meaning of critical words like "achievement" is understood properly by the reader of the questionnaire. Hofstede has argued that in some languages Western concepts like achievement cannot even be translated, and that there is no word in those languages that captures the meaning of the concept. While there are no magical or universal equations that would motivate anyone, anywhere, at any time, the findings from the research support the proposition that people seek to have their needs met, and when they have these needs met, they are motivated.

McClelland found that no matter where one travels, there are people to a larger or smaller degree who will be motivated by the need to achieve. In cultures where achievement is not a primary value, the likelihood of having a workforce with an innate orientation to work hard and achieve goals will be low. Thus, in such cultures, expatriate managers will need to focus on ways to meet their workers' needs and link those needs to motivation. Expatriate managers must learn the strengths of their host-national employees, and adjust their motivational strategy accordingly. The key for expatriates is to learn under what circumstances their employees perform well, and under what circumstances they perform poorly, and to learn what kind of tasks they like and dislike. Though it is difficult, expatriate managers must learn to understand the real nature of their workers and then manage accordingly. Expectancy theory seems to hold a strong potential for application in the cross-cultural work-setting once a manager understands the needs of his/her subordinates. In cross-cultural settings, it requires significant study, observation, and insight to be able to clearly understand the needs of one's workforce.

SUMMARY

- *Leadership and motivation in a global context* examines the leadership styles and a range of theories and beliefs about what motivates people in an organisation.
- Great leaders have existed throughout history and can be found in all cultures.
- While leadership is exhibited in all societies, cultural norms influence what kinds of leadership are appropriate in a particular culture.
- There are certain important norms that influence leadership behaviour in different countries.
- Employees can be motivated both as individuals and as members of a group.
- Motivation principles and practices vary across cultures.

REVIEW QUESTIONS

1. Compare and contrast leadership in France with leadership in the Arab World.
2. In a country that is high on power distance, people generally expect and accept differences in power as appropriate. Discuss equity theory in the context of a high power difference society.
3. Discuss the relationship differences in leadership and motivation across cultures to the need for careful selection of expatriate managers.

16

IHRM Issues Trends and Future Challenges

Objectives

- To understand why strategies focus so much attention on the issue of organisational capability.
- To explain the role of centres of excellence and shared service centres.
- To discuss intellectual and social integration by looking at the role that knowledge management and global networks play in developing IHRM professionals.

INTRODUCTION

The fundamental change in the international economy captured under the label of economic globalisation has changed the context of employment systems for firms all over the world. The World Development Report (1995) documents that the world economy is integrating and that working conditions of workers are changing all over the world. Globalisation is increasing the involvement of MNCs in national economies and has created new opportunities for local firms to export their products in global markets. Increased involvement of MNCs in developing countries is affecting firms and their employment systems in a number of ways. The easy availability of imported goods in developing countries which are often of better quality or lower cost is forcing domestic firms to become more competitive and match quality and price of imported goods. Further, with increased involvement of MNCs in domestic markets, the local firms now have to compete with their corporations that have better access to technology and financial resources. The removal of trade restrictions of other countries has created new export opportunities for local firms but to avail this, they must be globally competitive.

ORGANISATIONAL CAPABILITY

Trends of globalisation, market liberalisation, deregulation and technical evolution, are challenging global markets and traditional approaches to gaining competitive advantage. It is only the possession of specific capabilities and resources that now enables firms to conceive and then implement strategies that can generate what economists describe as above average rates of return (J.B. Barney, 1997). Ulrich and Lake (1990) brought together perspectives from the fields of management of change, organisational design and leadership, and argued that organisational capability was about competing from inside out.

Organisational capability focuses on the ability of a firm's internal processes, systems and management practices to meet customer needs and direct both the skills and efforts of employees towards achieving the goals of the organisation. IHRM has to gear up to meet various challenges in this regard. A distinction can be made between the developments that affect the overall nature of IHRM inside organisations, and the actual role of international HR professionals. Around fifty per cent of HR managers across Europe feel that they are proactively engaged in the development of corporate strategy (C. Brewster, 1994). There is evidence to show that the degree of representation at the board-level HR function is still relatively weak in corporate headquarters across most European countries. With more and more globalisation of activities, mergers and acquisitions are on the rise and the role of IHRM professionals seems to be losing its clarity.

Organisational capability has its roots in the argument that in an environment characterised by the globalisation of markets, changing customer demands and increasing competition, it is the people and the way they are managed that are more significant than other sources of competitive advantage (P.M. Wright, G.D. McMaban and A. McWilliams, 1994). They argue that competitive advantage is derived from both internal knowledge resources and the strategic resources or capabilities of the firm. These resources are generally considered to be complex, intangible and dynamic.

In addition to the management of people, developing organisational capability includes the means by which organisations implement policies and procedures. These means are centred around economic and financial capability, strategic/marketing capability, and technological capability. As the HR profession becomes more involved in developing organisational capability, it has to build alliances. Strategic or marketing capability is based around offering uniqueness to customers. The marketing perspective has been, in fact, a significant driver of approaches to talent management. The second alliance is based around technological capability. Perceived customer value is a result of responsiveness (meeting needs more quickly than competitors), the formation of endearing and enduring relationships, and the pursuit of service quality through guarantees.

Many multinational firms have a 'capability recognising' perspective, i.e., they possess some unique knowledge-based resources. However, these resources are typically treated as being based on the home country or somehow belonging to the corporate function and top team. There is a possibility that foreign national units could take a major strategic role within the multinational firm. What is needed is a 'capability-driven' perspective – a strategy based on how multinational firms attempt to build, protect and exploit a set of unique capabilities. It is based on three grounds: (a) strategies of international expansion or global integration; (b) the necessity to continue generating competitive advantage or to innovate through global learning; and (c) skills and activities operating at the business-level or corporate-level routines that integrate these skills across operations.

Tallmen and Fladmoe-Lindquist's work (2002) makes it evident that globalisation is a strategic effort to treat the world (or a significant part of it) as a single market. This does not, however, imply creating single research and development or production centres, unitary logistic networks or, indeed, HR systems and processes. Rather, it is the international networking that surrounds these activities and the conduct of these activities in the global context that provides significant organisational capability. The world becomes an important source for new knowledge as well as new markets.

Another opportunity for a more strategic role in this process of capability development comes from the process theories. Montealegre (2002) developed a model of the process skills needed to provide such development of capability. Five key resources were used throughout the process – all things that international HR managers can help build. These are:

- leadership – through the expression and subsequent articulation of strategic intent
- organisational culture – through the mobilisation of supporting routines already embedded in the culture
- information technology – not in the sense of technical investments but more in the way that these investments are leveraged to create unique resources and skills that improve the effectiveness of the organisation
- long-term view – developing a longer-term view of the strategy by developing and nurturing commitment
- social networks – through the cultivation of strong relationships with stakeholders inside and outside the organisation.

In the context of globalisation, organisational capability involves managing the conflicting demands of corporate control, and global coordination and standardisation of HR processes. This does not imply building totally standardised HR processes on a global scale but it does entail building a degree of common insight into the nature of shared HR processes and adherence to the design of these processes. The mantra of organisational capability, supported by developments in both the use of technological capability and marketing capability has, in some firms, begun to dominate the activity of international HR professionals.

UNDERSTANDING AND BUILDING CENTRES OF EXCELLENCE

In practice, multinational organisations have increasingly dispersed activities. They have relied on specialised and often network-based structures to coordinate these activities. The corporate headquarters typically adjusts its level of coordination and control to reflect the role of the subsidiary and the strategic importance of its mandate. A variety of missions can be assigned to subsidiaries. One particular type of subsidiary, the centre of excellence, has of late gained more prominence. These take on a strategic role in the global organisation that reaches beyond their local enterprises. Centres of excellence have to be tightly integrated with their surrounding technical or professional communities. They tend to be established as a general consequence of a long and slow internationalisation process within the organisation or as part of a deliberate aspect of organisational design where the managers at the headquarters decide to grant autonomy to units that have also been given a specific strategic mandate. A centre of excellence must have both high competence and high use of its competence throughout surrounding units.

Increasingly, small teams or units within subsidiaries are taking a leading role in one area of the centre of excellence, with other units taking the lead in different areas of capability. Indeed, although the leadership of a centre of excellence might still be vested in a physical location, the actual centre itself may be quite virtual, spread across networks of teams in many different geographical areas. In many cases, experts argue that these centres actually need to be quite loosely tied into the organisation and coordinated with other units if they are to help search for new knowledge and augment the capability of the MNC (W. Kuemmerle, 1999). Control typically varies between being direct or indirect and through personal or impersonal mechanisms – What Harzing calls centralised personal control, formal bureaucratic control, output control or control through socialisation and networks. Recent research suggests that controlling these centres of excellence through socialisation proves to be dysfunctional (A. Ambos and W.D. Reitsperger, 2002). Understanding and building these more globally distributed centres of excellence into viable operations has, therefore, become a significant challenge.

There is now available a fair amount of insight into how such centres should be fostered. Holm and Pedersen (2002) found that they must be more than just specialised in their knowledge. They have to be able to maintain one or several critical fields of knowledge that have a long-term impact on the development of activities in the other subsidiaries and units of the MNC. In the longer-term, global HR functions which establish their own centres of excellence will begin to learn from the research that has already been conducted and from other technical centres of excellence already established.

STREAMLINING HR SUPPORT FUNCTIONS

Lot of attention has been paid to the development of shared services in an organisation. Shared services are created when the organisation chooses to concentrate its administrative personnel activities into a centralised 'back office' function. Administrative processing is carried out separately from the main HR group. The central organisation of HR resources comes hand-in-hand with local tailored advice policy and practice designed around business needs. Administrative functions may be centralised but decision making remains decentralised.

The relevance of this development to international HRM gives considerable shared service thinking that represents a course for fundamental realignment of the HR function. It carries implications for the level of centralisation and devolvement evidenced across countries, regions, and corporate headquarters. Moreover, it changes the economics of HR services provision and introduces competing dynamics not only for the standardisation of HR processes but also the potential for mass customisation. Few international HR functions will be able to ignore this development.

Separating out those elements of the HR function that are concerned with business strategy from those elements that are concerned with service delivery, will have deep implications for the skills and competencies of HR professionals. The radical perspective also links the development of shared service structures to parallel changes in technology that have enabled greater outsourcing of HR activity. Although technology (notably organisational intranets, web-based portal, interactive voice responses, and document and information management systems) has been an important part of the equation, it is a facilitator rather than a driver of change. Technical innovation has enabled organisations to consider a much wider range of HR services on a common basis around the globe. However, the reasons for introducing shared services have more to do with cost, quality and the general nature of organisational change.

Issues that involve cross-national working and interpretation are of course more likely to be escalated upwards to international specialists or centres of HR excellence. Shared services, then, can change the way in which international HR professionals are sourced within their work, and can also bring with them new control systems to govern and monitor their response. One more implication of the move to shared services is that the structures of HR at the country level change. By the end of 1980s, most multinational organisations had decided that splitting up the HR function on a country-by-country basis when the rest of the organisation was increasingly aligned with the global aspects of the business, was not helping HR to achieve its objectives. However, concerns about diversity in employment law and the continuance of strong national influences on employment relationship meant that total alignment of the HR function with other business processes remained problematic. As a compromise, many organisations installed global HR directors as an extra layer in the reporting structure in order to create a position that acted as a strategic business partner.

OUTSOURCING OR INSOURCING HR

The issue of outsourcing the transactional aspects of HRM has been a source of considerable debate in recent years. Advocates of outsourcing HR activities[1] point to reduced costs, increased service quality produced by greater economies of scale, increased incentives and accountability for service providers, and increased access to experts in specialised areas. The most common targets for outsourcing are those HR activities that can easily be ring-fenced, and include payroll, training, recruitment, and benefits administration.

The global context requires deep, tacit understanding of the national culture and therefore should not be considered either for operating through shared services or indeed for any subsequent outsourcing. Organisations must make sensible assessments of these tacit knowledge constraints.

MANAGING TALENT

Intellectual, social, and emotional integration play a key role in the work of international HR managers. To these three types of integration, a fourth role is identified by Scullion and Starkey (2000) – the effective management of international management talent. They note that the management of senior managers and high-potential people identified as strategic resources is vital to the future and survival of most international operations. Talent management on a global basis is a far broader concept than plotting a series of international assignments for young high-potentials. In practice, talent markets still operate in a national way and even global organisations find that their relative positioning varies markedly from one country to another. Those organisations that are consistently in the top ten tend to maintain local recruitment strategies, but they mix this local strategy with a more global transfer of information and best practices. This is because the talent itself has become more mobile and organisations have to, therefore, coordinate the way they manage it on a global basis. Competition has also become more generic – global organisations do not just compete with the best local employers but also with each other.

MNCs are concerned with their 'talent pipeline'. They want to know who their top people are and what their key roles within their business. They are also concerned with developing a much deeper understanding about the links between the business agenda and the capabilities of the most talented people in the organisation, and also understand the mobility around these people. When they conduct such a 'calibration' of talent on a global basis, they have to ask what this means for a planned business development. In short, when global lines of business are introduced, there is a more immediate relationship between the international HR professional and the global leadership teams within major business functions or markets.

As marketing strategies become obsolete quickly due to rapid changes occurring across the globe, it is becoming more and more difficult to attract and retain the most desired talent.

In order to attract and retain the best talent anywhere in the world, an organisation must have a strong and positive employer brand. Therefore, many MNCs put in considerable effort in developing an 'Employee Value Proposition' (EVP) by identifying the most important features of working for them.[2] EVP is generally used to drive attraction and retention behaviour. This challenge for MNCs is to decide what the overriding message is – as to who they are and what they stand for.

As the world gets smaller, MNCs need to make sure that the way in which they are perceived as a company is similar wherever they go. What do their consumers want from them? What do current employees think? This involves the constant reselling of proposition to employees as to why their organisation is the place they should work. Therefore, the HR challenge is to understand what makes a really good person stay with them globally. The answer affects the development of people, which is a key driver of retention, and finally impinges on how the organisation recruits, designs compensation and benefits, and performance management systems.

GLOBAL KNOWLEDGE MANAGEMENT

The development of intellectual integration through the creation of shared knowledge bases is the next integration activity that the IHRM function can pursue. Although much attention has been paid to the issue of knowledge management in recent years, there is yet to be a significant attempt for looking at the issues of managing knowledge across borders. Perhaps, the most critical component in terms of IHRM positioning lies in the role it plays in championing knowledge management. In a global environment, physical and cultural distance presents powerful barriers to successful knowledge transfer among HR professionals. Choosing the most effective technological platforms, but most importantly, deciding the content of the knowledge to be shared and creating knowledge networks is, therefore, an essential factor in the HR function's globalisation efforts.

The HR function also has to grapple with the intrinsic stock of knowledge held in people's heads which is often the key to competitive advantage. Hence IHRM takes on responsibility for the conscious development of operating networks, both as practitioners within the HR community and as facilitators elsewhere in the organisation.

In reality, technology in the form of global intranets and knowledge management systems enables, but does not cause, the required connections and sharing. There is considerable 'social capital' within these communities (that is, a lot of importance given to the connections and relationships that each professional can call upon and the resources that they can mobilise). In order to build on the individual social capital, IHRM has to build the relationships across the broader HR community. This requires considerable face-to-face contact. HR professionals from around the world will have to work together if they have to solve mutual and pressing business and human needs.

MANAGEMENT THROUGH GLOBAL NETWORKS

Thus, building of the agenda for capability building in IHRM is often more concerned with up-skilling a business function and spending more time with the leadership teams of these functions. Global networking is one of the ways in which the IHRM function can help build this capability across international operations. This is now considered to be critical because of the organisational changes taking around. Historically, global information, insight into local conditions and best practices have all tendered to be shared just by conversation through the process of IHRM – getting groups of people together within the organisation to facilitate some transfer of learning. Indeed, IHRM has to set-up informal networks all the time – and this is generally one of their key objectives. It is much easier to have a network in place working on a significant HR issue from the start. With a network, there a greater chance of moving quickly, producing higher-quality HR services and providing a better business focus. Networks also suit a more decentralised model of international HRM. Global networks are generally not just put in place for the purpose of knowledge transfer; but are also used increasingly to cut through bureaucracy and to act as important decision making group. They serve several important purposes:

- providing a forum to encourage innovation and growth throughout the business, and a vehicle to get the right people on to the right teams in order to make this happen;
- encouraging HR professionals and line managers to think beyond their 'own patch';
- creating a situation whereby membership of the network provides advantages in terms of better quality implementation for both line managers and HR professionals;
- getting stakeholders (the senior HR community, presidents in businesses) to buy into business changes; and
- forcing the business agenda in forums outside the networks in subtle ways based on shared insight within the network.

At a practical level, management takes place through networks and the focus on knowledge management puts pressure on company intranets and on the technology needed to support such activity. Consequently, most of the future developments in the shared service models are likely to come about through technological change. A part of the response to the pressure on IHRM is the pursuit of better ways to do things. A key challenge facing HRM is the new information and communication technology which is changing ever so fast. This applies across the board, but its impact on global HRM could be immense. The ability to get HRM information to and from line managers' desks without a formal HRM intervention opens up new and exciting possibilities, allowing HR to focus on its capability and business development roles. Importantly, this e-enablement is being engineered on a global basis.

Technical changes are seen as an enabling factor, not a driving factor in the move towards more global models of HRM.

Web-enabling of HR activity, both transactional and transformational HR work, is therefore, seen as an essential step towards helping HR professionals to advise business leaders on the competitiveness of the firm. Even transformational HR work can be e-enabled. This is where more sophisticated HR practices, such as the recruitment and selection process, or the appraisal and performance process, are themselves offered in more innovative ways through web-based solutions. Current online access rights and limited up date rights are expected to be a stepping stone to managers authorising pay changes and performance management data, and to employees providing not only factual data about their preferences but also more dynamic and interactive information around skills and personal aspirations. Computing power is being directed at developing what are called 'proactive full technologies'.

But according to Reilly[3], 'speed of progress will probably not be determined by technological capability but by culture', that is, the organisational culture and extent to which this supports the conduct and practice of management. This statement can be extended to management within national culture as well as to cross-cultural management. Nonetheless, organisational and customer needs are already altering, and in future, will alter more radically in response to the globalisation of business and the internationalisation of resources within organisations. Nationally-based services are slowly being replaced by cross-national operations. For example, the advent of the Euro led to the drive to harmonise reward structures on a pan-European basis, and this work was considered to be best supported by commonly shared service centres in most multinational organisations. The environment will be one in which global firms will:

- extend the shared service concept to other parts of their business operations, subsidiaries and satellite companies;
- use it as a force for integration across recently merged or acquired business or joint venture operations; and
- seek common platforms for the HR, finance and logistics shared services.

So, sooner rather than later, these developments will take place and will signal two major shifts in focus of the HR role:

- The HR and IT functions increasingly work in collaboration, so that HR provides the IT function with HR practices to ensure that its people have the talent, discipline and accountability to design and use effective technical information systems; and IT provides HR with the technological infrastructure to deliver HR efficiently and effectively.

- The HR function can advise as to which processes can be standardised and which must remain localised, and who are the knowledge agents who transfer ideas across business functions and geographical boundaries within the global firm.

Exhibit 16.1

International HR Competencies

- Being a strategic thinker, articulating the benefits of having an effective HR process and capability, and the risks of both personal and business objectives of not having one.
- Having available strong personal networks inside and outside the organisation and the ability to build some structure into this collection of relationships.
- Being a provider of information and advice within this business network, based on personal expertise and credibility.
- Becoming a broker of appropriate knowledge, learning and ideas across a loose connection of people. Being seen as the owner of important new dialogues within the organisation.
- Displaying the capacity for and tolerance of the ambiguities and uncertainties inherent in new business situations, such as working through confused leadership.
- Being a resource negotiator, persuading managers to invest and capturing unassigned resources.
- Being a process facilitator, with diplomatic sensitivity to complex organisational politics and power struggles.
- Mobilising the energy and engagement behind ideas, maintaining pressure on people, managing the impact by under-promising but over-achieving.
- Having respect for the countries and communities being dealt with. Showing insight into their needs both as consumers (as employees) and as clients (as global business functions).
- Showing an appreciation of the ways in which culture influences core organisational behaviours.
- Possessing the capacity to work virtually.

Source: C. Brewster, H. Harris and P.R. Sparrow, (2002). *Globalising HR, Executive Brief*, London, Chartered Institute of Personnel and Development.

To deliver these competencies, IHRM needs to be able to understand, develop an insight into, and take an overview of, the links between HR processes and effective business performance across a global network of operations. However, in the light of the global re-positioning of HR functions that is taking place, international HR professionals have also to act as the guardians or caretakers of national culture.

MANAGING INTERNATIONAL PROJECTS: HR PERSPECTIVE

The success of project management calls for performing the basics of planning, organising, and controlling with specific challenges of managing human resources. The primary factors in global projects are cross-cultural settings that call for special attention, as nationals from different nationalities will be working together. The important requirement is to identify competencies and skills of employees to be employed in the projects, and integrate them into teams till the completion of the project.

In international projects, success depends on those factors that are primarily vulnerable to cross-cultural settings and building a team capable of dealing with the challenges. The challenge in international team-building boils down to developing and facilitating communication and understanding between people of different national cultures.

Development of a suitable project culture should have an objective, a schedule, and a development plan. Factors such as beliefs, feelings, informal behaviour patterns, group norms and values strongly affect behaviour of project managers and team-members. In short, cross-cultural team-building must take place so that individuals' can be channelled to meet the project goals.

The success of a project equally depends on the project leader and also on the dynamics of the project team. A dynamic team is a high performing team, which has certain characteristics, such as:

- Building upon individuals strengths.
- Supporting leadership and each other.
- Developing team culture.
- Resolving disagreements and communicating openly.
- Making objective decisions and evaluating a team's effectiveness.

HR ETHICS AND CORPORATE SOCIAL RESPONSIBILITY

Ethics and the question of corporate social responsibility are complex and the source of much controversy. In the domestic context, debates about corporate social responsibility have focused on whether a firm should adopt non-economic goals. Those who argue for a narrow view of corporate social responsibility believe that a firm's only responsibility is to maximise profits for shareholders within the law. Proponents of a broader view of corporate social responsibility argue that firms should adopt the role of a "good citizen" and balance the interests of shareholders with the best interests of society. When business is conducted across national and cultural borders, the debate about corporate social responsibility takes on added layers of complexity. In particular, perplexing questions about the existence of universal ethical standards are raised. This is especially problematic when multinationals operate in host countries with different standards of business practice. The questions of ethical relativity and corporate social responsibility arise not only in the context of different home and host country employment practices but also in the central operations and policies of multinationals.

Bribery and corruption tops the list of most frequent ethical problems encountered by international managers. Bribery involves the payment to agents to do things that are inconsistent with their position or office in order to gain an unfair advantage.

Application of core human values to specific duties of multinationals include the adoption of adequate workplace and environmental health and safety standards, the payment of basic living wages, equal employment opportunity, refraining from the use of child labour, providing basic employee training and education, and allowing workers to organise and form unions. Many multinationals now place considerable emphasis on being regarded as good global citizens and have initiated actions to address public concerns about the environment and human rights.

Ethical issues are also people issues and thus the issues raised above have direct implications for the HR function. It is recognised that the HR function is responsible for many of the activities that build a sense of corporate identity such as staff selection and training.

To achieve the goal of corporate social responsibility, HR professionals in multinationals may be required to:

- minimise the exposure of employees to corrupt conduct by assisting in the development, publication, and implementation of appropriate codes of conduct;
- ensure training programmes cover areas of ethical concern – such as bribery, human rights, justice, and the common good – in a manner consistent with the multinational's objectives in this regard;
- align performance appraisal and compensation systems so that they support the ethical stance taken;
- be conversant with the type of requests that may be made of staff operating internationally – not just expatriates but also those who visit foreign markets in various capacities – and provide the necessary training so that they have the requisite negotiating skills to handle problem situations that may arise; and
- ensure that employees understand the difference between corrupt bribery payments, gifts, and allowable facilitation payments. Given the strong positions taken by governments on ethical behaviour, it is important that all staffs are fully briefed on their responsibilities in this regard.

In particular, the foreign subsidiaries should mainly discharge their social obligations in the following areas:

- Adulteration and loss of quality for any reason.
- Environment and pollution control.
- Employment of women, children, and minorities.
- Employment of local citizens.

- Personal issues including remuneration, pension or severance benefit.
- Taxation and financial controls.
- Purchase of local and foreign materials.
- Purchase lease, and location of buildings and plant.
- Management-union relationship.

In the domestic context, debates about corporate social responsibility have focused on whether a firm should adopt non-economic goals. Those who argue for a narrow view of corporate social responsibility believe that a firm's only responsibility is to maximise profits for shareholders. Proponents of a broader view, on the other hand, argue that firms should adopt the role of a "good citizen" and balance the interests of shareholders with the best interests of society. The debate about it takes added layers of complexity especially when business is conducted across national and cultural borders. In this regard, perplexing questions about the existence of universal ethical standards are raised. The questions of ethical relativity and corporate social responsibility arise not only in the context of different home and host country employment practices but also in the central operations and policies of multinationals.

Many American companies have developed social responsibility programmes in South Africa under the guidance of the Sullivan Code. Its contributions have been found in various educational, community, and health projects. Tata Steel, largest private sector steel company in India, is a shining example of ethical practices and corporate social responsibility. JRD Tata said, "every company has a special continuing responsibility towards the people of the area in which it is located and in which its employees and their families live". It is one of the few integrated steel plants in the world to have a well-managed township for rendering various welfare services to their employees, family members, and to the community.

SUMMARY

- *IHRM issues, trends, and future challenges* emphasises on current strategic developments in IHRM, and their role in future.
- Organisational capability focuses on the ability of a firm's internal processes, systems, and management practices to meet customer needs and direct both the skills and efforts of employees towards achieving the goals of the organisation.
- The role of IHRM in the development of centres of excellence will be to manage the internal location of staff and to provide advice on the best HR strategies to coordinate and control such activities, and to understand and build networks of HR experts within these areas on a global basis.

- There are five key resources in the process of developing organisational capability in which HR can help, namely: (a) leadership, (b) organisational culture, (c) information technology, (d) long-term commitment, and (e) social networking.
- The mechanism of integration includes operational integration through standardised technology; intellectual integration throughout the creation of a shared knowledge base; social integration through the creation of collective bands of performance; and emotional integration through a sense of shared identity and meaning.

REVIEW QUESTIONS

1. How could an organisation obtain the benefits of a centre of excellence without having to declare a whole subsidiary to be such a centre? What are the alternatives?
2. Are shared services models going to represent a new force for standardisation of HR practices on a global basis, or will they result in more localised and customised policies and practices?
3. What type of knowledge do global HR expertise networks need through transfer?

REFERENCES

1. B. Klaas, J.A., McClendon, and T.W. Gainey (2001), *Outsourcing HR: The Impact of Organisational Characteristics*, Human Resource Management, Vol. 40, No. 2, pp. 125-38.
2. E. Michaels, H. Handfield-Jones, and B. Axelrod (2002), *The War for Talent*, Boston, Harvard Business School Press.
3. P. Reilly (2000), *HR Shared Services and the Realignment of HR*, Institute of Employment Studies Report, Brighton, IES.

Glossary

Acquisition: It is the procurement of one organisation by the other. The purchasing organisation becomes more dominant and plays a powerful role.

Assertiveness: The degree to which society encourages people to be tough, confrontational, assertive and competitive rather than being modest and tender.

Attribution: The way you perceive yourself and the way you perceive others.

Base salary: The amount of cash compensation that serves as a benchmark for other payments.

Bicultural teams: In this type of team two or more members represent each of two distinct cultures.

Bribery: A bribe in one culture is a gift in another. In many cultures, it is normal to pay a commission to people involved in a transaction.

Categorisation: Bombarded with more perceptions than we can keep distinct or interpret and therefore, we categorise perceived images into familiar groups to simplify our understanding. This allows us to function in a complex world.

Cluster organisation: Clusters or teams developed to carry-out specific key tasks which are permanently based around key activities rather than being *ad hoc* teams.

Collectivism: it measures the degree of 'social ties or bonds' between individuals.

Commuter assignments: Special arrangements where the person concerned commutes from the home country on a weekly or bi-weekly basis to the place of work in another country.

Competitive advantage: Any feature of a business firm that enables it to earn a high return on investment despite counter pressure from competitors.

Contractual assignments: Used in situations where employees with specific skills vital to an international project are assigned for a limited duration of 6-12 months.

Cross-cultural communication: Communication not only on different national cultures but also on the basis of race, religion, education, and economic backgrounds.

Cultural assimilator: A programme learning technique that is designed to expose members of one culture to some of the basic concepts, attitudes, role perceptions, customs, and values of another culture.

Culture: The way we do things here; the complex whole which includes knowledge, belief, art, morals, law, custom and other capabilities and habits acquired by a person as a member of the society.

Didactic training: Information about working conditions, living conditions, and cultural differences.

Direct compensation: Pay received directly in the form of cash.

Diverse workforce: Refers to multiracial, multiethnic, and multilingual workforces who have different lifestyles, values, beliefs, ideals, and practices.

Diversity training: A training which includes attitudes, skills, knowledge, and emotions.

Dunlopian model: An industrial relations system comprising of actors or parties; certain contexts; an ideology; and a body of rules.

Employee performance: Refers to planning, monitoring, developing, rating and rewarding of employees for their work.

Ethical relativist: A belief that there are no universal or international rights and wrongs, it all depends on a particular culture's values and beliefs.

Ethical universalist: A belief that there are fundamental principles of right and wrong which transcend cultural boundaries and that multinationals must adhere to these fundamental principles or global values.

Ethics: Is a study of the general nature of morals and of the specific moral choices to be made by a person.

Ethnocentrism: A way of believing and saying by people who tend to believe that their way of doing something is always best/right, and try to impose such beliefs on others.

Ethnocentricity: An approach in which all important positions in MNCs are filled by PCNs in the early stages of internationalisation.

EU: The European Union works toward an overseas economic and political integration of its member states with a common currency and a common central bank.

Evaluation: Means judging whether someone or something is good or bad. In this, we use our own culture as a standard of measurement, judging what is like us as normal and good and that which is unlike us as abnormal and bad.

Expatriate: An employee working and residing in a foreign country during his/her tenure of foreign employment. They include: (a) foreign employees working in domestic companies, (b) parent country nationals working in a MNC's subsidiary, (c) third country nationals working in MNCs, and (d) host country nationals working in the parent country of the MNC/TNC.

Extrinsic compensation: Is the monetary compensation in all forms.

Feedback: Formal sessions between appraiser and appraisee which includes positive and negative feedback.

Feminity: Refers to the concern for people and quality of life pertaining to societies in which social gender roles overlap.

Franchising: A franchise is a business arrangement under which one party (the franchiser) allows another (the franchisee) to operate an enterprise using its trademark, logo, product-line, and methods of operation in return for a fee.

Geocentricity: An approach strategy wherein managers can be recruited from any country and can be assigned to work in any other country irrespective of geographical location.

Glass ceiling: Refers to the barriers faced by women who are attempting or aspiring for senior positions in an organisation.

Globalisation: Refers to a growth of trade and investment in international business resulting in an integration of economies around the world.

Global mindset: Is the ability to scan the world from a broad perspective, always looking for unexpected trends and opportunities that may constitute a threat or an opportunity to achieve personal, professional, and organisational objectives.

Global strategist: Is the one who studies the environment under which the subsidiary operates, identifies the opportunities for new products/services and new markets, analyses the related strengths and possible weaknesses, and formulates the best strategy based on SWOT analysis to achieve the subsidiary goals.

Glopats: Managers who are highly mobile and focus on business-building or trouble-shooting; their assignments tend to be short or medium term.

Goals: Objectives or outcomes that an organisation seeks to achieve, maybe explicit or implicit.

Greenfield strategy: Refers to starting of the operations of a company from scratch in a foreign market.

Gifts: Every culture expects its members to give presents in certain circumstances such as weddings or birthdays. Some cultures extend gift-giving to everyday business meetings.

Guest employees: Foreigners with distinctive and rare skills who are invited to perform certain activities during a specified period.

Home country/Parent country: Is the one where the headquarters of a MNC or TNC is located.

Host country: Is the one where the subsidiary/branch of a MNC/TNC is located.

Host country nationals (HCNs): Are employees of a MNC/TNC's subsidiary/branch who are the citizens of the country where the subsidiary/branch of the MNC/TNC is located.

Indirect compensation: All kinds of deferred income, such as pension, insurance, and also benefits like a company car and certain allowances.

Individualism: Refers to a culture with a heavy emphasis on the individual taking responsibility for themselves and their family as compared to societies with a collective social emphasis.

Inpatriate: Are those employees transferred from subsidiary to headquarters and include parent country nationals, host country nationals, and third country nationals.

Intercultural communication: The process of communication between individuals from different cultures.

Intrinsic compensation: The non-financial compensation which is related to the nature of the work and career prospects.

Knowledge management: Management of the knowledge available to the organisation from all sources in such a way as to allow the creation of new knowledge and the sharing of existing knowledge.

Licensing: Is an agreement that allows one party to use an industrial property rights in exchange for payment to the other party.

Masculinity: Reflects the degree to which a society is dominated by masculine tendencies or, by contrast, feminine characteristics.

Merger: A merger is the joining of two organisations of equal status and power. Their union is mutually decided.

Mission: An enduring statement of the purpose for which, or reason why, an organisation exists. It comprises statements of shared purposes and shared values.

Multicultural teams: In this type of teams, members represent two or three ethnic backgrounds.

Multinational Corporation (MNC): An organisation which operates in more than one country.

NAFTA: US, Canada and Mexico entered into the North American Free Trade Agreement, the largest free trade area and richest market in the world.

Norms: Are established rules of what is accepted and appropriate behaviour.

Offshoring: Transfer of work and/or employment to another country typically where employment costs and benefits are lower.

Organisational culture: Refers to the set of values, beliefs, and behavioural patterns that forms the core identity of an organisation.

Outsourcing: Using an external organisation to provide one or more internal functions.

Parent country nationals (PCNs)/HCN's: Are employees of a MNC/TNC who are the citizens of home country/parent country of that MNC/TNC.

Parochialism: An expectation from others that they will readily adopt to their standards of behaviour.

Particularism: A belief that unique circumstances and relationships are more important considerations in determining what is right and good than abstract rules.

Perception: Is the process by which individuals select and organise stimuli in the environment to provide meaningful experiences to them.

Polycentricity: An approach in which the PCNs occupy positions at HQ, the HCNs are recruited to manage the subsidiary units in foreign locations.

Power distance: Refers to the degree to which people accept authority and hierarchical organisation as a natural part of their culture.

Pre-departure training: Is a training that is provided mostly in the areas of culture, language, preliminary aspect of the job, and business environment in the destination countries.

Regioncentric approach: A regional approach which relies on the region-specific recruitment and selection policy.

Repatriation: Return of the expatriate to his or her country of origin after completion of the foreign assignment.

Restructuring: Involves a top-down approach of cutting up assets, laying off staff and removing layers of management.

Roles: A set of norms that apply to specific groups of people in a society.

Rotational assignments: Employees commute from the home country to a place of work in another country for short, set period followed by a break in the home country.

Rumour and gossip: Rumour is typically regarded as unsubstantiated talk that is not supported by evidence or authority. Gossip, on the other hand, is commonly held to have a factual basis of some kind.

Social learning theory: A model which uses the concept of attention, retention, and reproduction and applies them in motivating learned expatriate behaviours in a foreign location.

Stereotype: A generalisation, based on limited experiences, about a class of people, objects, or events that are widely held by members of a given culture.

Strategic alliance: A cooperative and collaborative approach between two or more competitive international business firms in order to serve a global market.

Strategic planning: A process of determining an organisation's basic mission and long-term objectives, followed by a plan of action for attaining those goals.

Strategy: A unified, comprehensive and integrated plan designed to ensure that the basic objectives of the enterprise are achieved.

Strategic management: A continuous cross-functional process aimed at keeping an organisation as a whole with appropriate matching to its environment.

Takeover: A general term referring to transfer of control of a firm from one group of shareholders to another group of shareholders.

Talent management: A strategic and integrated approach to developing a skill and competent workforce, involving targeted recruitment, development and retention.

Tax equalisation: In this approach, the company pays both the home and host country taxes of the expatriate.

Tax protection: In this approach, the company reimburses the difference of payment to the expatriate, if the actual home tax plus the host country tax is greater than the hypothetical tax calculation.

Theory X: Assumes that employees dislike work, are lazy, dislike responsibility and must be coerced to perform.

Theory Y: Assumes that employees are creative, like work, seek responsibility and can exercise self-direction.

Third Country Nationals (TCNs): Are employees of a MNC/TNC or their subsidiaries/branches, and are citizens of those countries other than the MNC/TNCs home country and/or host country.

Training needs analysis: Consists of three inter-related aspects – organisational analysis, task analysis, and individual analysis.

Transnational bargaining: Unions identify the annual interests of diverse labour markets and go for transnational bargaining due to diversity of international business firms.

Transnational Corporation (TNC): An organisation that produces, markets, invests, and operates across the world.

Transnational process: Reflects the firm's ability to effectively include representatives and ideas from many cultures in the planning and decision making processes.

Transnational representation: Refers to the multinational composition of the firm's managers and executives.

Transpatriates: MNCs with global approach, recruit the people from any country and such employees' are termed as 'transpatriates', replacing the term expatriates.

Virtual expatriates: Are those people who live in their home country, but perform the work of a company that is located/operating in a foreign country.

Turnaround strategy: Is a strategy to reverse organisation's existing phase of decline by way of bringing radical change in organisational structure and policy.

Uncertainty avoidance: The extent to which the members of a culture feel threatened by uncertain or unknown situations.

Universalism: A philosophy where people believe that what is true and good can be discovered, defined, and applied everywhere.

Values: Basic assumptions held by a group of people about themselves, others, and the world.

Virtual teams: In such teams, members need not travel at all; they work across national and international boundaries aided by communication technologies.

Vision: A statement of purpose and philosophy that empowers and guides everyone throughout the company. It is a picture of what the organisation will be like at some point in the future.

Work permit: A document issued by the government of the country concerned (mostly by the department of immigration) granting right to foreigners to seek employment in the country concerned.

Bibliography

Adler, N., *International Dimensions of Organisational Behaviour*, South-Western Thomson Learning, Canada, 2002.

Bhatia, S.K., *International Human Resource Management*, Deep & Deep Publications Pvt. Ltd., New Delhi, 2005.

Black, J.S., Gregersen, H.B. and Mendenhall, M.E., *Global Assignments: Successful Expatriating and Repatriating International Manager*, Jossey-Bass, San Francisco, 1992.

Boxall, P., Purcell, J., *Strategy and Human Resource Management*, Palgrave Macmillan, New York, 2003.

Buckley, P.J. and P. Ghauri, eds., *The Internationalization of the Firm: A Reader*, Academic Press, London, 1993.

Clemente, M.N., and Greenspan, D.S., *Empowering Human Resources in the Merger and Acquisition Process: Guidance for HR Professionals in the Key Areas of M&A Planning and Integration*, Clemente, Greenspan & Co., 1999.

Daniels, J.D., Ogram, E.W., Radebaugh L.H., *International Business Environment and Operations*, Addison Wesley, 1982.

Dowling, P.J., Welch, D.E., Schuler, R.S., *International Human Resource Management: Managing People in a Multinational Context*, 3rd edition, South-Western College Publishing, Cincinnati, OH, 1999.

Dowling, P.J. and D.E. Welch, *International Human Resource Management: Managing People in a Multinational Context*, 4th edition, Thomson Learning, 2005.

Famularo, J.J., *Handbook of Modern Personnel Administration*, McGraw-Hill Book Company, New York, 1972.

Harris, H.C., Brewster and P. Sparrow, *International Human Resource Management*, London: Chartered Institute of Personnel Development, 2003.

Harris, J.E. and Morgan, R.T., *Managing Cultural Differences*, Gulf Publishing, Houston, TX, 1979.

Harzing, A.W. and Ruvsseveldt, J.V., *International Human Resource Management*, Sage Publications, London, 2004.

Hendry, C., *Human Resource Strategies for International Growth*, Routledge, London, 1994.

Hodgetts, R.M. and Luthans, F., *International Management: Culture, Strategy and Behaviour*, Tata McGraw-Hill, New York, 2003.

Hofstede, G.H., *Cultures and Organisations: Software of the Mind*, McGraw-Hill, London, 1991.

Mace, Myles L. and George G. Montgomery, *Management Problems of Corporate Acqusitions*, Division of Research, Harvard Business School, Boston, 1962.

Mead, R., *International Management*, Blackwell Business, UK, 1998.

Mendenhall, M., Punnett, B.J. and Ricks, D., *Handbook of Global Management*, Beacon Books, New Delhi, 1999.

Mitchell, C., *International Business Ethics*, Atlantic, New Delhi, 2009.

Nonaka, I. and Takeuchi, H., *The Knowledge Creating Company*, Oxford University Press, Oxford, 1995.

Phatak, A., *International Management: Concept and Cases*, South-Western College Publishing, Cincinnati, OH, 1997.

Punnett, B.J., *International Perspective on Organisational Behaviour and Human Resource Management*, Prentice-Hall of India, New Delhi, 2004.

Schuler, R.S., S.E. Jackson and Y. Luo, *Managing Human Resources in Cross-border Alliances*, Routledge, New York, 2003.

Shaw, J., *Cultural Diversity at Work: Utilising a Unique Australian Resource*, Business and Professional Publishing, Sydney, 1995.

TEE L. *Guidotti, Global Occupational Health (ed)*, Oxford University Press Inc., New York, 2011

Trompenaars, F. and Hampden, T.C., *Riding the Waves of Culture: Understanding Cultural Diversity in Business*, McGraw-Hill, New York, 1998.

Weather, J.F., *International Business Management: A Conceptual Framework*, McGraw-Hill, New York, 1969.

Index

Name

A

Adler, N., 119, 125
Adler and Ghader, 4
Argyris, C., 27

B

Barney, J.B., 234
Bartlett, C.A. and Ghoshal, S., 28, 37
Bean, R., 130
Bernardino Ramazzini, 196
Blace, 52
Black, S. and Gregerson, H.B., 61
Blake and mouton, 221
Blyton and Turnbull, 120
Bolon and Crain, 224
Brady, 209
Brewster, C., 233
Broon and Yetton, 221
Bruner, 190

C

Charles Turner Thackrah, 196
Chenn and Hsich, 96
Clemente and Greenspan, 157
Coyle and Collins, 52

D

Dodd, 188, 189
Dorfman and Ronen, 224
Douglas and Douglas, 134
Dowling, P.J., 14, 18, 25, 26, 122
Dowling, P.J. and Welch, D.E., 29, 51, 131
Dunlop, J.T., 129
Dwyer, 96

E

Evans and Lorange, 6

F

Ferrall and Fraedrich, 209

G

Garland, Farmer and Taylor, 215, 216
Gregerson, 52
Gross and Wingerup, 96

H

Hall, E.T., 165
Hamill, 130, 131
Harris, H., 64
Hedlund, 28
Herzberg, 229
Herzing and Ruysseveldt, 4, 93
Hixon, 59,120
Hofstede and Bards, 96
Hofstede, G.H., 169, 170, 172, 185

K

Khadra, 226
Kochan, T.A., 130
Kyosei, 211

L

LaPalombara, J., and Blank, S., 130
Likert, R., 221

M

Marschan, R., 77
Maslow, A.H., 228
Max Webber, 223
McCllelland, D.C., 229
McCormick, E., 7
McGregor, D., 221
Mendenhall, M., 76
Michael, Bogdan, 210
Morgan, P., 5-7
Murdock, 166

N

Norman Bowie, 210

O

Oddou and Menden Hall, 191

P

Paauwe and Dewe, 6
Paul, Sparrow, 5
Perceival Pott, 196
Perl Mutter, 30
Porter, M.E., 19
Priandis, 190

R

Rantanan, 199
Ratan Tata, 160
Reilly, 241
Reynolds and Bennett, 63
Roberts, 130

S

Schelur and Ragovsky, 96
Scullion and Starkey, 238
Smith, Adam, 20

T

Taylor Fredrick, 231
Tung, R.L., 53,75

W

Welch and Welch, 33
Williams and Adam Smith, 134
Wyld, 57

Y

Yoder, Dale, 129

Subject

A

Acquisition
- after, 156
- before, 155

Advertising, cross-national, 56
Analysis
- organisational, 38
- SWOT, 38

Appraisal, 360 degree, 110
Approach
- going rate, 92
- balance sheet, 93
- budget, 93
- hybrid, 93

Assessment centres, 60
Attributions, faulty, 190

B

Behavioural response, 191
Bhopal incident, 214
Biases, perceptual, 189
Business strategy, 32

C

Codetermination Act, 142
Collective
- bargaining, 133, 136
- culture, 170
- societies, 170

Collectivism, 170
Confucian, dynamism, 172
Contextual criteria, 110
Contract manufacturing, 3
Contractual mode, 33
Cooperate mode, 33
Cultural
- awareness, 75
- sensitivity, 165, 167
- shock, 166

Culture
- host, 76
- native, 76
- shock, 18

D

Diverse workforce, 174, 175
Domination societies, 173
Downsizing, 21

E

E-commerce, 21
Empathy, 222
Employee value proposition, 239
Equity theory, 230
Ethics
- business, 217
- code of, 219
- corporate code, 211, 212

Ethnocentric, 30, 31, 41, 43, 131
Expatriate selection, 71
Expectancy theory, 230
Exporting
- direct, 41
- indirect, 41

F

Femininity, 172
Franchising, 3, 42

G

General Agreement for Tariff and Trade (GATT), 20
Geocentric, 30, 31, 131, 132
Globalisation, 2, 4, 17, 20, 21, 174, 179, 235
Global mindset, 73
Grievance redressal, 133
Guest workers, 218

H

Hard criteria, 109
Heterarchy, 28
Hierarchy of needs, Maslow's, 228
Holding company, 27
Home country, 9, 63, 69, 78, 89-91, 93, 105, 120, 121, 125, 126, 131, 174, 204
Horizontal integration, 45
Host country, 7, 9, 12-16, 18, 29, 43, 54, 60, 69, 72, 73, 75, 77, 78, 80, 91-93, 107, 108, 120, 121, 131, 174, 177, 204
Host environment, 109
Host government, 11, 13, 15, 216
HRM strategy, alignment, 32

I

ICFTU, 140
ICOH, 204, 205, 207
Individualism, 170
International Labour Organisation (ILO), 12, 140, 148, 197, 198, 202-204, 207
International Monetary Fund, 179
International relocation, 14
International taxation, 14

J

Job analysis, 7
Joint venture, 29, 43, 45, 73

K

Kinesics, 188

L

Labour director, 144
Labour market, characteristics, 88
Licensing, 42
Lifetime employment, 137

M

Management board, 145
Management contracts, 3, 43
Managerial autonomy, 92
Managerial differences, cross-cultural, 182
Managing expatriates, 120
Masculinity, 172
Matrix structure, 27, 28
Mergers and acquisitions, 44
Mitbestimmung, 142
Mixed structure, 28
Monochromic, 165

N

Needs theory, McClelland's, 229
Network organisations, 29
Nuclear accident, Chernobyl, 214

O

OECD, 140, 148
Outsourcing, 30, 44

P

Parent country, 7, 62, 79, 88, 90, 108, 132
People's committee, 146
Performance management cycle, 101
Polycentric, 4, 30, 31, 131, 132
Polychromic, 165
Power distance, 170

Q

Quality of worklife, 141

R

Rater
  bias, 106
  competence, 105
Regiocentric, 30, 31, 132
Relativism
  cultural, 210
  individual, 210
Retrieval, 190
Role
  discretion, 53
  novelty, 53

S

Sheikocracy, 225
SMART, 102
Soft criteria, 110
Stereotypes, 191
Strategy
  concentration, 44
  conglomerate, 45
  differentiation, 41
  global, 37
  growth, 44
  international, 37
  low cost, 40
  multidomestic, 37
  niche, 40
  retrenchment, 45
  transnational, 37
Sullivan code, 245
Supervisory board, 143, 144

T

Tax
  equalisation, 96
  protection, 96
Third country, 7, 120
Time and distance, variation, 105
Tips, leadership, 227
Train and sell, 151
Transnational organisations, 29
Turnkey operation, 43
Two-factor theory, Herzberg's, 229

U

Uncertainty avoidance, 171
Universalist, 210, 211
Universals, 166

W

Wider nationalities, 17
WFL, 140
Workers'
  council, 145
  self-management, 145
Works council, 143, 144
World Health Organisation, 197-199, 203, 204, 207
World Trade Organisation, 17, 20, 179

13

5